Discourses in place

Discourses in Place develops the first systematic analysis of the ways we interpret language as it is materially placed in the world.

In this book Ron and Suzie Scollon argue that we can only interpret the meaning of public texts like road signs, notices and brand logos by considering the social and physical world that surrounds them. Drawing on a wide range of real examples, from signs in the Chinese mountains to urban centers in Austria, France, North America and Hong Kong, this textbook equips students with the methodology and models they need to undertake their own research in 'geo-semiotics', the key interface between semiotics and the physical world. The book is highly illustrated, containing real examples of language in the material world.

Including a 'how to use this book' section, group and individual activities and a glossary of key terms, *Discourses in Place* is essential reading for anyone with an interest in language and the way we communicate.

Ron Scollon is Professor of Linguistics at Georgetown University, USA, and Editor of *Visual Communication*. His previous publications include *Mediated Discourse* (Routledge). **Suzie Wong Scollon** is Research Coordinator, Associated Socio-cultural Research Projects, Georgetown University, USA. Ron Scollon and Suzie Wong Scollon have co-written *Intercultural Communication: A Discourse Approach* (second edition) and (with Yuling Pan) *Professional Communication in International Settings*.

Discourses in Place

Language in the material world

**Ron Scollon and
Suzie Wong Scollon**

Routledge
Taylor & Francis Group

LONDON AND NEW YORK

First published 2003 by Routledge
11 New Fetter Lane, London EC4P 4EE

Simultaneously published in the USA and Canada by Routledge
29 West 35th Street, New York, NY 10001

Routledge is an imprint of the Taylor & Francis Group

© 2003 Ron Scollon and Suzie Wong Scollon

Typeset in Perpetua by
Florence Production Ltd, Stoodleigh, Devon
Printed and bound in Great Britain by
Biddles Ltd, Guildford and King's Lynn

British Library Cataloguing in Publication Data
A catalogue record for this book is available from the British Library

Library of Congress Cataloging in Publication Data
A catalogue record for this book has been requested

ISBN 0–415–29048–1 (hbk)
ISBN 0–415–29049–X (pbk)

Contents

Preface

In their book *The Social Life of Information* (2002) John Seely Brown, Chief Scientist at Xerox Corporation and Paul Duguid of the University of California, Berkeley argue that in our enthusiasm for the massive increase in information in today's world we have neglected to understand that, as they put it, 'information and individuals are inevitably and always part of rich social networks' (p. xxv). Their thesis is that information only becomes knowledge when it is grounded quite concretely in the social, material world.

There are just three ways a sign such as a word, a sentence, a picture, a graph or a gesture can have meaning in semiotic theory. It can be a picture of the thing in the world. In that case we call it an *icon*. The little picture of a happy face made by email users out of a colon and the right parenthesis (:)) is an icon. It shows us a schematic picture of a smiling face. A sign can also be a completely arbitrary representation of the thing in the world. In that case we call it a *symbol*. A green traffic light means we can continue driving. There is nothing inherent in the color green that 'means' move ahead or keep going. It is an arbitrary association. Finally, a sign means something because of where and when it is located in the world. In this case it is called an *index*. An arrow pointing one direction down a street is an index which shows the exact direction in which traffic should go.

There is a difference among these three types of signs, though. Icons and symbols can exist independently and can encode independent although entirely abstract meanings. The property of indexicality, however, is a property of all signs. Icons, symbols, and indexes are all three of them also indexes. This difference between indexes and the other two categories is the substance of this book *Discourses in Place: Language in the Material World*.

All signs, whether they are icons or symbols are also indexes. That is because all signs must be located in the material world to exist. Information and knowledge must be represented by a system of signs — icons, symbols, and indexes; information and knowledge cannot have any independent existence. The familiar stop sign on the street corner is a symbol in several ways: The letters 'S', 'T', 'O', and

'P' symbolize the English word 'stop' which itself symbolizes the meaning 'to progress no further'. It also symbolizes this meaning through the conventional use of a red color on a hexagonal background. Until it is placed in the world, this sign only means to stop in the abstract. On the sign painter's bench it does not mean that he should stop painting. It only means that a car should stop when it is placed physically in the world at a place such as a street intersection. This shift from abstract meaning potential to actual, real-world meaning is the property of indexicality. The sign abstractly symbolizes 'to stop', but it indexes where and how and who in what container is to stop in the real world only when it is grounded in the material world of cement roadways, curbs, and metal poles. You can get a ticket for passing up a stop sign placed at an intersection but not for doing the same to a stop sign in the back of the worker's truck or on the painter's bench. Indexes have meaning in the real material and social world in which we live.

This is what Brown and Duguid are talking about when they say that we neglect at our peril this situatedness or groundedness of the signs of our information highway. *Discourses in Place* is a book about the situatedness of signs in the world. In it we outline a preliminary grammar of the 'placeness' of discourses in place by combining sociocultural theory, semiotic theory, and ethnographic studies of signs in place.

Fifteen days after Christopher Columbus sailed to the New World to colonize its spaces for Queen Isabella of Spain, Elio Antonio de Nebrija presented the Queen with his *Gramatica Castellana*, the Grammar of Castilian Spanish. Ivan Illich describes this work as

> a tool for conquest abroad and a weapon to suppress untutored speech at home (1981: 35)

> a tool to colonize the language spoken by her own subjects (1981: 4)

Finding the Latin spoken in Spain too corrupt a language to be worthy of the name, young Antonio went to Italy to learn proper Latin, published a grammar of it, then upon returning home proceeded to engineer the vulgar speech he heard in Spain into what he regarded as a proper language, Castilian Spanish. The result was the first grammar in any modern European tongue. Thus the first great move in the integration of language and the forces of social control within the nations of Europe was made.

Nebrija was distraught at the degeneration of ancient Latin and at the diversity of tongues that had found their way into print by way of the new invention of the printing press. He proposed to Queen Isabella that she standardize the language with his grammar and that she declare the printing of any vernacular to be against the law. Illich terms this 'a system of scientific control of diversity within the entire kingdom' (1981: 36). In the introduction to his grammar, Nebrija wrote,

So far, this our language has been left loose and unruly and, therefore, in just a few centuries this language has changed beyond recognition. If we were to compare what we speak today with the language we spoke five hundred years ago, we would notice a difference and a diversity that could not be any greater if these were two alien tongues.

(Illich 1981: 38)

Now more than 500 years later we have come to take the standardization of language for granted and to think of it as a simple necessity for teaching people to read and for schooling. The original aim, however, was to control the reading of the populace, who Nebrija wrote 'waste their time on novels and fanciful stories full of lies.'

(Illich 1981: 39)

He proposed to restrict printing to Castellano, spoken by no-one including the Queen, as a way to control what appeared in print and require citizens to be educated in order to be able to read or write. With this move, printed language disappeared from the commons and fell under the control of the nation state.

Language indexes the world. We speak and listen, write and read not only *about the world* but *in the world*, and much of what we understand depends on exactly where we and the language are located in the world. 'We would like you to read this' uses indexical expressions such as the pronouns 'we', and 'you' and the demonstrative 'this' but we cannot know *who* 'we' are or *who* 'you' are, or *what* 'this' is until we know how this sentence is physically located in the world on paper and in the hands of a reader.

Much more important than this simple indexing of 'you' and 'me', of 'here' and 'there', of 'this' and 'that', language indexes who and what we are in the world as we use it. We are writing and publishing this book in English. This is an observation that is almost entirely invisible until we call your attention to it. Our writing in English and your reading it in English indexes us as members of a particular social group with particular forms of power in the world in just the same way that Nebrija's grammar was used by Queen Isabella to control diversity and produce social uniformity within her nation. It must be remembered that the year 1492 saw not only the voyage of Columbus and the grammar of Nebrija but also the expulsion of 'the Moors', Muslims, from Queen Isabella's territory in one of history's most infamous cases of ethnic cleansing. A person who does not read English is indexed by the very choice of language in this book as an outsider to this discussion even as we index ourselves as insiders.

Geographers have been concerned with making a distinction between the concept of space and the concept of place. Harvey (1989) in his widely read *The Condition of Postmodernity* comments that the spaces of our earth have been carved out and mapped to reflect systems of command and control. As in the case of Queen Isabella, one of the major means by which this sociopolitical control of the spaces in which we live is produced and maintained is through the control of the discourses in those spaces. Everywhere about us in our day-to-day world we see the discourses which shape, manage, entice, and control our actions. Instrumental to the process of shaping those discourses are the objects by which we index our own positions and identities in the world. The traffic light at a busy intersection not only narrowly manages the flow of automobiles through the intersection, it also indexes the municipal regulatory powers and apparatus that have placed the traffic light and which maintain its functioning. Furthermore, as we approach the light and make our choices about stopping or driving right through it, we index ourselves in respect to those regulatory powers and that municipal power apparatus. Mostly, of course, we index ourselves as law-abiding citizens by stopping when instructed to do so.

Geosemiotics is the study of the meaning systems by which language is located in the material world. This includes not just the location of the words on the page you are reading now but also the location of the book in your hands and your location as you stand or sit reading this. It includes the urban planning designs by which the streets in your city are laid out as well as the signs placed on those streets. It also includes the many forms of what Erving Goffman calls the interaction order – the ways we organize ourselves as single individuals or as conversational partners out for a lunchtime walk – through which we interact with these many semiotic systems of the world around us.

Professionals, travelers, advertisers, and government officials in our globalizing world economy communicate daily with people who are very different from themselves. Developing a brand name for a product, speaking on the phone to a colleague on the other side of the world, reading the road signs on an interstate highway, or the sign on the door of a shop, we can no longer just trust our own intuitions of how to read the systems of indexicality in the world around us. In many cases we cannot read either what sociocultural or political powers are being indexed or the ways in which our own actions are positioning ourselves within those structures of meaning and power. A pair of pants bought recently by Ron for camping has zippers which allow the user to remove the lower parts of the legs to produce a pair of shorts. A tag that came with the pants noted that this would allow adjustment between pants and shorts 'as needed by the weather or by the local culture'. While clothing now may allow this adjustment we still have very few clues about how to read the discourses in place around us when we are in spaces that are in some way not 'our own'.

There are many books on intercultural communication, including our own, but scant attention is focused on the question of how the physical/material charac-teristics of language in the world give meaning to communications and how those meanings may be radically different from place to place in the world. Based on an extensive body of research into geosemiotics conducted by ourselves and our students in several countries including China and Hong Kong, Finland, the United States, the United Kingdom, Ireland, Austria, Germany, Brazil, Hungary, Lebanon, and France, this book develops the first systematic analysis of the ways we interpret language as it is materially placed in the world. We bring together research from our own fields of linguistic anthropology and social psychology as a contribution to the understanding of discourses in place in studies of communication and intercultural communication, sociolinguistics, cultural studies, semiotics, visual anthropology and sociology, and cultural geography. Geosemiotics as we conceive the field here is also directly useful in graphic arts and design, art and architecture, urban planning, public relations, advertising, and marketing because of the insights it provides for practitioners working across cultural-semiotic boundaries in designing public spaces and communication campaigns.

When Quebec asserted its wish to be independent from Canada this was written across the Province in the names of roadways, of government offices, and of stores and services. French was placed above English or any other language in all bilingual signs. When Estonia, Ukraine, and the other former Soviet Republics emerged from under the control of the central state one of the first displays of political independence was seen in the public commercial and government signs with Estonian or Ukrainian or even English placed in the privileged position over the formerly dominant Russian. In our own research projects we plotted the political currents of change in Hong Kong and China during the period in which sovereignty over Hong Kong returned from Britain to China. Our interest in this book began as we saw that whether it was the name of a post office, of a fashion boutique, or a food court, how and where those words were placed, the letterforms of those words, and the materials out of which they were made were a central part of their sociopolitical meaning.

We quickly realized that it was not simply a matter of the signs and lettering of signs in public places that we were investigating. We found that we needed to develop a broad and systematic analysis of how language appears in the material world, whether that language is on the lips of two people having a casual conversation or engraved in stone on the face of a national public monument. In each case one very important aspect of the meaning of language is based on the concrete, material, physical placement of that language in the world.

From the study of what we called the literate design of discourse in public we have now come in this book to a broad analytical position we call *geosemiotics*. We have begun with the classical research of Edward T. Hall and Erving Goffman on the ways in which we position ourselves in relationship to each other as we take up and perform what Goffman called the interaction order. This is the fundamental basis of indexicality – the quality of language that it makes reference to things in the world by pointing to or locating itself on or in them and in doing so positions us within that world.

We then turn to the visual semiotic framework of Gunther Kress and Theo van Leeuwen as the basis for our analysis of the signs and pictures themselves as semiotic structures. We believe that much of the meaning structure of signs and pictures derives from the more fundamental systems of indexicality of the social interaction order. A close-up photograph of a person's face signals a close relationship between the person in the photo and the viewer of the photo because the close-up is analogized on the social relationship of intimate or personal distance as observed by Hall and Goffman.

The main substance of *Discourses in Place: Language in the Material World* comes out of our own research projects. Using prior research such as that we have presented in the first sections of the book, we present a system for analyzing code preference when there are two or more languages or codes used in a picture, a system for the analysis of inscription – the material substance of signs, and a system for analyzing emplacement – the when and where of the physical location of language in the world. The final two chapters bring this analytical framework together to argue that all instances of language in the world occur in semiotic aggregates – very complex systems of the interaction of multiple semiotic systems. Human action is enabled only through the semiotic systems we use. We close our *geosemiotic* analysis by pointing out that any human action is a process of selection among many semiotic systems which are always in a kind of dialectical dialogicality with each other. Indexicality – the meaning of signs which is based on their material location – is the key to the analysis of any human action.

A project that spans many countries in several continents incurs a large debt to people everywhere we have gone. Since we began the research projects on which this book is based six years ago we have researched, lectured, given conference papers, taught classes, and simply traveled with our cameras in many countries of the world. Everywhere people have been generous with their ideas and it would be impossible to include the names of so many people who have been willing to discuss these ideas with us. In the first project we were joined by our colleague Dr Yuling Pan and our daughter, Rachel Scollon. Dr Yoshiko Nakano, our colleague at City University of Hong Kong, was also very helpful particularly in discussing the ways in which Japanese visual semiotics has penetrated into contemporary China in the form of Japanese popular culture. Dr Lucia Pan of Fudan University spent many hours with us researching problems of code preference in Hong Kong and China. Beatrice Chan was our always able research assistant on the Hong Kong projects and assisted us in transferring our archives to Washington, DC.

Our students at Georgetown University, Alex Johnston, Ingrid de Saint-

Georges, Sigrid Norris, and Alla Yeliseyeva have conducted their own geosemiotics projects and the results of these are cited in the bibliography. Their contribution goes much beyond such academic citations in that we enjoyed many hours of discussion of these topics with them. Students in R. Scollon's Public Discourse class in 1999 (Najma Al Zidjaly, Susan Chen, Elisa Everts, Shiraz Felling, Cynthia Gordon, Andy Jocuns, Gia Ann Russo) and again in 2002 (Jessica Bauman, Michael Blasenstein, Shanna Estigoy, Philip LeVine, Meaghan Nelson, Jackie Novak, Brendan O'Connor, Phil Piety, Aida Premilovac, Shana Semler, Margaret Toye, Veronika Zielinska) suffered through the first rough drafts of these ideas and it would be impossible to have arrived at this stage without their careful consideration and criticism of the ideas we present here.

Photos 4.15 and 8.02 are used by permission of Virginia Zavala-Cisneros who was one of the very first 'geosemioticians'.

1   Geosemiotics

Geosemiotics: Discourses in place

A website on California nudist beaches posts the following clarification of legal requirements:

> Before the citations were issued it's clear there's an ordinance in place and there were notice signs in place and people were clearly violating those posted notices.

'Ordinance in place', 'signs in place', 'people were clearly violating': these are crucial concepts in law and in life, whether we are thinking of nude bathing, crossing against a sign saying 'Do Not Walk', or driving through a red traffic light. There is a social world presented in the material world through its discourses – signs, structures, other people – and our actions produce meanings in the light of those discourses.

This book is about the 'in place' meanings of signs and discourses and the meanings of our actions in and among those discourses in place. A municipal ordinance prohibiting nude bathing or driving above a certain speed limit is an outcome of a complex and lengthy legal discourse. Meetings are held, investigations made; ordinances are drafted, opened for public comment, passed, and finally posted. All of this legal discourse becomes binding law when and where the signs are posted, when and where the signs become discourses in place.

Or we could put this the other way around: signs are designed by sign-makers, they are made in the shops and workplaces of sign-makers, they are taken out to the relevant site, and finally, some worker puts them up and they become 'signs in place.' The sign saying that nude bathing is prohibited has the same words, the same sentences, cites the same ordinances, and all the rest while it is riding in the back of the truck of the worker taking it out to the beach to be posted. During this time the sign may have abstract linguistic meaning but it does not have any binding 'in place' meaning until it is actually posted firmly in place at the beach.

This book is called *Discourses in Place: Language in the Material World.* It is a book which deals with *geosemiotics* – the study of the social meaning of the material placement of signs and discourses and of our actions in the material world. With this title we are trying to capture this 'in place' aspect of the meanings of discourses in our day-to-day lives. When we cross a street corner we encounter a complex array of signs and discourses. There are signs regulating vehicular traffic, there are signs regulating pedestrian traffic. We see lines painted on the street: some for pedestrians, some for automobiles, some for electrical workers who are to pull up a manhole to repair the lines underneath. We see commercial advertisements, public official notices, street and building identifications, graffiti, and pasted up notices for legal and even illegal goods and services. As we walk we may be chatting with a friend. This friend and all of the others present are also signs in place which we 'read' in taking our actions.

All of the signs and symbols take a major part of their meaning from how and where they are placed – at that street corner, at that time in the history of the world. Each of them indexes a larger discourse whether of public transport regulation or underground drug trafficking.

But this does not only apply to the signs and other symbols posted here and there about our worlds as we go through daily life. Our own bodies make and give off much of their meanings because of where they are and what they are doing 'in place'. A person who is wearing no clothing on a public beach is a 'nude bather' (whether legal or not). A person who is wearing no clothing in the privacy of his or her bathroom is simply a person preparing to take a bath, hardly a 'nude bather'.

Discourses in Place: Language in the Material World is a book about how we use language in concrete, physical instances: A heavy brass sign means this company is here to stay; a hastily made cloth banner means this sale will not last long; you'd better buy now. *Discourses in Place* gathers together insights from a wide variety of fields from linguistics to cultural geography and from communication to sociology into a perspective we are calling *geosemiotics*. We begin with the problem of indexicality.

Indexicality and the indexable

'What is that?' cannot be understood unless we look at the world outside of language to fix a meaning for 'that' and unless we look at where exactly in the world the person saying this is located as well as what he or she is doing. The meaning of 'What is that?' is anchored in a person (who is the speaker?), a social relationship (who is the hearer?), a social situation (what are the speaker and hearer doing – looking or pointing at something?), and a physical world (what is a potential 'that' within the spaces of those people?).

The meaning of a sign is anchored in the material world whether the linguistic utterance is spoken by one person to another or posted as a stop sign on a street corner. We need to ask of the stop sign the same four questions we would ask of a person: Who has 'uttered' this (that is, is it a legitimate stop sign of the municipal authority)? Who is the viewer (it means one thing for a pedestrian and another for the driver of a car)? What is the social situation (is the sign 'in place' or being installed or worked on)? Is that part of the material world relevant to such a sign (for example, is it a corner of the intersection of roads)?

This is the property of language called indexicality. Indexicality has been known to be a universal characteristic of language at least since the turn of the past century in the work of Charles S. Peirce, regarded by many as the founder of the field of semiotics. Indexicality is the property of the context-dependency of signs, especially language; hence the study of those aspects of meaning which depend on the placement of the sign in the material world. In geosemiotics, as in all branches of semiotics, the word 'sign' means any material object that indicates or refers to something other than itself. Of course language and discourse are our primary interest and so in that case we would speak of this sentence, this paragraph, or this book as a sign albeit a very complex sign. But we also include signs in the more conventional sense of shop names, traffic regulatory devices, and even the built environment such as roadways – a 'sign' that one can and should drive in this particular space. And, of course, we cannot forget that we ourselves are the embodiment of signs in our physical presence, movements, and gestures.

Because indexicality has been most fully studied in relationship to language, we begin with indexicality in language. Language indexes the world in many ways. The most frequently noted indexicals are personal pronouns ('I', 'we', 'you', etc.), demonstratives ('this', 'that'), deictics ('here', 'there, 'now'), and tense and other forms of time positioning ('smiles', 'smiled', 'will smile'). Our understanding of both spoken utterances and written texts must be anchored in the material world. To understand a sentence such as, 'Would you take this over there,' we need a provisional location for myself (the speaker – a meaning for here), for 'you' (my addressee), for the object ('this'), and for the goal intended ('there').

While anthropological linguists such as Haviland, Hanks, and Silverstein have dealt with the question of how indexicality is structured within languages of the world as a universal characteristic of language, sociolinguists have remained a bit reluctant to enter into the study of the semiotic systems in the material world apart from grammar which must necessarily be called upon for users of language to perform indexicality. To understand the phrase, 'As we have written above' we rely upon a semiotics of written objects which tells us that 'above' must index text written within the same document, that it will not be a comment scribbled in the margin but rather in the same general text portion of the pages, and so forth. It does not literally mean 'above' (in the air or on the ceiling) if we are writing on a table surface or if it is being read horizontally.

More to the point of this book, to understand the meanings and negations of the sign in image 1.01, we need a theoretical framework which first can take into consideration the telegraphic language of 'TRAFFIC LIGHT OUT OF ORDER' to tell us *which* traffic light is out of order – normally it is the next one the driver will encounter. Hence we need a theory of motion through space and the use of public spaces which will tell us where traffic lights are conventionally located. We also need a theory which will tell us that this sign is negated – it is *not* to be read (because of its physical position away from the flow of traffic, on the other side of the fence, and in a 'blocked' orientation.)

We are calling this theoretical framework *geosemiotics* to make reference to the social meanings of the material placement of signs (semiosis, to use Peirce's term) particularly in reference to the material world of the users of signs. For us, as linguists, the primary sign system (semiotic system) is language, though as we have noted above and as we will see in the chapters which follow, mostly we focus on rather simple signs. This narrowing of focus is for two reasons. In the first place,

1.01

the signs we find around us in daily life are extremely abundant though they have rarely been taken up for analysis by linguists and other specialists in language, discourse, and communication. Everywhere in our world are the logos and brand names on the products we use in daily life and on the shops that line our streets and malls. Wherever we go we see the sociocultural, sociopolitical regulatory apparatus of our worlds in the traffic regulations displayed in painted lines on streets that indicate where we may drive or walk and we see this apparatus in the traffic lights at intersections. We see signs for infrastructural work such as the electrical boxes that run the street lights and we see announcements and notices of events taking place. We see signs saying 'Post No Bills' and we see graffiti. The meanings of all these signs depend on forms of indexicality we will take up in the chapters which follow.

While linguistics has given us the most thorough foundation for the study of indexicality in signs, our primary interest in this book is not indexicality in language. This has been and is being widely studied within linguistics. Our interest here is in the ways in which this sign system of language indexes the other semiotic systems in the world around language. That is, we are more interested in the *indexable world* than in the systems of indexicality in language.

A restaurant in Kunming, China has the sign in 1.02 posted above the door.

Native speakers of English generally read this sign as saying, DNALIAHT followed by some Chinese characters. They can make no sense of it. People

1.02

who are from Taiwan, China, or Hong Kong, however, read this sign as saying 'King of Dai food [*Tai Wang Ge* in Chinese] or THAILAND [TAI WANG GE] THAILAND'. For them it is a straightforward sign telling them this is a Dai National Minority restaurant.

What makes some readers try to read this sign in a universalized left-to-right reading path while others read the sign starting from the Chinese characters over the central doorway and then read outward from center toward the margins? Part of this reading is based on knowing Chinese characters, of course, and that is the subject of many books on translation. But more fundamental than the question of translation is knowing *how* to read the sign in relationship to its placement above the door of a restaurant. Before we can think about *what* we are reading we have to have a principle to tell us *how* to read it. We have to know whether we should read from left to right, right to left, or from the center outward. This example illustrates that the first principle in the interpretation of language is to solve the problem of indexability – to locate language in the physical world.

A 'grammar' of indexability

Most of the semiotic systems which we index in daily life are completely transparent and invisible to us. Of course the language we use is invisible in this way, at least until it is made painfully visible in those grammar classes in school which so many of us resisted. This does not mean, however, that these all but invisible systems of meaning are unimportant in our lives. On the contrary as Michael Billig has noted in his book *Banal Nationalism*, it is just these invisible, almost banal, systems of meaning which form the sociopolitical systems that so closely define us and our actions in the world. Billig notes, for example, that we may not talk at all about our nation or even feel that there is any question about nationalism involved in such a simple daily event as the weather report, but as the map appears on the television screen here in the United States we see that there is a sharp boundary between the US and Canada on the north and between the US and Mexico on the south. Canada has no weather, nor does Mexico. The fronts and sweeps of climate are entirely 'national', represented as starting sharply at the borders on the map. Sadly for those of us who live in Alaska and Hawaii, both states of the United States, these are also not part of the weather picture. The contiguous 'Lower 48' as it is said in Alaska indexes 'the nation' in these weather reports in which Hawaiians and Alaskans are marginalized right along with Canadians and Mexicans. With a weather map a political concept is framed; with the definite article *the* in 'the nation' a political entity is flagged as surely as if it flew the red, white, and blue colors of the national flag.

Much of the substance of this book is taken up with the fairly straightforward description of the systems and sub-systems which can be indexed by language and by which language becomes indexable in the material world. Because of the rather compressed nature of this analysis which covers a very wide range of semiotic systems, we cannot in each case also dwell on the ways in which each of these semiotic systems indexes the sociocultural and sociopolitical structures of power in the world around us. Is it of value in and of itself to develop this comprehensive analysis? We believe it is, for two reasons. First of all, as has been well established in the field of linguistics, the grammatical systems of language are among the most visible external manifestations of human cognitive capacities. That is, grammar has been regarded by psychotherapists and cognitive scientists as well as by linguists as a window on the human mind. We believe that it will prove to be highly productive to extend the studies of semiotic systems beyond the analysis of the grammars of languages into the grammars of 'texts' taken in the much broader sense that we use here.

Our second reason, however, is for us the more important one. All semiotic systems operate as 'social semiotic' systems as we have suggested above in making reference to the ways in which nationalism is flagged in such a simple matter as the production of a weather map. In producing meanings we must make choices; as we make choices we preference one option over another. All semiotic systems operate as systems of social positioning and power relationship both at the level of interpersonal relationships and at the level of struggles for hegemony among social groups in any society precisely because they are systems of choices and no choices are neutral in the social world. This is a point well established in the work of M. A. K. Halliday and many other social semioticians, the analytical tradition within which we place this book.

In this book, of course, we cannot do more than show how three broad systems of social semiotics are interconnected at any site of social action – the interaction order, visual semiotics, and place semiotics. Research in critical discourse analysis has shown abundantly that texts themselves are among the most powerful tools for the production of social power relations. The systems of text, however, we will simply have to leave implicit in our discussion here, largely because they have been so widely studied elsewhere. We do not mean to dismiss the role of textual analysis, however; we simply mean to focus on these other three systems which have as yet not been so extensively studied and almost never in interaction with each other.

For the first of these three broad systems we use Goffman's term 'the interaction order' though, of course, we mean to include any of the research within a broad range of disciplines from social psychology and interactional sociology to communication, sociolinguistics, and conversational analysis which develops an understanding of the ways in which humans form social arrangements and produce social interactions among themselves. It is taken as central in these fields of study that discourse is a major organizing system in this interaction order though it is important to recall Goffman's caution that we should take the inter-action as primary, not the language.

For the second of these systems we use Kress and van Leeuwen's term 'visual semiotics.' Here our purpose is to focus on all of the ways in which pictures (signs, images, graphics, texts, photographs, paintings, and all of the other combinations of these and others) are produced as meaningful wholes for visual interpretation. Again, this focus would necessarily want to include art history, typography, visual design, and any other area of study or discipline which takes as its main object to understand how we produce meanings through visual artifacts. Our use of Kress and van Leeuwen's framework is studied in that we feel their framework fits well with our overall social semiotic understanding of semiotics, but we do not intend to exclude the very much wider range of work that might have been included were there more space to do so.

The term 'place semiotics' is a coinage of sorts here without intending in any way to elevate this broad set of meaning systems to any sort of theoretical prominence. All we mean to indicate here is the huge aggregation of semiotic systems which are not located in the persons of social actors or in the framed artifacts of visual semiotics. This would naturally have to include architecture, urban planning, landscape planning and analysis, highway engineering, and so many other fields of analysis as to be positively daunting. Cultural geographers are working very actively in coming to productive analyses of such 'place semiotics' and we hope here to signal an interest in bringing about some future integration of these three very broad systems of semiotics into a more comprehensive framework.

Geosemiotic systems

The three main systems of geosemiotics, then, are the interaction order, visual semiotics, and 'place' semiotics. This last system is far from a single or internally unitary system, as we have said. As we shall see in Chapters 6 through 8, there is really a continuum that runs from the semiotics of code preference in signs that use multiple codes such as street signs in bilingual communities through to the meanings that are the result of where a sign is physically placed on the ground as is the case with the stop sign positioned on a street intersection.

Image 1.04 gives a schematic diagram of how we see these three systems grouping as the main semiotic systems of any form of social action. Any and all social actions take place at some intersection of the interaction order (a conver-sation, a meeting, a walk with a friend in a city park or square or in a shopping mall, a single reading a newspaper in a café) of visual semiotics (the design, layout, and production of all the signs, pictures, books, newspapers, posters, and other images which are either being used by the interaction order or being ignored by them), and place semiotics (the built environment along with the 'natural' landscape within which the action takes place). While all of these separate semiotic systems have been studied to a greater extent elsewhere (greater for the linguistic study of texts or the social psychological and interactional sociological studies of social interaction; lesser in the case of the semiotics of public squares), this book brings these factors together within the single framework of geosemiotics.

The example below will to help to make these relationships clearer at the outset though each of these areas of study will be taken up separately in the chapters which follow. We begin with the interaction order in Chapter 3. In Chapter 4 we give a necessarily selected summary of Kress and van Leeuwen's (1996, 2001) grammar of visual semiotics. Then in Chapters 6 through 9 we outline in sequence our grammar of place semiotics: the code preference system (Chapter 6), the inscription system (Chapter 7), the emplacement system (Chapter 8), and then the properties of the semiotic aggregates which are the intersections of all of these subsystems in which social action takes place (Chapter 9).

In photo 1.03 we see a corner section of the busy and elegant Stephansplatz in Vienna. Here in front of St Stephen's Cathedral are banks, fashionable shops and cafés, pedestrians and, as in this case, a street performer. Dressed as a statue, this performer stands motionless until passersby make donations in a box placed on the

1.03

ground in front of him. At that point he very slowly bows and extends a hand toward the donor. In some cases the donors will take the hand and give it a slow and solemn handshake before the 'statue' returns to his immobile position.

This small scene of social action entails all of the elements we will discuss even though there is no actual speech exchanged between the street performer and the audience. There are the social interactions both among the various people passing by and between at least some of them and the performer. There are the visual semiotics of the kiosk of posters we see to the side of the street performer which taken together form an important part of the sense of this public place. They link this place to the theater and other performances taking place currently throughout Vienna. Then there are the 'place' semiotics of the performer who teases the distinction between being part of the built environment on the one hand and being a social actor on the other. He is a social actor who embodies himself as the built environment as his performance.

The relationships among semiotic systems can be sketched as we have done in image 1.04. Of course there are many social actions going on just within the frame of this photo and many more in the proximal environment. If we just focus on the couple standing watching the performer we can say that the action (at the moment)

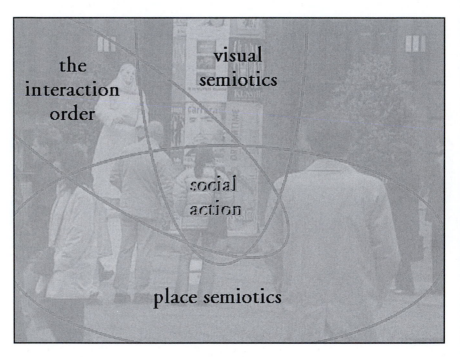

1.04

is just that of watching. Another photo not included here shows the man in this couple bending over to make a donation. This social action of watching is taking place within what Goffman calls a 'with' (Chapter 3). That is, it is a small group of two who are 'together' and can be seen to be together. We see another 'with' moving off toward the left and not watching the performer. On the right side is another 'with', a couple, who are reading the posters on the kiosk and in the foreground is a single who is somewhat indeterminately watching the scene which includes the two 'withs' and the performer. The performer himself together with the observers forms the unit of the interaction order that Goffman calls a 'platform event'.

The fact that we can relatively simply write about 'the couple' or 'the with' and have confidence that the reader can identify who we are writing about suggests that this structured bit of social interaction – what Goffman calls the 'interaction order' (Chapter 3) is directly indexable. That is, we can point to this bit of structured social interaction as a semiotic object in this photo. The photo consists of discernable objects – the couple watching, the couple moving off to the left, the couple looking at the kiosk, the single watching the scene in the foreground, the street performer, the kiosk, the tree, the posters which we can take pretty much at face value when we index this scene. The interaction order, then, is itself a semiotic object in the world to which we can point and about which we can talk. This is the property of being indexable which we will discuss in Chapter 2. This indexability that is provided by the configurations of social interactions within any social scene is what we mean by the interaction order aspect of geosemiotics.

Any social action must be somehow positioned within the interaction orders appropriate for the society within which it takes place as we will see in Chapter 3. It is this very complex aspect of geosemiotics with which we begin because it is the social-interactional ground on which all of our actions in the world take place.

We might use the term 'visual semiotics' to refer to any and all of the ways in which meaning is structured within our visual fields, but in this book we prefer to use the analysis provided by Gunther Kress and Theo van Leeuwen in their books *Reading Images* (1996) and *Multimodality* (2001) and restrict ourselves to the semiotic systems of framed images and pictures (graphs, charts, books, posters, photos, art works, scientific illustrations, shop signs, or advertisements). In this photo the main visual semiotics is available for interpretation on the many posters pasted on the kiosk at the center of the photo. In the same way that the street performer forms a semiotic object that we can recognize when we say 'the couple is looking at the street performer', the kiosk of posters forms a similar visual focus for attention. In the case of the couple we are looking at here, the two who are watching the street performer, the visual semiotics of the poster kiosk is being disattended. As we will discuss in Chapter 9, a crucial aspect of geosemiotics is negative in the sense that we believe we must not only account for the semiotic systems currently in play but for those which are currently set aside for disattention.

We are extending this interest from Goffman's notion of 'civil inattention' which we discuss in Chapter 3. In that case he points out that a crucial part of forming a 'with' is that members of the 'with' do not engage in interactions with people who are not part of that 'with' (except, of course, as spectacles which the 'with' may watch as in the platform event we are looking at here). Similarly, to give a full account of the semiotics of social action, we argue, we need to account for not only what systems are being given attention at any particular moment, but also what systems are being treated with a kind of 'civil inattention'. As in any system of social semiotics, there is a choice implied in all actions. In order to watch the street performer the couple must *not* look at the kiosk. A major piece of the semiotic work that the street performer performs is to accomplish exactly this capturing of the attention of the audience.

Finally, there are the broader considerations of what we have loosely called place semiotics. In Chapter 9 we will discuss what we call the semiotic aggregate – multiple semiotic systems in a dialogical interaction with each other. This is certainly a case of a semiotic aggregate. There is a street performer to watch, there is a poster kiosk to read, just to the left of this picture is the very striking St Stephen's Cathedral, and throughout the square are people doing a multitude of things, not least of which is observing each other as part of the very enjoyable city square scene. Each of these elements has an internal semiotic organization – the performer's performance, the events announced by each of the posters, the collective meaning of all of them which forms up the poster kiosk as a poster kiosk – and together they form the place semiotics which we call a nice afternoon in Stephansplatz in Vienna.

Geosemiotics is an integrative view of these multiple semiotic systems which together form the meanings which we call place. The interaction order, visual semiotics, and place semiotics have largely been studied up until now as different disciplinary interests. In each case the other aspects have been thought of as the context in which something happens. In studies of social interaction, for instance, the semiotics of texts, posters, images and the like as well as the meanings of the places in which these interactions occur are just part of the context of the focal interest – a conversation, for example. Cultural geographers, on the other hand, have given progressively more acute analyses of the ways in which places in time and space come to have subjective meanings for the humans who live and act within them. At the same time, however, the social interactions which occur within places are largely relegated to issues of context which are, perhaps, too fine-grained a focus to take into direct consideration. Studies of visual semiotics have largely treated the structures of meaning that lie within the frames of pictures and left what occurs outside of that frame for further study elsewhere. It is our goal in this book to provide an organizing sketch of how these three main systems might be integrated within a single perspective.

From social interaction to images to action in the world

As we have said there are three ways in which language can be located in the material world: the interaction order (including speech, movement, gesture), visual semiotics (including text and images), and place semiotics (all of the other non-linguistic symbols that directly or indirectly represent language). Geosemiotics analyzes the semiotic systems among which we take actions in the world. In that sense it is closely related to an action perspective on how meanings are made. What we would like to do in this book is to begin to make a linkage among work in discourse analysis, linguistics, and communication on the one hand and studies in other fields such as human geography (or cultural geography) which have taken as their primary focus the analysis of time and space in a broader perspective – what Lemke (2000a, 2000b) might call a slower timescale. Studies of discourse have focused primarily on two main entities – face-to-face social interactions and written texts. For good theoretical and methodological reasons the physical world in which social interactions occur has been summarized as being the context in which these social interactions take place. Text analysis, on the other hand, partly because it derives from literary analysis, has tended to focus on just what could be analyzed within the bounded frame of the text. Our interest in this book is to use a geosemiotic perspective to try to bring together the study of texts – albeit mostly very simple ones – the study of social interaction, and the study of the material world in which human actions take place. We speak of this intersection of multiple discourses as the semiotic aggregate which we will introduce and develop in Chapter 9.

In this sense our analysis here picks up and extends work begun in the 1940s by the Swedish geographer Torsten Hägerstrand. He set out eight principles by which human action could be related to the place of humans in time and space. Many geographers point to this work as the first modern attempt to integrate time as well as space into an analysis of place. Giddens (1984, 1991) also takes Hägerstrand's work as a point of departure.

The eight principles set out by Hägerstrand (1978: 123–124) were:

1   the indivisibility of the human being (and of many other entities living and non-living);
2   the limited length of each human life (and many other entities, living and non-living);
3   the limited ability of the human being (and many other indivisible entities) to take part in more than one task at a time;

4   the fact that every task (or activity) has a duration;
5   the fact that movement between points in space consumes time;
6   the limited packing capacity of space;
7   the limited outer size of terrestrial space (whether we look at a farm, a city, a country or the Earth as a whole); and
8   the fact that every situation is inevitably rooted in past situations.

He goes on to say,

> Life requires that the individual successively and without interruption associates himself with sets of entities emerging from his surrounding. Some elements are actively sought, others cannot be avoided. . .
>
> 1   other individuals,
> 2   indivisible objects (such as other living organisms, machines, tools),
> 3   divisible materials (such as air, water, minerals, foodstuffs), and
> 4   technology and other institutional domains.

In *Discourses in Place: Language in the Material World* our focus is somewhat more sharply defined than that of cultural geography. Our primary interest is in the ways in which language or discourse is part of this perennial weave of individuals, objects, time, and space. Here we refer to this as geosemiotics to emphasize that indexicality, action, and identity are all anchored in the physical spaces and real times of our material world.

Geosemiotics takes four elements to be central to our understanding of human action in the three-dimensional and multiply discursive spaces in which we live and act as we have noted above:

- social actor
- interaction order
- visual semiotics
- place semiotics

The social actor

The concept of human action begins, of course, with the acting human being. This is not quite as straightforward a concept as it might seem to us in ordinary life. Bateson (1972) pointed out many years ago that if there is one thing virtually all psychologists can agree upon it is that we do not have much conscious knowledge about the sources of our own actions. These sources are largely unconscious to us, always very partial, and largely rationalized after the fact. Since the 1930s and onward such thinkers as Freud but also Elias, Nishida, Piaget, and

Vygotsky, and more recently Bourdieu, have used the concept of *habitus* to cover what are really three separable aspects of the human person: sociocultural-psychological knowledge, the social actor or agent, and the physical body in space and time.

From the point of view of geosemiotics we want to keep in mind all three of these aspects of the human being in action in the world. In the first place a person brings into any moment of action all of his or her history of experience, knowledge (whether conscious or unconscious), and interests, motivations, and dispositions. This is important to geosemiotics because it is here we see that there is in all cases already a history of the meaningful use of any sign at the moment a person encounters it anew.

In the second place, the person is a social actor. Although it is strongly debated just how much agency (active, rational, conscious intention) any social actor might have in any situation, the position we take is that in most cases our actions are only vaguely purposive and conscious, and almost always they are multiple and complex. When we cross a busy intersection we might keep open a small window of attention to the traffic in the street and another small window on the pedestrian signal, but at the same time we are carrying on a conversation with a friend about things that happened at work the day before. As we shall see in Chapter 3, one of our main concerns in such cases is often simply showing ourselves to be a certain kind of person in a particular role performance – a sophisticated urbanite having a lunchtime conversation with a friend. To put this another way, whether or not the person consciously undertakes any particular action, that action will 'give off', as Goffman puts it (Chapter 3), a personal identity and a position in the social world that is available to others to see and to respond to. We simply cannot act in the world without indexing our own habitus on the one hand and the sociocultural and sociopolitical structures among which we act on the other.

Finally, as Hägerstrand pointed out six decades ago, a person is also a unified physical body moving in the physical world. Whether or not he or she intends to do so, as we have just noted, this body 'gives off' expression to anybody who is within view. A person who is extremely tired 'gives off' the expression of fatigue; one who is nervous 'gives off' this nervousness. A sophisticated urbanite out for a lunchtime walk 'gives off' irritation at a few drops of rain falling on his or her work clothing. A physically big person 'gives off' different mammalian signals from a physically small person, and, of course, we mostly 'give off' race, sex, and age through whatever other social role performance overlays we might choose to enact.

To summarize, we see humans in the physical world as bundles of histories – of language, of discourses, and experiences, of social and political performances, as juggling multiple social roles and performances, largely unconsciously, and as being physical bodies which carry and express genetic, social, and momentary dispositions which are never possible to fully occlude behind those socially constructed performances.

The interaction order

As we shall see in Chapter 3, we live our lives within elaborate socially constructed worlds of discourse and social interaction — what Goffman called *the interaction order*. This interaction order consists of the current, ongoing, ratified (but also contested and denied) set of social relationships we take up and try to maintain with the other people who are in our presence. Near the end of his life Goffman identified 11 main types, beginning with the single — a person alone in social space — through the conversational encounter among two or more participants, to a platform event in which one or more people produce a spectacle for the observation of others as we have seen in image 1.03 above. Each of these types of social encounter is a recognizable way of being together with others in the social space as a set of agreed upon social arrangements to maintain a kind of social interaction. While there is much sociocultural variation in the recognizable forms of the interaction order, in any society people recognize the difference between a casual conversation with friends and a ritual performance such as a wedding or funeral. And while these types of social interaction vary widely from society to society both in their structure and in the 'rules' for a good performance, there is no society that does not distinguish quite a variety of ways in which people come together within some interaction order for that society.

The 11 types of the interaction order that Goffman proposes are not universal in all societies, of course, as we have just said. They are constructed out of a very full repertoire of resources which are available in complex combinations in all societies. There are resources including the sense of time displayed by social actors, perceptual spaces, interpersonal distances, and the personal front embodied by social actors. In Chapter 3 through the early work of Edward T. Hall and Erving Goffman we will look at just some of the meaning systems which are available in any place we might find ourselves in the world. Hall, for example, distinguishes among five kinds of space:

- visual space
- auditory space
- olfactory space
- thermal space
- haptic (or tactile) space

From the point of view of a small conversational encounter the structure of auditory space is very important. We like to be able to talk comfortably without either shouting on the one hand or feeling like we need to whisper to keep from being overheard on the other. For a dinner party olfactory space is very important; a restaurant with offensive odors quickly loses its business.

Goffman uses the term 'sign equipment' for all of the meaningful signs (in the most general sense) that are available for participants in a social interaction out of which they can build their actions. This would include not only the 'atmosphere' of a good coffee shop or a restaurant or the busy environment of a city center shopping district, but all of the many discourses available in the form of other people's discourses, signs, shop logos, designed spaces for sitting out or relaxing, and passageways to get between destinations.

Our interest in the interaction order in *Discourses in Place*, then, is as a semiotic system of discourses in place. We are interested in the ways these different structures of social interaction are used by people to produce discourses in place – where do they feel comfortable having a chat and with whom, and how are these structures of social interaction themselves part of the 'world' for others who are in that same physical space? A conversation in an almost empty coffee shop can feel very different from that same conversation in a crowded coffee shop. The difference is not so much within the conversation itself but in the other conversations also occurring in the same place. *Those* discourses in this place are part of *this* discourse in the place.

All of these semiotic systems which we find 'in place' are part of the sign equipment we can and do use to produce our actions in the world. Our study here in *Discourses in Place* focuses primarily on this sign equipment and how it works, through indexicality, to produce meanings for our social actions (Chapters 4 through 9).

Visual semiotics

A conversation over coffee can be depicted in various ways within a visual frame. In Chapter 4 we examine how objects are constituted as visual wholes, whether two-dimensional pictures or sculpted figures, in the semiotics of visual space. Taking Halliday's social semiotic approach to grammar as a means of representing meaning potential, Kress and van Leeuwen (1996) analyze the compositional structures of visual images in terms of different interpretations of experience and different forms of social interaction. This 'grammar of visual design' is intended as a step toward training in 'visual literacy', which they see as quickly becoming a matter of survival in contemporary life, in the workplace in particular. Though global to the extent of being spread all over the globe, their visual semiotic is not universal but culturally specific, with a history of some five centuries in 'Western' cultures. With their examples of paintings, photographs, diagrams, and other two-dimensional representations as well as sculpture, they hope to stimulate the study of visual communication in non-Western societies, anticipating that elements such as center or margin, top or bottom will convey meanings and values differently where writing proceeds from right to left or top to bottom.

Rather than a mere extension or illustration of verbal text, Kress and van Leeuwen see the visual component of text as independently organized and structured with its own grammar. As we discuss in Chapter 4, systems represented may be narrative, with participants and vectors of action, or conceptual, including classificational taxonomies, analytical and symbolic processes, such as models in poses depicting classes of personal attributes. People, places, and objects in these systems are represented participants, in contrast to interactive participants – the human writers, artists, graphic designers or readers and viewers who produce and interpret images. Interactive participant systems include relationships between producer and represented participants, between represented participants and viewers, between producer and viewer. Types of representations include contact, with poses suggesting demand or offer, social distance whether intimate, social or impersonal, and attitudes of power or involvement. Visual semiotics allows among other things the analysis of social actors in the interaction order as represented pictorially.

Truth and reality are constructed visually through markers of modality such as color saturation, color differentiation, color modulation, contextualization, depth, brightness. In our society, truth is associated with naturalism or a high degree of correspondence between what we see with the naked eye and the visual representation of an object. Abstraction is generally associated with low modality, but in science and education abstract and decontextualized representations often convey a deeper truth.

The layout of text and images is seen to follow principles of composition with information value distributed in terms of center vs. periphery or polarized so that given information is presented on the left with new information on the right, or images of the ideal at the top of a painting with the real at the bottom. Salience may be conveyed through size, foregrounding, color, sharpness of definition, and other features. A third key element of composition is framing, with varying degrees of connection of information units.

Represented participant systems, modality, and composition all help make up the semiotic landscape of visual images and thus shape interpretations of personal experience and social interaction. Our interest in visual semiotics is in how the interaction order is represented visually on the one hand and in how placement of visual symbols affects their interpretation on the other.

Place semiotics

Geosemiotics considers 'non-semiotic' spaces where signs are prohibited as well as semiotic spaces which facilitate pictures, discourses, or actions. Of course any human action must take place somewhere in the material world of the physical universe. With the exception of a few astronauts we all live our lives here on the earth and the central thesis of geosemiotics is that exactly *where* on earth an action takes place is an important part of its meaning. It should not be surprising, then, that the 'natural' world is a central aspect of geosemiotics.

As we will see in Chapter 5, however, we should not be seduced by the word 'natural' into thinking that there is anywhere a world that is untouched by human meaning-making processes. Perhaps it might be argued that to a physicist or a chemist there is such a world, but from the point of view of human action there is not. As we discuss in Chapter 5, in some parts of this natural world such as in traditional China writing on the rock surfaces of mountains is felt to make them *more* natural; in other parts this is considered to be defacing their natural appearance. In western, science-based society we tend to think of the directions, north, south, east, and west as somehow pure and independent of any human construction. We have simply forgotten the source in an overlay of a kind of pure-science logic. Many people in the world tell their directions in reference to rivers: upstream, downstream, away from or toward the river. Island people such as those in Honolulu in the Hawai'ian Islands tell directions as Mauka (toward the mountains) and Makai (toward the ocean), Diamond Head (to the left if facing Makai – the ocean) and Ewa (to the right if facing Makai – the ocean).

From the point of view of geosemiotics everything from our location among mountains and rivers, oceans and deserts, cities and farms is part of the world which may be called upon by humans in taking particular actions. Spreading a white cream on the skin may 'mean' a very different thing on a beach in Hawai'i and in the streets of Helsinki in December to someone simply observing the action. A few days of vacation in Namur, Belgium during which the sun shines without a break gives very different meanings to the place, one's actions, and one's memories than a possibly more 'normal' few days of unrelieved rain.

Of the three geosemiotic systems, the interaction order, visual semiotics, and place semiotics, none of these is new or really newly developed here. What is new is the taking up of these three elements within a single and, we hope, coherent framework. In this way *Discourses in Place: Language in the Material World* tries to integrate well established work in psychology, social psychology, communication, discourse analysis, and human geography into a single framework by which we can consider the role of all of these working together in the production of human action. From this point of view, then, geosemiotics is the study of the role of the interaction order, visual semiotics, and place semiotics in discourses found in the material universe. In this sense it goes beyond the 'social situatedness' of social interaction research to a kind of geo-situatedness.

An outline of geosemiotics

Here we outline in full detail the three systems as they will be taken up in the following chapters as indicated.

The Interaction Order (Chapter 3)	Visual Semiotics (Chapter 4)
Resources	*Represented participants*
the sense of time	narrative
urgency	conceptual
monochronism/polychronism	
(multitasking)	*Modality*
perceptual spaces	color saturation
visual	color differentiation
auditory	color modulation
olfactory	contextualization
thermal	representation
haptic	depth
interpersonal distances	illumination
intimate	brightness
personal	
social	*Composition*
public	information
personal front	centered
sign equipment	circular
civil inattention	triptych
	center–margin
Units of the interaction order	polarized
single	left–right (given–new)
with	top–bottom (ideal–real)
file or procession	
queue	
contact	*Interactive participants*
service encounter	producer – image participants
conversational encounter	image participant – image
meeting	participant
people-processing encounter	image participant – viewer/reader
interview	
screening	
examination	
platform event	
celebrative occasion	

Place semiotics (Chapters 5 through 9)
'Non-semiotic' spaces (prohibition; 'naturalized')

(*Chapter 5*)
Semiotic spaces
      pictures
          code preference (*Chapter 6*)
              center — margin
              top — bottom
              left — right
              earlier — later
          inscription (*Chapter 7*)
              fonts, letterform
              material qualities
                permanence
                  or durability
                temporality
                  or newness
                quality
              layering: add-ons or
                extensions
              state changes
          emplacement (*Chapter 8*)
              decontextualized
              transgressive
              situated
                exophoric
                situated ('feng-
                  shui')

spaces (*Chapter 9*)
    frontstage or public
        exhibit/display
        passage
        special use
        secure
    backstage or private
discourses
    regulatory (e.g. municipal)
        vehicle traffic
            cars
            buses and
                trucks
            bicycles
            horse-drawn
                carts
        pedestrian traffic
        public notice
    infrastructural (e.g. municipal)
        public functional notice
        public label
    commercial (e.g. advertising)
    transgressive (e.g. graffiti)

The structure of *Discourses in place*

We live and act, we speak and we write in a world of real spaces and of real time. Indexicality is the pre-eminent feature of language and of semiotic systems that make reference to the real-time concrete spatial world in which we live. Geosemiotics is based on this understanding of indexicality. While virtually any and all signs are indexical, in Chapter 2 we focus on just three types of indexicality: space ('here', 'there'), social relationships ('I', 'you', 'we'), and time ('now', 'later', 'at 12 o'clock'). This provides the point of reference for the following chapters which turn their attention to the indexable world which is indexed by language.

Chapter 3 begins our geosemiotic analysis with the interaction order, the embodiment of indexicality in the human body. That is, we study the ways in which we use our bodies as social actors in the presence of others to produce meanings through four primary semiotic resources: the sense of time, perceptual spaces, interpersonal distances, and the personal front. Face-to-face communication is both the source of much of the indexicality of language in the material world and one of the main indexables. As we speak among friends we both talk about the world around us and we produce ourselves as something to be indexed by others. We not only have a conversation; others see that we are a conversational 'with' (to use Goffman's term).

The social groupings that we make as we communicate can be indexed through ordinary discourse or they may be represented in images and texts. Chapter 4 uses the visual semiotics of Kress and van Leeuwen (1996) as a theoretical model from which to develop a semiotic analysis of the images and signs that appear all around us in the world. We are particularly concerned with four of their sub-systems of meaning: represented participants, modality, composition, and interactive participants.

Chapters 2 through 4 provide us with the background understanding of social interaction on the one hand and the semiotics of representation of images and text on the other. Chapter 5 then provides a pivot from those studies to the central interests of geosemiotics, place semiotics or the ways in which the placement of discourse in the material world produces meanings that derive directly from that placement. Chapters 6 through 8 introduce three elements of place semiotics: code preference, inscription, and emplacement.

Signs in which multiple languages are used index the social worlds in which they are placed. In Quebec by law French appears in the upper position and in a more salient presentation than English or other languages. In Hong Kong it is English which is given preference in signs that are regulated by the government such as the signs naming streets. Chapter 6 takes up this system of code preference and extends features of Kress and van Leeuwen's visual semiotics to analyze the placement of linguistic codes in a sign as a way of signalling these legal and social relationships among languages in the speech community.

Inscription is to the non-human material world what embodiment is to the human world of discourse. In Chapter 3 we discuss the ways in which the personal front (clothing, posture, gesture and the rest) are used to signal role performances. In Chapter 7 we consider the material out of which a sign (or other semiotic system) is constructed as a meaning system. We consider four of these systems: fonts, physical materials, add-ons or extensions, and state changes.

Chapter 8 lies at the very heart of geosemiotics in that it is an analysis of the three systems of emplacement. A sign (or other form of discourse) may be decontextualized (it signals a complete independence of its placement in the world – brands and logos are good examples), situated (it is shaped by and shapes the material world in which it is placed – an exit sign derives its meaning from the exit and the exit is found because of the sign), or transgressive (it is in the wrong place or in some way violates conventions on emplacement – graffiti are the most obvious example).

We could look at discourses in place in the material world from one of two perspectives. From one point of view, if we pick a specific place on the earth, we will find at that place a semiotic aggregate of many discourses all in interaction with each other. This view is a kind of centripetal one that focuses on the gathering in of discourses to produce a particular place as a unique place on earth because of the multiple discourses which are found there as well as the unique actions which are afforded because of these discourses.

On the other hand if we take the point of view of a particular discourse we see that it is distributed very widely across many different times and places. This centrifugal view would show that whatever might be found in any single place would lead out into many other places and times. From this point of view what is unique about any particular place or time or action is the construction of that moment out of elements all found elsewhere but in different combinations of semiotic interaction.

Chapter 9 takes up these two points of view – a *place orientation* and a *discourse orientation* – to argue that the meaning of any discourse or any place must take into consideration other discourses in that place as well as other places where that discourse leads.

Finally, in Chapter 10 we bring the book to a close by returning to an *action orientation*. We iterate three fundamental principles of geosemiotics:

1   the principle of **indexicality**: all semiotic signs, whether embodied or disembodied, have as a significant part of their meaning how they are placed in the world.

2   the principle of **dialogicality**: all signs operate in aggregate. There is a double indexicality with respect to the meaning attached to the sign by its placement and its interaction with other signs. Each sign indexes a discourse that authorizes its placement, but once the sign is in place it is never isolated from other signs in its environment, embodied or disembodied. There is always a dynamic among signs, an intersemiotic, interdiscursive dialogicality.

3   the principle of **selection**: any action selects a subset of signs for the actor's attention. A person in taking action selects a pathway by foregrounding some subset of meanings and backgrounding others. Action is a form of selection, positioning the actor as a particular kind of person who selects among different meaning potentials a subset of pathways.

How to use *Discourses in place*

Each of the chapters of *Discourses in Place* except for Chapters 1, 5, and 10 has two sections, an opening section on Theory followed by a section on Practice. The Theory section introduces the central ideas of the chapter. The Practice section gives supplementary material as well as suggestions for activities to be done by students. There are many more activities given in the Practice sections of the book than can be accomplished by students within an academic year. In our teaching we have found it useful to vary our use of these activities. All of the Practice sections and activities should be read as there is both review and new material given in them.

Some of the activities can stimulate interesting class discussions with relatively little preparation outside of class. Other activities work very well as small group fieldwork projects, and ample class time should be allocated for presentation and discussion. In some cases students have found it useful to organize a full term project by doing a sequence of two or three activities from different chapters and making a coherent single presentation later in the course. In our experience many readers have found the activities we have given here stimulate their thinking about new projects we had not imagined. We believe that the Practice sections of these chapters should be treated very flexibly by making up new or replacement versions of these activities.

Finally, we have compiled a Glossary of the main terms we have used in *Discourses in Place*. This glossary will provide not only a quick reference for terms found in the text but it also will provide a short handbook of geosemiotics. We have carried just this glossary with us on field trips as a way to stimulate our thinking as we made observations of language around us in the world.

2 Indexicality

In Middle English the word 'discourse', from Latin *discursa*, meant 'running to and fro'. As speech and images now speed willy-nilly around the globe, it is a task of geosemiotics to tie language and the meanings it runs after to space, social relationships, and time. A plot of land in what is now named British Columbia has been called 'Place where Happiness Dwells' from time immemorial by Dunne-za and Cree Indians. With Treaty 8, signed in 1899, it became known as 'IR-172' (Ridington 1990). Discourse about the 'Place where Happiness Dwells' became a nightmare in a court trial that lasted 40 days, with the outcome that 'IR-172' was not recognized by federal law as Indian land.

It is not our purpose to deplore or explicate or even try to summarize the history of geopolitical transfer of land ownership. All we can hope to do in this book is to outline the geosemiotic systems, the grammar of place indexicality, by which such battles have been fought. In our own research in Hong Kong, for example, we documented the return of Hong Kong to Chinese sovereignty with photographs of signs which index spatial, sociopolitical, and temporal relationships (Chapter 7). Like the signs prohibiting nude bathing, these point to actions in the social order using visual semiotics to relate these actions to places on earth. This property of language, that it makes part of its meaning because of where it is in the world, is called 'indexicality'.

Icons, indexes, and symbols

Icons, indexes, and symbols are the full inventory of the ways in which we can signal our meanings to others. To put it briefly, a sign can resemble the object (icon), it can point to or be attached to the object (index), or it can be only arbitrarily or conventionally associated with the object (symbol).

Icon

The pictures along the base of an escalator in image 2.01 tell us iconically what actions are expected or not expected when ascending the escalator. We are told, through these icons, to hold the handrail with one hand while holding a child with the other, to stand straight and not to put our feet on the side rails, to hold packages with one hand and the handrail with the other, and not to try to transport large objects. Two of these are direct iconic signs. That is, they are pictures of the world that is meant by the sign. Two combine the icon with the symbol 'X' (in red) which cancels the meaning of the icon: The 'X' does not look like anything in the world; it only conventionally or arbitrarily means 'Do Not'.

2.01

Index

An **index**, the second type of sign, points to its meaning. Maybe the most common sort of index in daily life, at least in signs in public life, is the arrow. In photo 2.02 we see a sign that includes both an icon and an index. It shows a picture

2.02

of a train, an icon, and an arrow showing the direction in which the trains can be found, an index.

Another type of index, of course, is the simple gesture of pointing. In Chapter 3 we will come more directly to the question of the ways meanings are embodied by humans.

Symbol

Symbols are the third type of sign. They are completely arbitrary or conventional signs that do not resemble their meaning and do not point to it. We have already seen the red 'X' on the escalator sign which cancels the iconic meaning in the picture. The most common symbols in our lives are those of written language. We see so many of these, and this book consists so much of these arbitrary symbols, that we can easily come to think of them as the most fundamental form by which we make meanings. Since Ferdinand de Saussure it has been emphasized by semioticians that the relationship between signs and the objects they represent is entirely arbitrary, but this arbitrariness may be only on the surface. Certainly symbols such as Å, ζ, or Ⴊ seem opaque to us even though they are available on the word processor we are using to write this text. Unless we know what they mean and how to use them to create further arbitrary signs – words – they basically mean nothing to us.

We should not forget, though, that even though these symbols are largely arbitrary to us and even though we use them arbitrarily, some or all of them once had iconic meanings. For example, the letter we now call 'd' was once a drawing of a tent door, the name of which began with that sound; the word delta maintains a slight memory of this history. Likewise, the letter we now call 'g' was once a drawing of the hump of a camel. The word 'camel' is derived from this letter, called 'gimel' in Hebrew. While symbols may be arbitrary or purely conventional, often this is only because their history and iconicity have been forgotten. This reminds us that our current icons might rather quickly become purely arbitrary.

A good example of this process can be seen in this shot of the 'icons' on the desktop of the computer being used to draft this chapter in 2.03. The 'computer' icon does look like a computer, but not like *this* computer which is a laptop model. The telephone looks like a telephone, but not like any telephone in this house, and certainly it does not look like a cell phone. The 'icon' for the photo-editing software uses an oil painter's palette, but of course there is nothing of the sort involved in the CD and book which were the only physical objects connected to that software.

2.03

Icons, indexes, and symbols; iconicity, indexicality, and symbolism

We have said that there are three types of signs, but there is a major problem with thinking that signs come in three classes. This may lead us to think that any sign must be classifiable within one of these three classes, and of course we might then go so far as to think they cannot also be classified in any of the others. In fact, as we have already seen, signs often come together in combinations of all three types of signs. And as we will see further, in many cases, perhaps in all cases indexicality is involved in the making of any meanings at all. In a sense it might be more accurate to say that there are two types of signs, icons and symbols, and that all signs achieve their meanings through properties of indexicality.

The sign in 2.04 from the Mass Transit Railway in Hong Kong uses an icon of a hamburger and a soft drink with the international 'prohibition' symbol – the red

2.04

circle with a diagonal line across it – to indicate that no food or drinks are allowed. This part of the sign, then, uses both an icon and a symbol. Beyond that, though, there is also a further message. In English it says, 'Let's keep the train clean' and the equivalent in Chinese above that. In this way it uses the symbolic systems of two languages to make this highly redundant message.

Incidentally, to anticipate our discussion in Chapter 4 on visual semiotics, the iconic part of this sign is in the upper (ideal) section of the whole sign and the linguistic part of the sign is in the lower (real) section which indicates the maker of this sign considers the text the 'real' or more significant part of this message. The photo does not show it clearly, but this interpretation is borne out by the very fine print at the bottom which cites the municipal regulations that are the basis of this prohibition.

There is an aspect of indexicality in this sign which is the most important for us in the long run. That is this: *the sign only has meaning because of where it is placed in the world.* Image 2.04 which prohibits food on the MTR does not specify *where* (in the image part at least) this prohibition is to apply. It is because the sign is fixed on the inside of the train that we read this prohibition to apply in this place, not elsewhere.

Signs that identify businesses are more clearly indexical in this manner. In photo 2.05 we see a sign which tells us that the business under that sign is 'Pacific Coffee'.

The sign uses an icon in the center – a steaming cup of coffee – and the symbols in the phrase 'Pacific Coffee Company' as well as 'the perfect cup' within the circle around the icon to identify itself. But the sign achieves its main meaning through the indexicality of being located above the entrance door to the shop. This sign does not only mean 'there is such a thing as "the perfect cup"', or 'one can find the perfect cup at Pacific Coffee Company'; it means 'This place here where

2.05

this sign is affixed is the Pacific Coffee Company' (presumably where one will find
the perfect cup of coffee).

This is the aspect of indexicality that is of greatest interest to us in this book.
Whether a sign is an icon, a symbol, or an index, there is a major aspect of its
meaning that is produced only through the placement of that sign in the real world
in contiguity with other objects in that world. This is the focus of the field of
geosemiotics.

Finally two more signs will make clear that indexicality is part of the
interpretation of any sign in several ways. In images 2.06 and 2.07, fire exit signs,
the running figure iconically shows a person escaping from flames. The arrow
shows, through indexicality, which way to run. But the icon itself is also indexical
in that it shows the figure running in the same direction as the arrow. That is, in
our data of many examples from a dozen countries of this fairly universal icon for
emergency exit, we have never seen this running figure facing in the direction

2.06   2.07

opposite to the exit. The figure is not only iconic in showing running, it is also indexical in pointing the direction. This is a question to which we will return, however, in Chapter 4 when we look at the question of the information system in signs and then again in Chapter 8 when we take up the problem of emplacement and situated semiotics.

There is a third indexicality involved here in these two signs which has to do with the physical placement of these signs in the world (Chapter 8). Not only do these signs mean 'run in this direction away from the flames', they mean this from the point where the signs are placed. While the signs were being painted in the paint shop or being carried up to be placed here in this location it would be absurd to take them as meaning to run in the direction they happened to be laid on the painter's table or on the workman's cart. Only when they are affixed to the appropriate wall does this indexical meaning come into force. 'Run that way from this point.' This is the meaning we have tried to capture in the title of this book: *Discourses in Place*.

Indexicality in language

The questions: 'What is this?' or 'What is that?' show the problem of indexicality in language. To get the meaning of 'this' or of 'that' the listener must look to the world in the environment of the speaker to locate a potential meaning. This meaning might be clued by a gesture (the speaker is pointing at something or holding up something to view) but even so, the object or space indexed also requires a semiotic analysis.

It is said that the name 'Canada' was exactly this sort of mistake. The explorer gestured down from the hill on which he was standing and asked, 'What is this place?' 'This' in the mind of the explorer was intended to mean 'this place: What do you call this land?' but the answer given was 'a group of huts or teepees'. While this may be apocryphal, it tells us that even a gesture alone cannot solve the problem of knowing what the language is indexing.

Anthropological linguists have studied indexicality in many languages of the world. Although it is fair to say that every utterance in language is indexical (along with its other meanings), the main systems of indexicality that have been studied are demonstratives, deictic adverbials, personal pronouns, and tense. The demonstratives ('this', 'that') depend for our interpretation on whether or not we can establish what in the real world is being indexed. The personal pronouns, ('I', 'you', 'we', and so forth) likewise must look to the context for their interpretation. Who is it saying 'I'? Where is the gaze directed when the speaker says, 'You'? Deictic adverbs ('here', 'there', 'now', 'then') take their meaning from some common and presupposed reference point which is the only basis for interpretation. When the speaker says, 'We won't have time to do that now,' does he or she mean within the next sentence or two, within this social event, within this calendar year? A mother said to her child, 'We'll do that sometime,' and the child's retort was, 'I know what "sometime" means; it means never. I want to do it now.'

Of course tense – the sense of past, present, and future – depends on some commonly indexed notion of when is the present. When she asks, 'What are you doing?' and he answers, 'I'm cooking dinner,' is she being fair to complain, 'No, you're not; you're reading the newspaper'? The answer depends on when in the real world we are to understand the present tense ('cooking dinner') to apply. Is it during this period of time, even though he will also do other things, for example, while the pot comes to the boil?

Major indexicals in language

The main indexicals which have been studied by linguists are demonstratives and deictic adverbials, personal pronouns, and tense and time adverbials.

Demonstratives and deictic adverbials

We often take indexicality in language for granted. Demonstrative pronouns in English are dispensed with fairly summarily in *Harbrace College Handbook*.

> **demonstratives** Four words that point out (*this, that, these, those*) (Hodges et al. 1990: 558)

There is a simple distinction between an object which is 'here' and one which is 'there', between singular and plural. These distinctions are put forward in this handbook as if there is nothing at all complex or problematic in knowing how to use them. It is assumed that it is outside of the purview of a handbook on language to worry about how we know what 'this' or 'that' might refer to, or to look at the related deictic (pointing) adverbs, 'here' and 'there'. It seems these are quite outside the interest of someone concerned with correct usage of language.

Nevertheless, as Hanks (1990) points out, these ideas of here and there are far from simple. The sentence

I've been very busy since I've been here.

might mean since I came to the office today. It might mean since I came back from vacation this past summer. Or it might even mean since I came to the US from abroad. Pinning down just how wide the scope of the meaning of 'here' is will depend on further contextualizations. It depends on knowing specifically for people who use these words how big the circle of here is, how wide the boundary between here and there is, and how many concentric circles of here there might be that can be indexed. In other words, our interpretation of the indexicals 'this' and 'that', 'here' and 'there', depends on also having a meaning system of the indexable in the world – what we call a geosemiotic analysis. As Hanks has said, in every case the concreteness of 'here' or 'there' (anywhere that is not 'here') is a sociocultural construction depending on how the users of language in that situation see the world and also how they see themselves in it.

The British newspaper *The Guardian* on Wednesday January 16, 2002 had a feature on their website awarding prizes in a competition to write a haiku on the theme of the new money of the European Union, the euro. As readers will know, the United Kingdom is a member of the European Union, but as of writing had nevertheless chosen not to join in the changeover to the new money. This leads to the ambiguous situation of being a member in one domain but not in another. This ambiguity was captured nicely by a haiku by Steve Wiseman as quoted in *The Guardian*.

> the euro is here
> but not actually here
> it's just over there

The deictics 'here' and 'there' are played with quite subtly in this haiku. The first 'here' is both here in time (as in the holidays are here) and here within the European Union. Thus, the euro is now the currency of the European Union, of which 'we' (the UK) are members. But then this 'here' is qualified: 'not actually here'. That is to say, not here in the UK. The domain has now shifted from the broader sociopolitical and geographical 'here' of the EU to the narrower nation of the UK. 'Just over there' is equally polysemous. 'Just over there' might be read as very close by in the sentence, 'It's just over there by you – not far away'. It might also be read as an exclusive 'just' as in 'it's only over there, not here'.

Schegloff (1972) made it clear that even when we move away from the purely indexical forms in language such as the demonstratives or deictic adverbs, any phrase which requires us to locate in space requires us to know or presuppose something about ourselves and others and our respective places in the world. If someone asks, 'Where do you work?' we might answer, 'Over at that desk', or we might answer 'At Georgetown University', or 'At a university in Washington, DC', or even 'At a university in the US'. The answer depends, through indexicality – or what is also called *situatedness* (Goffman 1959) as we will see in Chapter 3 – on whether we were in the general vicinity of my desk, within the university, in some area outside the university but within some social circle in which the name of the university would have a meaning, someplace outside of

Washington and among people who are not familiar with universities, or entirely outside of the US.

Even with these subtleties taken into consideration, demonstratives in English are relatively simple compared to those in some other languages. Demonstrative pronouns in Spanish are a bit more complex than English ones in that a three-way distinction is made. English indexicals imply an indexable world which has basically just two spaces, one close to the speaker and one at a distance. These are indexed by 'this' and 'that' (which correspond to 'here' and 'there'). Spanish demonstrative pronouns imply an indexable world of three spaces, one which is near the speaker, one that is near the hearer, and one that is at a distance from both speaker and hearer (Table 2.1). For our purposes here we are setting aside the marking of gender as well as singular and plural.

One of the things a person who speaks only English needs to learn when learning Spanish is how to sort out the world into three types of indexable space instead of two. Of course we can do this in English when we need to. We can correct a misunderstanding of 'there' by saying, 'No, right there next to you,' or 'No, way over there, see where I'm pointing.' We don't want to give the mistaken impression that we can only think in the terms given to us by the language, though it is clear that it is more trouble in English than in Spanish to be clear about the indexability of objects in the spatial world we are pointing to or talking about.

Other languages can be very much more complex than either of these European languages. Yup'ik Eskimo is spoken in the Lower Kuskokwim River area of Alaska which is a low, rolling to flat tundra plain that is laced with rivers and ponds running out to the Pacific Ocean. The built environment is relatively simple in that most buildings with a few exceptions in the city of Bethel are small houses of a few rooms. The public school is often the largest building within the daily

Table 2.1 Demonstrative pronouns in Spanish

Singular		Plural		Singular	Plural	English gloss
Masculine	Feminine	Masculine	Feminine	Neuter	Neuter	
éste	ésta	éstos	éstas	esto	estos	'this, these' (near speaker)
ése	ésa	ésos	ésas	eso	esos	'that, those' (near listener)
aquél	aquélla	aquéllos	aquéllas	aquello	aquellos	'that, those' (away from both)

Source: Duran *et al.* (1978)

environment of most people and these schools are mostly only about 20 or 30 years old.

We might also say that the weather in this region can be very severe both in terms of temperature and winds. There is often blowing snow, mist, and fog. Perhaps it is for these reasons that the Yup'ik Eskimo language indexes a world that makes considerably finer linguistic distinctions than are commonly made in English. For example, the 31 demonstrative pronouns in Yup'ik Eskimo (Table 2.2) divide up the indexable world of spaces into large expanses of land or water, closed, restricted or confined areas such as the inside of a house or building, and spaces that are not clearly visible, presumably because they are out of range of sight or because of obscuring conditions. The language also partitions objects into a group that are lengthy or moving, perhaps boats on water, and those that are stationary or, if moving, are doing so within a confined space. This indexable world also includes the distinctions of Spanish between a 'there' that is close to

Table 2.2 Demonstrative Pronouns in Yup'ik Eskimo

Extended	Restricted	Obscured	English gloss
man'a	una		'this' or 'the one near speaker'
tamana	tauna		'that' or 'the one near listener'
		imna	'the aforementioned one'
ukna			'the one approaching speaker'
augna	ingna	amna	'the one over there, going away from speaker'
agna	ikna	akemna	'the one across there'
qaugna	kiugna	qamna	'the one inland, inside, up river'
qagna	keggna	qakemna	'the one outside'
un'a	kan'a	camna	'the one below, toward river'
unegna	ugna	cakemna	'the one down river, on the coast, or by the exit'
paugna	pingna	pamna	'the one up there, away from river'
pagna	pikna	pakemna	'the one up above'
	kina		'who?, what person?'

Source: Reed *et al.* (1977)

the hearer and one that is at a distance from either speaker or hearer. As Reed et al. (1977) note,

> Demonstrative pronouns in the *extended* column indicate either large expanses of land or water, or objects that are lengthy or moving. Those in the *restricted* column indicate objects that are stationary (or moving within a confined area), fairly small in extent, relatively near, and visible. Those in the *obscured* column indicate objects that are farther away and not clearly in sight.
>
> (p. 257)

Personal pronouns

The demonstratives and deictic adverbs are focused on the sociocultural conception of the spaces we live in. In contrast to these, personal pronouns index the people with whom we are speaking. As we all know, and as we will discuss in much more detail in Chapter 3, it is essential in social situations to constantly monitor who is within the current social gathering and who is on the outside of it. When we are having a conversation at dinner in a restaurant, there is a clear difference in the currently ratified conversational roles between the diners at the table and the waiter who comes to take an order or to deliver the ordered dishes. If one says, 'Would you please give me another fork?' we know this to be addressed to the waiter and not to one's dinner partner. On the other hand, 'Would you please give me another chance?' is likely to be understood as a very intimate statement for the partner to hear and respond to and not to be taken up by the waiter, even if he should be within hearing range.

The personal pronouns such as the English 'I', 'you', 'he' index the world of people and social relationships through which we move much like the demonstratives index the physical spaces in which we live. It is equally important and difficult to specify what it is about these social worlds that is indexable by the personal pronouns. How do we *know* that it would be socially wrong for the dinner partner to go to another table to fetch a fork instead of the waiter, or for the waiter to answer, 'O.K., I'll give you another chance; what would you like to order?' Of course situational humor is based on exactly this sort of intentional misreading of the indexable social spaces of our worlds. Our purpose in Chapter 3 will be to show how those social spaces which are indexed by personal pronouns (and of course they are indexed in many other ways well) are constructed as complex but very intelligible semiotic systems.

The photos in 2.08, 2.09, and 2.10 show three stages of a lunch conversation which has been interrupted by a cell phone call. In the first (2.08) the man is listening to his partner and we see this in the downcast eyes and the orientation of his face and body in her direction. When he receives his telephone call he begins

2.08   2.09

2.10

to turn his body away from her and in 2.09 we see that both his face and gaze are focused at some distance from the personal space which the two occupy at the table. Finally, in 2.10 after he has closed his telephone conversation he returns his gaze to his partner at the table and their conversation resumes. This conversationalist has used body orientation and gaze to index the sharp division in the social relationships between him and his lunch partner on the one hand and between him and the caller on the other. It is this indexable social world of social relationships that the personal pronouns index along with gaze, body orientation, gesture, as well as other means which will be taken up in Chapter 3 on interaction order.

Before leaving the personal pronouns behind, we would like to note that there is an interesting twist on indexicality in a number of languages such as Navaho and Chipewyan, both grouped by linguists within the Athabaskan family. In English we make the three-way distinction among the speaker (or the speaker's group in the case of the plural 'we'), the hearer (or the hearer's group in the case of the plural 'you' – which of course is phonologically identical to the singular), and other parties which are not currently socially ratified as participants in the exchange. These are 'he', 'she', or 'it'.

In many languages of the world these personal pronouns are further complicated. Mandarin Chinese in Beijing distinguishes in many cases between an inclusive 'we' and an exclusive 'we'. That is, if I say 'we're' going to dinner, there is one pronoun to mean 'all of us who are here right now, including you the person I am speaking to'; there is another pronoun to mean 'those of us who are included within my own circle but not including the person I am speaking to.' There are, of course, many other languages which make this distinction. The indexable social world becomes one in which it is easy to make clear whether a person you are speaking to is being invited at the moment or not. Those of us who speak less complex languages would often like to have this pronoun to avoid uncomfortable embarassments.

In the Athabaskan language family, there is a third person indefinite pronominal prefix (in some cases called a fourth person), dji- in Navaho (Reichard 1951) and ts'e- in Chipewyan (Li 1946) which seems to have as its main function to dodge indexicality. This pronominal prefix is used specifically to dodge saying explicitly who you are talking to or about. While linguists have not fully specified what are the circumstances in which this third indefinite person is used, we do know that it is often used as a polite or indirect index in place of the more direct 'you'. At Arctic Village, Alaska, for example, some people who predominantly speak Gwich'in (Kutchin), another Athabaskan language, use the English third person 'he' in this 'fourth person' way. A man came to our house and said something like, 'I visited him earlier today but he wasn't at home.' Only after some time did we discover that he was speaking about one of the authors to whom he was speaking at the time. We might have expected, 'I visited you earlier today but you weren't at home.' Like many other forms in European languages such as the indefinite third person 'one', the pronoun is used to make an indirect indexing of some social participant, perhaps for reasons of politeness.

We should also note the use of 'someone' in colloquial uses of English as when we say, 'Someone left a package at the door.' Naturally this can be inverted to become highly indexical as when a mother might say, 'Someone isn't eating his breakfast quickly enough.'

Tense and time adverbials: Now and then

We discussed the deictic adverbs 'here' and 'there' above in connection with the demonstratives 'this' and 'that'. Those adverbials, along with the demonstratives, index the spaces within which we live. We have seen that these can be rather different from language to language, and hence, from culture to culture. There is another comparable relationship between tense (past, present, future) and the deictic time adverbs 'now' and 'then'.

We can imagine this conversation:

A: Shall we go for lunch now?

B: Well, I'm not quite ready. Let's go at 12 o'clock.

A: O.K., I'll see you then.

The indexicals here are the time adverbials 'now' and 'then', the future tense 'will see', and what might seem to be an absolute time reference, '12 o'clock'. We need to make reference to the world of these people, A and B, to know how large the expanse of 'now' really is; we only know that it does not include being ready for lunch. We can also see in the 'not quite ready', not in themselves thought of as indexicals, that we do have an indication of placement in time that is much different from saying, 'not at all ready'. 'Not quite ready' tells us that the distance from the 'now' is relatively brief; 'not at all ready' tells us that it is a much longer time until noon.

But the absolute clock time, '12 o'clock' is also indexical much in the same way that locatives can only be interpreted by positioning oneself in space. This absolute clock time cannot mean 12 o'clock tomorrow. This impossibility is constrained doubly by the language – 'not quite', the contrast to 'now'–and the sociocultural knowledge that A and B are talking about the next lunch, not some lunch.

Further tests of this groundedness in time of the time adverbials and tense as well as the absolute clock time could be seen in this hypothetical variation on the conversation above:

A: Shall we go for lunch now?

B: Well, I'm not quite ready. Let's go at 12 o'clock.

A: Uh, it's two minutes to twelve right now.

A's rejoinder tells us that the absolute time indication indexes a time significantly longer than 'in a few minutes'. If the lunch time is within the 'now', 'in a few minutes' would be appropriate. If the lunch time is within the 'then' (that is outside of 'now'), then absolute clock time can be used.

Of course it takes a rather full ethnographic study of the uses of time within a particular sociocultural group to establish these rings of time about the 'now'. For our purposes here, it is enough to see that in the same way that space is semiotically partitioned into some 'here' and some 'there', time is also partitioned into 'now' and 'before' and 'later'. These partitionings are very complex but must be understood among participants in a communication for the other meanings to work.

One final example of indexicality in time can be seen in a conditional road sign in Washington, DC (image 2.11). The readings are so complex that we were only able to work it out by taking a photograph and going home to study it.

The most fundamental message seems to be 'DO NOT ENTER' as this is established with the international symbol – the red circle with the prohibition bar. This is conditional, however, as the prohibition on entry is in force only Monday

2.11

through Friday from 6:00–10:15 am and not on holidays. Above that central prohibition are double arrows indexing the driver's direction of movement. In other words there IS entry into this road from 3:00–7:00 pm, again on Monday through Friday, holidays excepted. Finally, at the bottom we see that at all other times the road allows two-way traffic.

With time to study this sign it is possible to see that this road of two lanes has three conditions of travel at different times of the day, different days of the week, and depending on whether it is a normal calendar day or a holiday. Clearly the meaning of this sign is only interpretable by positioning the reader in time on three different time scales – the hour of the day, the day of the week, and the workday–holiday annual calendar.

It should be obvious to the reader that this sign is uninterpretable in real time for a driver who arrives at this point and tries to decide if it is safe or allowable to enter the road. Three points of indexability must be referenced first: What time is it now? What day of the week is it? Is it a holiday? We would guess that almost anybody would find that it takes a bit of reflection to be certain of all three of these time conditions of the current moment. Having that anchor point in time settled, then, of course there is the problem of sorting out how to read the other indexicals – the arrows on the sign.

Indexicality of the social actor

The uninterpretability of the sign in 2.11 derives from another source which is extremely important to a geosemiotic analysis. The driver of this car is positioned in time and space. The car is in motion at a particular speed, there are social prohibitions on stopping dead in the flow of traffic, and a decision must be made about the action to be taken. This places a real-time window on the driver's reading of this sign which in all of the cases we know about makes it a simpler decision to keep on driving without making a turn, or risking turning into oncoming traffic.

Here we have concentrated primarily on the indexicality of language and other signs in the world. At the same time, however, we want to emphasize that the interpreter of any sign is also in the world taking action in real time. Such indexicals as 'now' or 'that' are not just a matter of the world outside of the social actor, but are also indexical by the position and actions and psychological states of the social actor. As social actors move through time, time itself sets limits on interpretability. 'Now' becomes 'a few minutes' ago rather quickly. 'Here' becomes 'there' as one moves through space.

In Chapter 3 we will take up many matters having to do with the embodiment of meanings in the persons of social actors in the interaction order Goffman described. Here we want to remind ourselves in closing that indexicality works not as an abstract or objectivist system of reference but as a lived, real-time process by which meanings are made.

PRACTICE

Indexicality in space, social relationships, and time

Space

While there are many aspects of indexicality in language and in other semiotic systems, our focus will be on just three of these kinds of indexicality. The activities below focus on indexicality in space (deictic adverbials [here, there] or demonstratives [this, that]), in social relationships (personal pronouns [I, we, you, he, she, it, they]), and in time (time adverbials and noun phrases [now, then, later, at 12 o'clock]).

Assignment

Make a collection of deictic adverbs or demonstratives in news stories or in advertising copy and write a brief analysis for each item of what

must be known by the reader to determine the scope of each of these indexicals. Try to fill this out with evidence of how that can be known.

Alternatively, go about asking people questions that will require indexical clarification such as 'What's that?' and write a brief analysis of what sort of counter questions and other means are required to clarify the indexable objects in the world (such as, 'You mean that red one?')

Observations

If you do the alternate assignment, make careful observations of the ways in which people use their bodies in deixis – pointing, orientation of their faces, gaze, and so forth as they clarify the objects they are indexing.

Social relationships

We often think of the pronouns as operating only in face-to-face communications in which 'I' indexes the person speaking, 'you' indexes the person being addressed and so forth. In discourses which occur in public such as in advertising and public notices pronouns are also used and their interpretation is often quite ambiguous.

The hand-written sign in 2.12 tells someone that someone has *Real* Boston Cream Pie. Again, the interpretation of the 'we' here is based on seeing the sign posted on the window of a small family-style restaurant.

Assignment

Write a three-page analysis of a dozen or so signs. These can be public notices or advertisements. Indicate in your analysis what are the persons being indexed (both as producers of the signs or notices and as the receivers/viewers) and, more importantly, how this indexicality is determined.

Camerawork

Take pictures of public notices and/or advertisements. This is usually easiest to do in city centers or other public places where there is a high density of traffic. Be sure to include in your photos enough of the context to be able to determine the basis of the indexicality.

2.12

Observations

Your observations in this activity will be fairly simple. The main concern is to see enough of the context where the sign is posted to be able to determine the bases of indexicality for the interpretation of the sign. For example, if the sign says 'No Admittance' how is it determined *who* is prohibited from entering and who is allowed to pass?

Time

As we saw above, many communications, especially in public notices such as in 2.11, are time referenced. In order to know what it is legal to do, one needs to know what time and what day it is.

Assignment

Prepare a display of time-indexed photos you have taken or that you have clipped from magazines, brochures, or other news sources. Annotate your display from the point of view of how it is determined how to pin down the time. For example, 'today's' weather is time indexed on another part of the newspaper page where the day's date is given.

Observations

Be sure to observe how the time-indexing is established or confirmed. For example, 'Today's soup' on a restaurant window seen after closing time or before opening in the morning is ambiguous as it might mean 'the day now finished' or 'the day next time we're open'.

3 Interaction order

THEORY

The human body indexes the world

Our bodies as humans cannot fail to anchor us in the real, physical world in which we are performing as social actors. Whether we are actively trying to communicate a particular idea or position for ourselves or just trying to be nearly invisible, a 'fly on the wall' to some other social interaction, our bodies take up space, they take up particular postures, they make movements or are expressively still. Whatever we do, we communicate *something* to those who are there to view us as objects in their worlds. The general term which includes all of the ways in which we may be together with others in the world is the interaction order. We may be alone as what Goffman calls singles or we may be watching a sporting event together with hundreds of thousands of others in what he calls a platform event. However we organize ourselves, we cannot fail to project some set of relationships which group us together with some others in our vicinity and apart from the rest.

As we have said in Chapter 2, our language inevitably indexes us as well as the others in our world as we speak. A simple comment like, 'Look at that!' implies a place in space where the speaker is positioned, a place where the listener is positioned, and a third place where the spectacle to be looked at is located. 'Let's go,' implies a grouping of some sub-set of the people in the world as a social group which is indexed by 'us' in 'Let's'. Every utterance places us in some implied grouping of the interaction order at the same time that it places the rest of the world either to be included in that grouping or to be excluded from it. We simply cannot use language without implying the groupings of the interaction order.

Here in Chapter 3, then, we will first look at some of the resources by which we enact the social performances of the interaction order and then we will briefly enumerate the main units of the interaction order which have been identified and researched by sociologists and social psychologists. Our first focus is on the main

The Interaction Order

Resources

        the sense of time

                urgency

                monochronism/polychronism

        perceptual spaces

                visual

                auditory

                olfactory

                thermal

                haptic

        interpersonal distances

                intimate

                personal

                social

                public

        personal front

                sign equipment

                civil inattention

Units of the interaction order

        single

        with

        file or procession

        queue

        contact

        service encounter

        conversational encounter

        meeting

        people-processing encounter

                interview

                screening

                examination

        platform event

        celebrative occasion

semiotic resources out of which we construct the entities of the interaction order which are so central to the production and interpretation of discourses in place. There are four of these which we will discuss:

- the sense of time
- perceptual spaces
- interpersonal distances
- personal front

Each of these is a resource by which we take up social or psychological positions in relation to others who are present in the same social-physical space and time. Together they are the main elements out of which we produce what Goffman named the 'interaction order'.

Much has been written elsewhere on these systems in the pioneering studies of Edward T. Hall and of Jurgen Ruesch and Weldon Kees as well as, of course, the now extended line of research developed from their original insights; the fourth of these, personal front, makes reference to Erving Goffman's concept of the overall 'kit' or sign-equipment from clothing to wearable technology (wristwatches, pens, PDAs (Personal Digital Assistants), cell phones, stethoscopes, and the like) that one assembles to carry and produce the identities of daily activities. The non-personal side of Goffman's role performance, the situational front, is addressed as 'place semiotics' in Chapter 9 on Discourses in Time and Space and Chapter 10 on Indexicality, Dialogicality, and Selection in Action.

Our focus here in this chapter is not on nonverbal communication in itself as this is the subject matter of many other books. Our interest is in what is indexable – what language can point to – in the embodiment of language. To put this another way, our first purpose is to return to the classic nonverbal research to see that indexicality in language must necessarily make reference to such semiotic systems. Then we will move on in following chapters to examine how these somatic systems are at the root of much of the visual semiotics of image and graphic design. Then in the final chapters we will come to ways in which somatic meaning (nonverbal communication), visual semiotics (the grammar of visual design) and place semiotic resources come together when we move as social actors through physical spaces.

In most cases, of course, the different somatic or nonverbal systems work together simultaneously. The phrase 'camping friends', for example, indexes in the two academic colleagues in photo 3.01 aspects of their personal front in this situation such as their jeans and work shirts. The phrase also indexes their sense of time (relaxed – they stand and talk as if in no hurry whatsoever), the perceptual space (they are outdoors by a picnic table) and their position in relationship to each other (close to intimate personal distance).

3.01

Geosemiotics and Edward T. Hall

Edward T. Hall is one of the most influential anthropologists of our time. When Hall's *The Silent Language* first appeared in 1959 it seems it was read by everybody. In the subsequent 40 years much of his work has become part of the commonsense of our understanding of social life. When his book first came out the most striking points for most readers were probably that

1   culture *is* communication and communication *is* culture,
2   much of what governs our daily lives is outside our own awareness of the processes by which it is happening, and
3   the vast amount of miscommunication we experience when we deal with others is a result of this 'out-of-awareness' aspect of communication.

This point that that much of our communication happens outside of our own awareness of it, was not new, of course, as it is a primary tenet of psychoanalytical theory. Nevertheless, this has become a foundational basis for much of our understanding of cross-cultural and intercultural communication in the years since Hall's first books.

Probably what is best remembered of Hall's first work is his emphasis on the sociocultural patterning of time. In fact, one could think of his first book being about time and the second one, *The Hidden Dimension,* being about space, though both ideas are touched upon in both books.

The Hidden Dimension followed the *The Silent Language* by seven years in 1966; the paperback Anchor edition followed in 1969. Hall picked up and developed his concern with space in private and public and labelled the new study 'proxemics'. A simple example, which can now be examined because of changes in the intervening years, is that of the 'American' automobile. Hall noted that Americans are encapsulated within a private 'bubble' of territoriality. They do not like to be touched, bumped, or approached too closely except by intimates. He argued that the huge American automobiles of that time (the 1950s and 1960s) gave internal space to those individual 'bubbles'. The consequence, however, is very large cars with wide roads and the rest of the urban design that goes to accommodate them.

Europeans, by contrast, do not have such a large individual bubble of space, and so they can enjoy using much smaller cars, and consequently can use automobiles within old cities on narrow streets.

Since his book was first published the US experienced the 'energy crisis' of the 1970s. Small Japanese cars became the norm for many years, and this might seem to argue against Hall's thesis. Still, recently we have seen the return to cars which are considerably larger than anything known to Hall at the time, the SUVs, which may actually prove his point.

For the study of geosemiotics, discourses in place, we believe that three main 'hidden dimensions' first identified by Hall are important to develop:

- sense of time
- perceptual spaces
- interpersonal distances

and we take these up in turn just below. First, however, it is important to emphasize that our interests are somewhat different from those of Hall and from others who study nonverbal communication. Hall and others were mainly interested in the ways internal sociopsychological states were producing miscommunication between people who were different from each other for some reason. That is, if people from two different cultures were talking to each other, the intercultural question is: How does a difference in a sense of time or how does a difference in interpersonal distance lead them to misinterpret each other?

Hall noted about personal space, for example, that an 'Eastern Seaboard American' would have a tendency to stand just a bit farther away from a conversational partner than a 'Mediterranean'. This would feel uncomfortable to the Mediterranean who would move a bit closer. This would make the ESA move back just a bit which would, in turn, make the M feel uncomfortable. Each person seeking his or her own most comfortable distance would produce a sort of dance with the ESA backing away from the M which could result ultimately in the ESA coming to feel the M was 'aggressive' or 'pushy' or too intimate and the M feeling that the ESA was 'withdrawing' or 'evasive'.

Such insights are, of course, very important for discourses in place, but for our purposes here we are concerned with the indexable in relationship to somatic expression. That is, we are concerned with knowing how internal social, psychological or cultural states are displayed on the body, how they become somatized, if you like, so that they can be 'read' by others as resources for the production of the interaction order. Furthermore, we are interested not just in how they are read in lived social circumstances, but how they may be depicted as visual images or other representations so that those representations themselves can come to be used as discourses in place.

The sense of time

In Chapter 2 we saw that time and space interact with each other. In photo 2.11 we examined a sign that gave the conditions for passing on a particular road. To interpret that sign the driver would have to place himself or herself at a time of day, at a day of the week, and in addition would have to know whether this particular day was on the regular or holiday calendar. Naturally, parking prohibitions that say such things as 'No Parking between 7:00 am and 10:00 pm' are of the same kind. The space is only a parking space in relationship to a time. In order to interpret the sign the person must establish where he or she is against a clock standard.

The internal psychological sense of time is very complex as Hall and subsequent researchers have shown. For our purposes two aspects seem most relevant, *urgency*, and *monochronism–polychronism*. In what follows, however, we are departing somewhat from Hall's analysis, which is rooted in the point of view of the social actor, the individual person who is taking some social action. A person's sense of duration, how rapidly or slowly time is passing, is derived from at least two factors:

- urgency – the more urgently I want something to be done, the more slowly time seems to pass by.
- monochronism (monofocal activity) – this is doing one thing at a time. This is contrasted with polychronism or multitasking (polyfocal activity).

The geosemiotic questions here are:

- How do we index these internal psychological states through language, and
- How are psychological states embodied in the material world so they can be 'read'?

Some of these states are indexed by words such as 'walk', 'crawl', 'stroll', 'mean-der', or 'stride'. 'Stroll', for example, indexes a relaxed body posture, a relatively slow motion without a fixed line of direction, possibly with the gaze moving from place to place in the environment of the stroller. 'Stride' indexes a more tensed body posture, more erect, longer steps, a rather direct line of movement at a faster pace than a stroll, with the gaze directed ahead in an instrumental way (to avoid collisions, etc.).

A sense of time urgency is embodied in more rapid body movements, by signs of 'impatience' such as 'nervous' tapping of the fingers, or by frequent and rapid changes of position. Likewise, a monochronic sense of time is displayed by gestures to wait until someone is finished with a task. A store clerk operating within a monochronic sense of time – that is doing one thing at a time – will studiously avoid eye contact with a customer who is not his or her current focal customer. A person 'not doing anything' will display this inner state with a laconic distribu-tion of eyegaze, slowly moving across scenes but not resting on any position that might suggest a primary involvement.

Ruesch and Kees (1956) noted that much can be read in a still photograph from posture, body and gaze orientation, and degree of equilibrium. A still photograph of a person running shows a body very much off balance that could not be held in that position but for a moment. A person whose gaze is tightly focused on a distant object with the body held with firm tonus is read as a person involved in an activity, perhaps as a spectator of a sporting event, whereas a person whose gaze is loose and vague with the body in a fully relaxed position is read as a person 'doing nothing'.

We index these inner psychological states including our sense of time and motion through our postures and movements and they can be read by others who are in the same social situation. Thus, as we will see in Chapter 4 on Visual Semiotics, these postures and gazes can be frozen in images and the images can be read as displaying otherwise invisible psychological states of the image participants.

Frederick Erickson, who studied with Hall at Northwestern University, has pointed out on many occasions that we can be very wrong in making our reading of these embodied psychological states. He observed a factory in which pieces of steel were cut at machine stations. As the pieces came off the machine they were placed in wooden crates. The crates were then stacked on a pallet. Erickson noted that as Anglo-American workers lifted each crate and placed it on the stack they held their bodies in an erect, taut, firm tonus and made jerky movements. African-American workers held a loosened and relaxed and flexible body tonus as they lifted each crate and swung it around in a smooth trajectory and placed it on the stack. Observers from the management judged the Anglo-American workers to be better workers and the African-American workers to be 'lazy', based primarily on these postures at these times. The actual performance counts showed that there was no difference in work accomplished by these different classes of workers.

Erickson's interpretation is that the Anglo-American posture between moments of work displayed a psychological state of monochronism – one thing at a time – of urgency and of a single activity. In contrast to this, the Anglo managers read the African-American posture as not paying attention to their work (polychronism). Thus we can see that words such as 'industrious' and 'lazy' often index presumed embodiments of inner psychological states and foci of attention. As we will see when we discuss Goffman below, social actors not only must participate in social interactions in a meaningful way, they must be seen to be doing so. It is this latter point that becomes difficult when gestures, postures, gaze, and body movements are no longer simple reflections (icons) of inner psychological states but are, in fact, symbols (conventional ways of displaying particular forms of social participation). This problem is particularly acute in intercultural communication.

Perceptual spaces

The physical spaces of our world are not clearly and discretely bounded. Hall's work, like that of Goffman, as we will discuss below, makes it clear that our senses produce boundaries around at least five different kinds of space:

- visual space
- auditory space
- olfactory space
- thermal space
- haptic (or tactile) space

Perhaps our visual space is the largest space, or at least when we are outdoors and the weather is clear we can see for light-years of distance. As the ancient Chinese philosopher Xunzi put it, however, our eyes only take us to the nearest wall; our ears take us to the end of the village. As we sit preparing this manuscript, we can see the moon which is outside of the atmospheric sphere of the earth. We can hear airplanes taking off and landing at Washington's National Airport two or three miles away. We can smell dinner cooking in the kitchen a few feet away. We can feel the warmth of the computer's motor and the chill of the winter air circulating near the floor at our feet.

Each of these senses demarcates a different kind of space within which the indexicals such as 'here' and 'there' take up their relevance. 'Do you hear *that*?' might make reference to a Secret Service helicopter at the Vice President's residence a ten minute walk away, but 'Do you smell *that*?' is most likely to make reference to the dinner burning in the kitchen while we write.

Geosemiotics takes it that all of these spaces are crucial in the location of discourses in place. 'It's dark', 'it's quiet', 'it stinks here', 'it's hot', or 'that's hot', all index different perceptual spaces; one looks to a different semiotic zone for the interpretation. Our preferred systems of representation tend toward visual and auditory senses, and so there is a tendency to undervalue smell, warmth, touch, or taste (perhaps the most inner of the perceptual spaces) when we try to index the meanings of the world around us.

One of the authors was working on mineral identification in a geology class some years ago. A particular rock seemed to be identified, but he wasn't certain. The teacher said quite simply, 'Lick it.' The salt taste was so powerful an identifier that it over-rode all other aspects of the analysis.

This dominance of the visual and the auditory in our thinking about meaning is so powerful that we have very long traditions of art history, of linguistics, and of other studies based on sound and vision. We now almost forget that a significant part of the meaning of any sign in the material world is also how it smells, what warmth it gives off, and how it feels. W. H. Auden said that he could not write poetry without two or three rotting apple cores in his desk drawer. We are not poets, but we continue to enjoy the feel of a well-made book in our hands when we are reading. We like the smell of ground ink in doing Chinese calligraphy. And in another type of occasion, we recently walked out of a coffee shop where we were planning to have morning coffee because it smelled of disinfectant, not of ground and roasted coffee.

Interpersonal distances

The best known aspect of Hall's work is the concept of four crucial distances that separate people in face-to-face communication and their meanings:

- intimate distance (touch to 18 inches)
- personal distance (18 inches to 4 feet)
- social distance (4 feet to 12 feet)
- public distance (12 feet to 25 feet)

It is important to note before going on that these are calibrated for what Hall called the 'Eastern Seaboard American'. The closest distance is the distance of love-making and wrestling (touch to 18 inches), as Hall says. Of course it is also the distance we find ourselves in on elevators, on crowded city streets, in fixed seats in concert or lecture halls, and in many other public situations. The interesting social problem is taken up by Goffman, as we shall see, in how we display our intentions to others about our relationships given that we have these social distances to work with as resources. Put another way, how do we display in an elevator that we *are not* seeking an intimate relationship with the person who is touching us shoulder-to-shoulder? Alternatively, how do we display an intimate relationship when separated by a personal or social distance?

Personal distance is the distance within which we feel we must engage in some kind of social interaction with the other person (18 inches to 4 feet). It is very difficult in many societies to ignore someone who is within this 'personal bubble' of space. Goffman notes that as many North Americans approach another person walking in public, we first glance into their eyes to display while still in social space that we see them, that we recognize them as socially present within the same space. But then we glance away to signal as we enter personal space that we are not seeking any further or closer relationship with them.

Social distance (4 feet to 12 feet) allows us to treat civilly but without interpersonal engagement someone else who is in the same space. It is also the distance between a lecturer and his or her audience members in most cases, though those in the back of a large lecture are at a public distance from the speaker (12 feet to 25 feet).

Obviously beyond 25 feet it is quite an exaggeration in most cases to say that this is an 'interpersonal' distance as the two parties are quite unlikely to be in any sort of social interaction.

Neither Hall nor Goffman made any attempt to relate their concepts of interpersonal spaces to indexicality in language. And it is not clear to us that this topic has been actually taken up in research in this area. But it is fairly clear that in languages such as Spanish where a distinction is made between 'here', 'over there by you', and 'over there away from both of us', these deictics are based on distances of the kind Hall wrote about. 'Over there by you' would mean 'Over there within your personal space bubble' (i.e. within 18 inches to 4 feet of you), all things being equal.

'All things being equal' is, of course, the central problem. The crucial point Hall makes is that, because our interpretations of these spaces are different in different sociocultural groups, we badly misunderstand what others are intending in their uses of space. As we mentioned above, Hall observed that 'Mediterraneans' talk to their friends standing on the inner edge of the personal range. That is, they tend to stand around 18–20 inches from each other. 'North Americans' tend to stand much farther out in this personal range, generally about 2½ feet or more from each other.

These differences in interpersonal distance index differences in social and interpersonal relationships. Because we express our relationships to others in part by where (and how) we stand or sit or touch, those postures can be 'read' by others to be signaling those interpersonal relationships. Interpersonal distances become, then, a crucial resource by which we geosemiotically embody significant meanings about ourselves and about others and about our relationships.

Goffman's 'frontstage' and 'backstage'

Sputnik's launch in 1957 began to transform how we think about the relationship between the earth and outer space. At nearly the same time Erving Goffman began to transform how we think about the self with the publication of his *The Presentation of Self in Everyday Life* in 1959. Four years later in 1963 his *Behavior in Public Places* further extended these ideas to lay a foundation for the analysis of the ways in which social life is constructed in an active dialectic between psychological selves and the material worlds of our lives.

Freudian psychology had convinced us that what we saw on the outside in a person's behavior might be very different from inner and invisible processes. Goffman's work of a lifetime, which he began to publish with the first of these books, was to show us that the outside or public or social self is itself displayed in a highly complex theater of performances.

Because places on the earth are always circumscribed socially, the study of discourses in place cannot really begin without some understanding of where the socially constructed public/private line is drawn and, more importantly, *how* this boundary is socially produced. As Goffman so enjoyed pointing out, all of the winks, nods, nudges, and other signals of collusion between team players while in full performance before their audience show that 'public' and 'private' are probably not as useful as his notions of frontstage and backstage regions and actions.

The sign on the fence in photo 3.02 marks not only a construction site, but also the social boundaries between social performances – laborer, city inspector, construction company owner on the inside of the fence and citizen, pedestrian, or nuisance photographer on the outside. Those social performances in turn mark the boundaries of the larger social institutions of our world – companies, banks, cities, and the social-scientific research academy.

Goffman's work is worth close attention in our view and it is often the case in his writing that a significant point will appear to be an off-hand suggestion. From that point of view, Goffman requires (and rewards) a careful reading. On the other hand he had rather specific goals in mind in his writing and one of those was apparently to avoid engagement with broader social questions of his society. It is in the spirit of using Goffman's work as a starting point that we introduce it here. In due time we will come to considerations that go beyond anything dealt with in his work.

Two quotations encode much of Goffman's argument:

> The expressiveness of the individual appears to involve two radically different kinds of sign activity: The expression that he *gives* and the expression that he *gives off*.
>
> (Goffman 1959: 2)

3.02

Performers can stop giving expressions but cannot stop giving them off.
(Goffman 1959: 108)

We imagine a third quote which, to our knowledge, Goffman never said but which is rather fully developed throughout the text. It might have been:

The performer who learns to control expressions he is apparently only giving off has achieved a higher level of social control over the performance.

What is important to us from the point of view of geosemiotics is that Goffman began to lay out the dynamics of the ways in which other people in the same social space form a major aspect of the physical world in which we live. Not only are our discourses in place positioned to the spot on the earth in which they take place, they are positioned in relationships, both social and physical, to the other humans who are also in those spaces.

To return to our interest in indexicality, as we have noted in Chapter 2 the pronouns 'I' and 'you' may seem to index speaker and hearer in a straightforward way, but Goffman's work shows that this 'I' is constantly under construction in lived social and physical spaces as a social performance and so is the 'you'.

Goffman made much of the distinction between 'frontstage' and 'backstage' performances. A waiter takes on a different face and demeanor as he passes through the kitchen door to enter the main dining room to attend to customers. When he returns to the kitchen to place the order he has received, his demeanor again changes; he relaxes, chats with the cook, perhaps he even speaks insultingly of the customer to whom he has just shown the utmost deference and respect.

Through many examples of this sort Goffman has clarified that our social selves are constructed on stages that consist of both the physical places we inhabit (kitchens, main dining rooms) and of the social roles we perform (waiter in service, waiter in the kitchen). And, of course, it is not far from this sort of example to cases in which the waiter winks or nods in collusion to another waiter and thus cuts across the public, frontstage performance to let a bit of the backstage performance leak through into the frontstage performance. These social roles and physical spaces constantly index each other and so neither can be left out of the analysis when seeking to understand how discourses are placed in our social, geosemiotic world.

The personal front

We have now looked at the sense of time, perceptual spaces, and interpersonal distances as discussed in the work of Edward T. Hall. With Erving Goffman's idea of the personal front we come to the fourth aspect of embodiment which is of importance for our study of the interaction order. In a few words, the personal front is a kind of identity kit that one assembles out of the mixed bag of what Goffman calls 'sign equipment', personal and physical characteristics and objects one might wear or carry. It includes the disposition of one's hair and the posture in which one holds the body. The personal front includes both the shoes one wears and the degree of shine buffed onto their surfaces. It includes the choice of eyeglasses or contact lenses or neither and whether one carries pens in the front shirt pocket. The personal front is virtually any visible or perceptible – because perfumes or their absence are also part of the personal front – aspect that a person carries physically into the presence of others, whether or not these aspects of the personal front are consciously controlled.

This distinction between *giving* and *giving off* expression is reiterated and developed in several places, largely to make certain that the reader understands that we are not thinking only of what a person *intends* to communicate. Whether or not we intend our embodied communications, our bodies continue to give off meanings for others to read.

Of course one could argue that all three of Hall's dimensions – the sense of time, perceptual spaces, and interpersonal distances – are actually components of the personal front. The important distinction to remember is that Hall's focus was on internal states – psychological and cultural ones. Goffman's focus is on external displays made to others present in the social situation. The concept of the personal front captures the sense of time through noting how a person conveys that sense through, say, repeated glancing at his wristwatch. In Goffman's terms, the wristwatch serves an important function as a tool in constructing the personal front of someone who might prefer to be elsewhere and not talking to the present interlocutor.

In 1963 Goffman introduced the very powerful idea of 'civil inattention' which lies at the heart of much of our interest in discourses in place. Perhaps only Goffman would have seen so clearly that the source of much of what happens 'in public' is the invisibility of what we silently agree not to pay much attention to. As we shall see in Chapters 8 and 9, much of the 'work' of making sense of our geosemiotic environments lies in what we do not bring to focal attention. The process of careful and social selection of what to pay attention to is central to our ability to make sense of the very busy and complex array of discourses we find in place in such simple social activities as crossing the street, entering a shopping mall, driving a car across town, or, in fact, carrying on a good conversation in a coffee shop.

What seems crucial in this overall analysis of discourses in place is 'fitting in'. Fitting in too much or too little carries meaning. As Goffman puts it, producing and maintaining the social order seems to depend on the participants all riding just on the surface of the social interaction. The main concern is:

> The conduct of individuals by virtue of their presence among others.
>
> (Goffman 1963: 242)

He makes reference to the person in ways that are very reminiscent of Hall's ideas on interpersonal distance. Though Goffman speaks metaphorically rather than in terms of specific distances, we believe that these spaces *can* be physically examined and determined. Goffman refers to

> 'circles of self' which persons draw around themselves, and for which the individual is obliged to show various forms of respect.
>
> (1963: 242)

The basic rule is to 'fit in' which breaks down into the sub-rules: do not cause a scene or disturbance, don't attract undue attention to yourself either through thrusting yourself on others or withdrawing from them, and keep the spirit/ethos of the occasion.

Fitting in is done largely through

1   the disciplined ordering of the personal front,
2   a readiness to attend to new stimuli in the situation, and
3   the alacrity of body motion displayed in responding to others.

Goffman's term for this is 'body idiom' (which he seems to prefer to either 'body language' or 'nonverbal communication'). There are two kinds of expressions, embodied and disembodied. The latter include writing, leaving footprints and the rest. Goffman has no interest in that (though he himself is a master of disembodied expression in the form of his books). Embodied expressions (also referred to as 'co-presence') have two very important characteristics: they are *naked*, that is they are not boosted by microphones, and they are reciprocal (if you see others you can be seen by them).

For our purposes this is the geosemiotic importance of Goffman's work: Discourses in place take their meaning in no small part from the physical co-presence of others in that same place. The embodied actions of any social actor are produced not only out of internal and personal motivations and meanings, but also in reference to and in conjunction with the actions of others within that same space.

Two aspects of 'fitting in' are important for our understanding of the embodiment of discourses in place, *involvement*, and *civil inattention*.

> the individual apportions his involvement among main and side involvements, dominant and subordinate ones, and . . . in each situation a particular apportionment will be defined as proper.
>
> (p. 64)

It's very important for discourses in public to get these concepts clear. Not only do we carry on our actions in the presence of others who are physically co-present, we display to them some range of involvements that are socially judged to be appropriate for those situations to receive their normative definition. One of the main ways through which this is accomplished is through civil inattention.

Goffman defines civil inattention as follows:

> One gives to another enough visual notice to demonstrate that one appreciates that the other is present . . . while at the next moment withdrawing one's

attention from him so as to express that he does not constitute a target of special curiosity or design.

(p. 84)

Nothing captures Goffman's concept of how social order is produced more succinctly. The trick is in the very delicate balance of glancing and looking away. Too much of a glance becomes a stare; too little becomes ignoring the other. The social order, the 'right kind of people', 'our group', and the rest of these social identities are produced through producing just the right amount of expression. This is the exchange that takes place as we pass another in public, first giving a glance while yet in social range and then looking away as we pass into personal range.

Naturally, that is taking on the personal front appropriate for strangers. In encountering a friend, we make the first identification often at public distance and then look away for most of the time we are moving toward personal space, at which moment we then re-engage the other and begin to exchange greetings as we arrive at personal space.

The interaction order

Finally, we arrive at Goffman's 'with', a social group that is very important for the study of geosemiotics. Goffman did not define the 'with' as such until 1971, but it is prefigured in earlier writings in his concept of civil inattention. Goffman defined the 'with' as:

A party of more than one whose members are perceived to be 'together'.

(1971: 19)

Once defined, Goffman used the term 'with' without quotes and we will follow that usage in what follows. Characteristics of the with are:

* civil inattention (to those who are not members of the with);
* ecological proximity (to other members of the with);
* the right to initiate talk and other interactions among members;
* availability of these interactions to all members of the with;
* ritual practices for joining and for departures;
* greater latitude in behavior than members would enjoy as singles in the same situation.

Deictics such as 'they' often make reference to a with, as when somebody might ask, 'Who are they?' glancing in the direction of two or more people who are together in some public space. For geosemiotics this concept captures the idea that the primary indexable human-social entities in the world outside of our language are the single and the with. A comment such as, 'I wonder why they are doing that here?' incorporates both kinds of indexicality – that of geophysical location ('here') and that of social co-presence ('they').

Goffman's development of what he called the interaction order began with this concept of the with. With the culmination of his career in his presidential address to the American Sociological Association, he itemized several kinds of interaction arrangements that may be taken on when we are in each others' presence. For us these interaction arrangements are useful for two reasons. First, as we have just noted, and as we shall see below, these groupings form semiotic units which become indexable social organizations in public (or other) places. Secondly, these groupings are the units in which we 'package' our own spoken uses of language as it occurs in the world. Naturally, it is important to remember that Goffman wrote from the point of view of the dominant ethnic majority of North America – Euro-Americans – and these ideas about the interaction order remain to be more clearly and contrastively elaborated for other sociocultural groups.

The 11 kinds of interaction units are:

- **singles** – a person who is by himself or herself in a social space among others.
- **withs** – two or more who are perceived as being together with each other as the main focus of their mutual attention.
- **files and processions** – groups which move together, whether more or less loosely formed as military parades or groups of tourists.
- **queues** – aggregates of people, mostly not known to each other, who coordinate their activities so that they will arrive at some transaction point in a sequence.
- **contacts** – the fleeting social interactions that are produced by glances of mutual recognition but which are not allowed to segue into more fully developed forms such as the with or the service encounter.
- **service encounters** – the social arrangements that occur when we procure and are delivered some service such as buying a cup of coffee at a counter or exchanging a bus ticket with the driver as we board a bus.
- **conversational encounters** – a with which has as its main focus of attention the production and the maintenance of a state of talk among a relatively small group.
- **meetings** – more tightly structured encounters which normally have a declared purpose with a ratifiable set of participants, relatively clear beginnings and endings, and most often a chair or facilitator.
- **people-processing encounters** – others have used the term 'gatekeeping encounters': social interactions which are polarized into those who have some

power to define significant outcomes for those others who normally must provide some account of themselves. Job interviews and the issuing of traffic violation tickets by the police are examples.

- **platform events** – someone or a small group performs as a spectacle for others to watch whether on an elevated platform or encircled by the group of watchers. Elsewhere we have called this a 'watch' to parallel Goffman's with.

- **celebrative occasions** – social interactions which are tightly ritualized such as weddings, awards ceremonies and the like where the actions of all participants are governed by prior scripts for performance.

Many social groupings in public places can be seen and it is a matter of further analysis to determine whether they should be included within one of Goffman's eleven categories or whether new categories should be added. For example, is a game of football played in a public park an example of a platform event? One might want to say that it is, but in a game the primary social interactions of the participants in the game are focused on the unfolding of their actions in relationship to each other, not in relationship to the watchers of the game. In a lecture or in many other forms of platform events, the main concern of the spectacle is with his or her interactions with the watchers.

This is not of major concern for us here, however. It should be fairly obvious that these eleven types of social interactions form indexable social arrangements when seen externally, and also form the primary ways in which discourse is organized in these social places. We are able to identify people seen at a distance in public on the basis of these arrangements of the interaction order and from that we are able to draw inferences about their social role performances at that moment and about the language they are using.

We can easily identify a queue in front of a theater or waiting for a bus. We can identify among that queue which of the people are in withs on the basis of their orientations to each other and their maintenance of a state of talk. In most cases a brief glance into a room can settle whether the people sitting there are involved in a conversational encounter or a meeting. Entering a coffee shop we can identify which of the people in that shop are singles, which are in withs, and which among them are service personnel. This is partly, to be sure, on the basis of positions in front of or behind counters and the wearing of uniforms, but it is also by the indexicality of their social interactions.

New media technologies bring into question whether or not we should extend the concept of the with to people brought together into social interaction through a medium such as the cell phone as we noted in Chapter 2.

Singles in public places often protect themselves against unwanted involvements by reading or otherwise being actively involved in something that at least appears

3.03

to occupy their full attention so that they may not be seen to be seeking involvement with strangers. In a library, however, social license is produced for
individuals to socially present themselves as singles for long periods of times as in
3.03 where a student with her book studies (her cell phone at the ready).

Of course some public places and events are so complex that they virtually defy
categorization within any one category. Photo 3.04 gives a glimpse of the inaug-
uration of an American president. At the center of the moment is the ceremonial
occasion being staged on the steps of the US Capitol Building. This event is
not at all visible from this distance. Intermittently placed throughout the crowd
on the mall are large television screens which produce this ceremony as a
spectacle. As we can see in the foreground there are also multiple singles and withs
and other social arrangements occurring simultaneously within this large-scale
social event.

3.04

This chapter has focused on the embodied forms of discourse found in what Goffman called the interaction order. In Chapter 4 we will turn to disembodied expressions of body idiom in the form of representations in images and signs of the interaction order with its variety of interaction units. The semiotics of the sense of time, perceptual spaces, interpersonal distances, and personal front are indexed by words, pictures, and other visual forms in the designed images so ubiquitous in the contemporary world.

PRACTICE

The embodiment of perceptual space, time, interpersonal distances, and personal front

The activities which follow are based on the theoretical section above. In doing these activities you are likely to find that some aspects of the interaction order are much easier to capture and to represent than others. For example, it is difficult to represent in writing or with a visual image how olfactory space works and an audiotape recording works best to represent auditory space.

Our examples both here and in the theoretical section have been limited by necessity to still images and text. Much of what we have been writing about could be much more easily understood by using video or by taking a walk through a shopping mall on a Saturday afternoon. You should not limit yourself in doing these exercises to still images and texts with their narrow constraints. We think it is worth trying to experiment to see what different kinds of representation you can find for the theoretical concepts we have discussed above and in the activities below.

Activity: Perceptual spaces

Hall talks about five types of perceptual space which are at the foundation of the distances we use to signal our interpersonal relationships: visual, auditory, olfactory, thermal, and haptic (or tactile). Almost any situation in which two or more people are in communication will make use of all five of these types of space, but certain conditions arise where one or more of these becomes crucial to the definition of the relationship.

Visual

Many authors have said rather emphatically that vision is the synthesizing perception, the sense which encompasses the most and at the greatest distance. From that point of view, vision is the sense which gives humans our greatest reach. Walter Ong commented that vision was distancing because of this quality but sound was involving as we associate sounds with things closer to us.

Auditory

Xunzi, a Chinese philosopher of the third century BC, said just the opposite of Hall, Ong, and others. He said that while we can only see to the nearest wall we can hear sounds to the end of the village. For him, vision is the involving sense and sound the formal, distancing one. These two very different positions are a good warning not to take the proclamations of either philosophers or scientists as final until we've surveyed the views of thinkers from very different traditions.

Olfactory

The sense of smell is more crucial in some social circles than in others, or at least conveys different things. Sales of soaps, perfume, breath cleansers and the rest are predicated on the assumption that olfaction is very central in social relationships as you can see in almost any advertisement for these products. The economist John B. Leeds in his 1917 Columbia University doctoral dissertation wrote:

Many people do not sufficiently realize the extent to which the increase in cleanliness of home and person contributes toward the growth of democracy. So long as the upper classes felt the necessity of using smelling salts whenever approached by one of the common people, just so long would they despise the vile-smelling yokels. Cleanliness is not only next to Godliness, but it is essential to the establishment of the Brotherhood of Man.

(Cowan 1983)

Thermal

The outside temperature influences the way we dress which, in turn, affects not only our thermal sense of distance and our olfactory sense (smell) but also the potential for tactile exchanges.

Tactile

Good friends often feel it is necessary to be able to approach their friends within touching distance to establish the appropriate relationship and we all know just how attracted children are to museum and zoo exhibits that allow them to touch objects and animals.

Assignment

Write a short report which investigates the five different types of perceptual spaces (and, of course, the relative roles of these different spaces in any one space). Which types of space are most suited to which types of social relationships?

Camerawork

Take either stills or videos of each of the five spatial perceptions. Much of the task will be taken up with trying to figure out how to get visual images that will represent non-visual perceptions such as olfactory, auditory, and thermal.

Alternative

Make a soundtrack on a tape recording to represent the five types of spaces. Which type of space is done more easily with a tape recording as compared to a still photographic image?

Observations

Use your camera and your observations to inform each other. That is, work in a cycle of thought, observation, camerawork, thought, observation, camerawork until you feel you can give a clear illustration in just five still photos of the role of each of the perceptual spaces in interpersonal communication.

Activity: Sense of time

Our sense of time has to do with at least four factors: urgency, monochronism – doing one thing at a time, activity, and variety.

Urgency

One imagines these people sitting on a bench eating melon seeds in the Fragrant Mountain Park near Beijing as in 3.05 have little current sense of urgency. Hall would argue that they would be quite comfortable with their sense of how time was passing.

3.05

3.06

Monochronism–polychronism

This woman in Beijing shown in 3.06 is standing in the traffic, has just hailed a taxi, and is making a telephone call while checking her watch. This is a perfect example of polychronism – doing multiple things at the same time. Hall argues that such polychronism gives a sense of time flying by.

Activity

Three men are working on breaking out a portion of the wall of a building in photo 3.07. The most active is the one with the hammer pounding in a steady rhythm. The other one dressed in jeans stands at the ready to help. The third, most likely a foreman, stands with his hands behind his back only observing. We would expect these three men to have different senses of how quickly time was passing in this

3.07

scene. For the man with the hammer it would be moving much more quickly than for the foreman.

Variety

The man in image 3.08 works from about 6:30 in the evening to about midnight selling soup in an outdoor food stall in Beijing. His activities are carried out in a very small space but he keeps up a constant round of taking orders from customers, dishing up soup, putting in condiments, taking payment and making change and throughout whenever he is not talking he sings out very loudly to come get his soup. One would imagine his evenings would fly by in this flurry of varied activity.

3.08

Assignment

Make a photomontage, a slide show, or a sound track which shows differences in the sense of time. Monitor your own sense of time for several days noting when it seems that time has just flown by and when it seems that it is dragging. Try to establish which of these four factors is most crucial to either the increased or decreased sense of time passing. The main question is: Can we *read* someone else's current sense of time from their actions and behaviors, their stances and postures?

Observations

Focus your observations mostly on your own internal sense of time as it is very difficult to get 'subjects' to clearly focus on their sense of time. Once you have some photo/video/audio illustrations you can show those to others to get their reactions.

Activity: Interpersonal distances

Territoriality is fundamentally mammalian as many researchers have pointed out. Still, as Hall, Goffman, and many others have shown, we humans have put our own overlay of sociocultural meanings to the spaces we like to make between ourselves and others when we talk. This activity is intended to give the participants the direct experience of talking under varying interpersonal distances.

When two people differ in their sense of what is the appropriate distance for a conversation their choice is to vary the distance or vary their sense of the relationship. Let's say person X prefers a slightly shorter distance than person Y. When X moves in on Y, Y either feels the need to move back or to decide that X is shifting from social to personal space or from personal space to intimate space. Y can either step back or become more intimate. If Y backs up then X feels Y is either moving too far away or becoming 'colder' (i.e. more distant). He or she has the same dilemma. These are not usually, of course, personal preferences but unconscious performance of the norms for our sociocultural groups.

Assignment

1   Make strings/ropes enough to pair up all the participants
   * Intimate (18 inches or under)
   * Personal (18 inches to 30 inches, close phase), (30 inches – 4 feet, far phase)
   * Social (4 feet to 7 feet, close phase), (7 feet – 12 feet, far phase)
   * Public (12 feet to 25 feet, close phase), (25 feet+, far phase)
2   Assign an 'information gap' task to the participants. This could be a set of questions such as finding out where they went to school or where they like to vacation or anything else that would be relatively easy for the participants to do but which would hold their attention.
3   Ask each member of a pair to hold the end of a string at the center of the chest. They should stand far enough apart to keep the strings relatively taut.
4   Start some of the pairs with the longest strings and others with the shortest strings, then shift toward the other extreme as the task continues.
5   Write a short report which summarizes your findings.

Camerawork

Take pictures, preferably video, of this activity. If you have enough cameras you could have teams of three, two to talk and one to shoot.

Observations

Most likely you will observe very lax strings at the longer distances as well as raised voices. At the shorter distances you will see embarrassment and holding the strings away from the chest to achieve more comfortable distances. Be alert to observe differences between men and women, tall and short, younger and older and so forth.

Present videos and still captures as discussion pieces for the group to talk about as a way to capture their subjective experience of these differences in space and the effect on their ability to enjoy the exercise.

Activity: Distances in public places

The previous activity was designed to give to participants a personal experience of the different interpersonal spaces we use in speaking to others. This activity is designed to use that experience to begin to 'read' the behavior of others in public places.

The man in photo 3.09 is speaking with much movement. He walks up and down as he speaks and gesticulates with very strong hand motions while speaking very loudly. His posture and movement suggest far personal or even social space is appropriate between him and his non-present interlocutor.

Assignment

Prepare a report which focuses on a single image (still or brief video clip) and gives an interpretation of what is seen in the image. Outline your reasons for the interpretation you have given to this observed behavior. Visit several different kinds of public places, particularly where observations of others can be made relatively unobtrusively. Places such as shopping malls or downtown shopping districts are good. Parks or sports stadiums also work fairly well, though in the case of stadiums people are often constricted by the fixed arrangements of seats.

Take pictures of people as you find them. If you have video, take stretches of several minutes at a time if possible as this will give you a chance to see if there are changes made in the distances people are using. It is particularly convenient to make observations from upper floors of malls down toward the lower floors.

3.09

Observations

You are observing strangers (in most cases at least) and so ask yourself how you *know* those two or three or several people are actually together. You can't really know that two strangers are a married couple except from what you see of their behavior, but you should be able to use your knowledge of proxemics to draw fairly accurate inferences.

Activity: Personal front

Goffman's dramaturgical view of social interaction sees us as constantly taking up and presenting personal fronts, that is, social roles that we put on and enact through the use of conventionalized sign-equipment, gesture, posture, dress, and the use of the material aspects and objects of our surroundings. The purpose of this activity is to sharpen up our ability to observe a variety of personal fronts in actual life.

The photo 3.10 shows a person displaying a recognizable 'personal front'. What is the 'sign-equipment' used to make this display? How is the setting exploited as part of maintaining this front?

3.10

Assignment

Take pictures (preferably videos) of people in public places. To the extent it is possible try to get the social-interactional equivalent of outtakes. That is, try to catch people at moments of realignments, of preparation of the front, of transition between front and backstage regions, or in out-of-character and discrepant roles.

   Make a photo-montage or slide show of a variety of personal fronts. Accompany this display with captions which indicate the principal bits of sign equipment (including of course gesture, posture, and the rest) which go into the production of these fronts.

Observations

Base your observations on what you see as you go about your day but also on the photos/videos you take. Pay particular attention to the inception and closure of fronts as these are the crucial transitional moments as the sign-equipment is changed.

Activity: Regions, back and front

The performances or personal fronts we take up are keyed to different regions, primarily frontstage and backstage. In the cell phone shop in 3.11 (in Beijing) the sales clerk stands behind the counter which is marked as a backstage region by the display case and the display of all of the telephones outward for the view of the shoppers.

3.11

Assignment

Draw a diagram with a short analysis of some backstage/frontstage configuration. In your analysis be sure to indicate both what features of the physical setting are used to construct the boundary of the two regions and what actions or behaviors on the part of players are keyed to the shift across this boundary.

Observations

In your observations be watchful of boundary movements and actions. Transitions will be shown by shifts in gaze, posture, ways of speaking as well as by the sign-equipment carried or set aside by the persons making the transition or by shifts and orientations in their clothing or hair. Do not neglect to observe time boundaries as well as physical ones. What shifts in front occur at opening or closing times or in the shifts from one event to another?

Activity: Public performances

Places are semiotic or sign complexes (or aggregates) which provide ample resources for the production of some performances while on the other hand they are extremely restricted in the extent to which they facilitate other performances.

In photo 3.12 we see the atrium area or galleria of the ICC Building at Georgetown University. What performances are playable in this space and which ones might be severely restricted? Why?

Assignment

Write a short analysis of some commonly available public place – a shopping mall or street, a park, a lecture hall, a museum – from the point of view of saying what resources are available to be exploited by people for producing particular performances. It might be useful to give, for example, a map or diagram of the place, a list of sign-equipment (mediational means) available, and a list of particular roles which use the available resources. Still photos giving central and peripheral areas, particularly boundaries will help in delineating the 'stage'. Of course photos of individuals performing in that space will give concreteness to your analysis.

3.12

Observations

In making observations, as in cases above, you might get the richest information from boundaries (either in space or time) as well as from the differences across performances and roles or from discrepant roles and out-of-character ones you observe.

Activity: The 'with'

One type of social arrangement is what Goffman calls the 'with'. He defines this:

> A with is a party of more than one whose members are perceived to be 'together'.

(1971)

The 'with' contrasts with the 'single' in Goffman's definition. As discussed above we recognize the with through tie-signs, principally

- ecological proximity
- civil inattention
- rights to initiate talk among the with
- the interaction is available to all members of the with
- ritual practices for joining and leaving
- greater latitude in behavior than in singles

The two photos, 3.13 and 3.14, show different withs. Examine them carefully to see which tie-signs of the withs you can identify.

3.13

Assignment

Make a photo or video collection of several withs in public places – parks, squares, street corners, and the like – where people go by or stand about in groups. Include a written key and analysis which will indicate the tie-signs by which you have assumed you are viewing withs.

3.14

Observations

Of course if you *only* look and make visual observations, you will not really know if the withs you identify are truly withs. That is, you cannot know if they are themselves together. A bit of interviewing just to verify your ability to identify withs can be very useful.

Activity: Involvements

Goffman defined four types of involvements:

- dominant
- subordinate
- main
- side

Waiting for a train might be a person's *dominant* involvement on a particular occasion and reading a magazine on the platform the *subordinate* involvement. Within that *subordinate* involvement of reading the magazine the *main* involvement might be 'reading' it (i.e. actually reading, turning pages, etc.) and a *side* involvement might be humming a tune, glancing around from time to time to see what other sorts of people are on the platform.

Perhaps any or all social occasions are made up of these multiple and complex involvements. Certainly the mix of dominant and subordinate, of main and side is likely to be part of the definition of the occasion. From the point of view of public discourse (discourse in public) it is important to know for any particular bit of discourse where it fits within some scheme of involvements or actions. The platform number in the train station might seem a rather insignificant bit of discourse (a large #2 for example) but from the point of view of the dominant involvement/action it is the most important bit of discourse. The magazine is quite insignificant in this case and is put away immediately when the train comes along the track.

The photo 3.15 shows a man doing something. Work out, if you can, which actions/involvements are likely to be *dominant*, which *subordinate*, which *main* and which *side*. A still photo, of course, gives far too little information to be conclusive about this and so the task is to dream up plausible cases. In the activities below you'll need to get further information. As a bit of context which isn't obvious from the photo, 3.15 is taken in a pub in Dulles Airport in Washington, DC.

3.15

Assignment

Find and observe one social situation and work out the several types of involvement which construct that situation. Once you've identified a particular social situation, use the camera (video preferably) to document the several involvements out of which the situation is constructed. A brief report along with a few photos should be sufficient to illustrate your points. Try to position discourse within this scheme of involvements. Is it the dominant or subordinate involvement, etc.?

Observations

It will probably be crucial to observe activity over a period of time as the shift from one level of involvement to another might not happen frequently. Of course you can assume a person waiting for a train or plane will change their involvement when the train arrives, but be sure to observe that moment as it will make clear which other actions are interruptible.

4   Visual semiotics

From real life to depicted life: Visual semiotics

In Chapter 3 we saw how we place our discourses in the world through a complex set of social performances. This interaction order, as Goffman calls it, is the way we accomplish our spoken, face-to-face discourse in the world and it is also the indexable world we use in this discourse. Now in this chapter we turn from the spoken, face-to-face discourses to the representations of that interaction order in images and signs.

In order to see our perspective here more clearly, we will return briefly to the picture of the street performer we looked at in Chapter 1 (1.03).

The scene is complex from the point of view of Goffman's interaction order. There is a street performer who stands as a statue until someone takes the action of donating money in his collection box. This is a typical platform event which we defined in Chapter 3 as:

> someone or a small group performs as a spectacle for others to watch whether on an elevated platform or encircled by the group of watchers.

From the point of view of the platform event the interaction order consists of the spectacle and the viewers or audience and their relationships are displayed through the performance of the event on the one hand and the appreciation as audience on the other. At the same time, however, we noted that the 'audience' does not consist of isolated singles but, rather, of at least one with.

In the same way we might note a queue of people formed up in front of a ticket window to buy tickets for a movie, a concert, or a train trip. The queue itself is a unit of the interaction order but within the queue might be several withs – people who have come to buy tickets together and who throughout the queuing might

Visual Semiotics

Represented participants
        narrative
        conceptual

Modality
        color saturation
        color differentiation
        color modulation
        contextualization
        representation
        depth
        illumination
        brightness

Composition
        information
            centered
                    circular
                    triptych
                    center–margin
            polarized
                    left–right (given–new)
                    top–bottom (ideal–real)

Interactive participants
        producer – image participants
        image participant – image participant
        image participant – viewer/reader

sustain a conversational encounter – yet another of the units of the interaction noted by Goffman.

We need to keep alert to the fact that the interaction order is almost always complex and will include units within units, withs within service encounters, conversational encounters within files and processions, or contacts within celebrative occasions. From spy movies we might remember a number of meetings held within the broader structure of a platform event as two agents conduct their business while appearing to watch a horse race, for example.

In what follows here in Chapter 4 we will be needing to watch our focus carefully so as not to become disoriented in our analysis. As we will see there are multiple relationships going on simultaneously much as there always are within the interaction order. There are relationships among the participants *within the picture frame*; there are relationships *among those who make the picture* and further *between those who make the picture and the participants within the picture*; finally there are also relationships *between those who are in the picture and those who are viewing it*. From this point of view a visual image is much like a sporting event or the statue street performance in Vienna (image 1.03). We need to be careful to sort out these multiple relationships in our analysis.

The term 'visual semiotics' makes reference to the work of Gunther Kress and Theo van Leeuwen, particularly as found in their book *Reading Images: The Grammar of Visual Design* (1996). Our interest in their work here in *Discourses in Place* has three aspects:

• the representation of real-world actions in visual images,
• the problem of how visual images index the real world in which they are placed,
• the problem of how social actors index these images which are so abundant in our world, constructing ongoing social performances as part of the social situation front.

Put more simply, we are interested in how images represent the real social world, in how images mean what they mean because of where we see them, and in how we use images to do other things in the world.

In the first place we are interested in how the real world of people acting in the presence of others is represented, particularly in visual images. For example, here we move from asking how we recognize a 'with' in the real world to asking how a with is depicted by means of a visual image such as a photograph, a painting, or a schematic diagram. Or we might want to know how such vague and internal psychological states as a sense of time can be captured as a visual image for the purposes of representation. As we shall see, for example, the sense of interpersonal distance is captured in images by the size of the image within the frame. Thus a close-up full-head shot visually represents Hall's 'personal' or even 'intimate' space, depending on just how large the close-up shot is. Alternatively, Hall's public space is represented in visual images by full, head-to-toe shots at some distance.

Kress and van Leeuwen outline a complex grammar of visual design which takes us a long way toward understanding the first aspect of our interest – how visual images do their semiotic work.

The second and third aspects we are extending from this basic framework, mostly through our own research projects in this area. That is, here in this chapter we cover a few of the semiotic structures outlined by Kress and van Leeuwen. Then after a brief interlude in Chapter 5 we will turn to the question of how visual images (photos, graphics, diagrams, street and shop signs, and the rest) take their meaning from where they are located in the world in Chapters 6, 7, and 8 on Code Preference, Inscription, and Emplacement. Finally, in Chapter 9 on Discourses in Time and Space and Chapter 10 on Indexicality, Dialogicality, and Selection in Action we will take up the question of how real world social actors index the plethora of images and signs in our world – the multiple systems of indexability.

Four semiotic systems

Kress and van Leeuwen focus their attention on what they refer to as 'pictures', i.e. composed images from works of art to children's drawings and from scientific textbooks to scribbled personal maps. They use the word 'pictures' in its broadest sense to include any form of constructed and framed image. It is important in thinking about this to remember that composition is a significant part of their thinking about visual semiotics. That is, they are not including in their analysis a simple snapshot of people doing things in the world.

It is one thing to analyze a snapshot of two people walking through a park and it is quite another to analyze a highly crafted advertising photograph of two models displaying clothing. In the first case we are primarily focusing on the actions and displays of the people in the world captured by the photographer. In the second case we are primarily focusing on the actions of the photographer who has choreographed the displays of the models as well as constructed the frame of the image within which their staged actions will be presented. To put this another way, in the first case we might draw reasonable inferences about the social performances of the people in the park and in the second case we might draw reasonable inferences about the social performances and intentions of the photographer. Reading the second type of image must be a very different process from reading the first type of image.

Naturally, it is difficult to know where and when to draw the line between a casual, documentary, or journalistic photographer with a skilled eye in capturing the social world in highly meaningful moments and the fully structured images of the advertising or fine arts photographer. Similarly we would find it hard to draw a firm line between the careful and intentional meanings of a master painter and the serendipitous, chance insights of his or her work. We must always work on this continuum, of course, but for this chapter and in the work of Kress and van Leeuwen we are discussing our primary focus is on the crafted and designed image, not the accidental snap of something happening in the world outside the designer's studio and outside the image frame.

This, then, requires a comment on many of the illustrations which we are using below. We have primarily used images caught in the real world to illustrate concepts more appropriately limited to constructed, designed images. There are two reasons for this. First, some of the most highly valued intellectual properties of our contemporary age are just the advertising and other professionally crafted images we would like to analyze. These are either very expensive or permissions to use them are impossible to obtain. Secondly, however, we have done a bit of work of our own in crafting these images to illustrate our points. For example, the four images below (4.04, 4.05, 4.06, and 4.07) were captured from a vacation videotape made by the authors and then produced as 'portraits' using photo-editing software. Thus they are not simple snapshots, but constructed images in the sense that Kress and van Leeuwen are interested in studying.

Image 4.02 is a bit different as this sort of posed group image is very common as an intermediate ground between people caught in the real world and the constructive work of the image maker. This is a case in which a real world group – a group of picnickers – voluntarily poses itself according to common social conventions for the photographer. They voluntarily take on the positions and characteristics of represented participants. They form themselves as what Goffman would call a platform event or a spectacle.

Kress and van Leeuwen's grammar of visual design is very complex and deserves to be understood in its full complexity. Here for our purposes, however, we must limit our focus to just four of the main semiotic systems they have presented because of our interest in seeing how the interaction order is visually depicted:

- represented participants
- modality
- composition
- interactive participants

Represented participants: Narrative and conceptual

Pictures (composed visual representations from printed texts to blueprints of architectural structures) carry meaning through a system for representing the participants within the picture. Here we follow Kress and van Leeuwen and use 'participant' to mean a construction element used in a picture. This might be an image of a person, but it would also include a block of text, or a chart or graph or a logo. These representational structures can be either narrative or conceptual. Narrative structures present unfolding actions and events or, perhaps, processes of change. Conceptual structures show abstract comparative or generalized categories.

Key concepts in representing participants in pictures are the participants and vectors which relate them. When one participant looks at or is oriented toward another, for instance, a vector (arrow of gaze in this case) is produced which shows how the one relates to the other. This is derived, of course, from our perception of vectors in eyegaze in the social world we have discussed in Chapter 3. The image portion of a shampoo advertisement from China taken several years ago (4.01) shows a narrative relationship in which gaze and the flow of water produce the narrative vector from man to woman.

Conceptual relationships among the participants are marked by the absence of such vectors as gaze or direction of movement. We might want to call image 4.02 *analytical* in that it shows or displays all of the high school students attending a Labor Day outing. The array of the bodies in rows produces something much like a diagram or a chart of the participants which is achieved through the suppression of any narrative actions.

It is possible to see that the narrative relationships among represented participants in Kress and van Leeuwen's visual semiotics derive directly from the display of personal fronts which we studied in Chapter 3. In their seminal work, first published in 1964, Ruesch and Kees outline several ways in which we 'read' action in the world:

4.01

4.02

- Motion (from point of origin to point of destination): this is read through such signs as the speed and the direction of motion.
- Path or trace: some moving objects leave traces (the wake of a boat or the tracks of an animal).
- Degree of balance of moving object: a person running is leaning forward; a person at rest must center the weight over a steady point or lean against an object to be steadied.

They mention other natural vectors: heat rises, water flows downward, wind-blown objects show the trajectory of the movement of the invisible air. Even our sense of gravity anticipates a downward potential for motion of a heavy object in a higher position. The growth of plants, on the other hand, anticipates an upward potential for motion over a very long period.

Football players in arrested motion also show vectors of action. In 4.03 one player is entirely off the ground and in the other we can read the frustrated attempt at catching from his suspension in air and the position of the ball below his grasping arms.

4.03

Modality

As Kress and van Leeuwen use the term, modality is based on the linguistic concept of modals. As they say, modality 'refers to the truth value or credibility of (linguistically realized) statements about the world' (p. 160). Linguistic modals include 'might', 'should', 'would', 'could', and the like.

Many years ago Margaret Mead commented that an interesting difference between Americans and the British is that the latter express deep sincerity by speaking carefully and fluently but Americans express the same sentiments by hesitations and disfluencies. On hearing of a person's loss of a loved one, for example, she felt that the British response would be to say just the correct thing whereas the American response might be to mutter, 'I hardly know what to say.' Whether this is the case now or not is not at issue; what is interesting is that she was expressing the cross-cultural finding that truth, veracity, or sincerity might be expressed in very different ways from one society to another.

Similarly, Kress and van Leeuwen note that what is seen as a 'true' representation in one case often seems very distorted in others. They do not tie this to social or cultural group differences, though that might be an interesting area of study. Following Bernstein they refer to this as the *coding orientation*. For example, in portraits or candid photographs, 'natural' coloration is seen as the most faithful to reality. The three modifications of the snapshot in 4.04 give different feelings about the reality being represented from the highly saturated second shot (4.05), the reversed colors of the third (4.06), and the black and white outlining of the fourth (4.07). In this case the original (4.04) would be said to have the highest modality.

In the world outside of images there is also a type of modality not discussed by Kress and van Leeuwen. For example, a very similar kind of 'veracity' is produced by the semiotics of National Parks in North America where 'authentic' wilderness means that there should be the absolute minimum of divergence from the 'natural' colors of the scene. Park signs and overall color schemes are in brown, yellow, and green to 'match' the natural semiotics of the wilderness area. This 'modality' is highly conventionalized and well known and, within some sociocultural circles, taken for granted. The central theme seems to be the 'untouched' or non-semiotized character of the 'natural' world.

Kress and van Leeuwen argue that in Western aesthetics the primary or default modality is *naturalistic representation*. All other things being equal, the truest visual representation is felt to be the one that comes closest to what one would see if one were on the spot in person to see it. This, of course, glosses over a host of variations in what people actually 'see' governed by differences in perceptual ability, sociocultural socialization, and common, practiced social role performances as we have suggested in Chapter 3.

The main indicators of modality in visual semiotics given by Kress and van Leeuwen are

- color saturation
- color differentiation
- color modulation
- contextualization
- representation
- depth
- illumination
- brightness

Any of these factors from brightness to color saturation may be used in the design of a visual image to produce greater or lesser degrees of modality. These will vary across the four principal coding orientations currently in play in Western visual semiotics: the technological, the sensory, the abstract, and the naturalistic.

Of course, we could examine a range of sources to see if we wanted to consider further coding orientations or sub-orientations to those proposed by Kress and van Leeuwen. For example, it is not entirely clear which coding orientation would be the right one within which to classify logos and brand names. They are very high

4.04

4.05

4.06

4.07

in color in many cases but nevertheless highly abstract. Should we consider establishing yet another coding orientation to encompass these kinds of images?

It is clear that modality is a feature of specific sociocultural groups and their coding practices and so this becomes an extremely important area for analysis in a globalizing world. In the history of western European art, modalities of drawing, expression, and proportion were tabulated and even numerically graded by members of the Royal Academy of Painting and Sculpture in Paris, founded in 1648. The ancients received the highest marks while Venetians, who overemphasized color, ranked low. Debates raged toward the end of the seventeenth century over Poussin's view that drawing, which appealed to the mind, was superior to color, which appealed to the senses. Followers of Rubens held that color was more true to nature and pointed out that drawing, being based on reason, appealed to the expert elite while color appeals to everyone.

We have found in our own research that high modality tends to be associated with reds in Hong Kong, China, and Taiwan but in Korea high modality tends to be associated with darker greens and brown. In Oman blue features as a color of high modality. This research needs to be further developed, but could lead to an area of important comparative insight.

Composition

The diagram in 4.08 indicates the overall system put forward by Kress and van Leeuwen.

margin	margin
ideal	ideal
given	new

center

margin	margin
real	real
given	new

4.08

Adapted from Kress and van Leeuwen (1996), page 208

An advertising designer asks, 'Why do we always put the logo down in the lower *right*-hand corner?' The answer Kress and van Leeuwen give to that question is: that is the position which signals the *real* and the *new* information. What appears in the upper portions of the image is the *ideal*, what is in the lower portion is *real*; what is on the left is *given*, what is on the right is *new*. The company whose brand or products are being represented 'naturally' wants to be seen as real and new. One might say that in any message the point of the message is to use what is given to present the new, to use ideal concepts to convey the real.

In Kress and van Leeuwen's analysis there are two basic information structures, centered and polarized and the polarized is, in turn, divided into two systems, the left/right (given and new) system and the upper/lower (ideal and real) system.

	centered	circular
		triptych
		center–margin
information		
	polarized	left–right (given/new)
		top–bottom
		(ideal/real)

These information structures are an important point in the Kress and van Leeuwen book and while we would want to develop these much further, particularly as they interact with other visual semiotic systems and as they are changed across sociocultural groups and practices, our own research has shown this analysis to be relatively robust. This information system of a visual image works together with *salience* and *framing* to form the full composition system as the examples below indicate.

While there is some cross-cultural variation, shop signs around the world make use of these informational systems as shown in the examples below.

For example, this noodle shop in Hong Kong places the name of the company in the central position (4.09). The name is flanked on either side by more specifics. On the left it says 'rice noodles', on the right it says 'wheat noodles.' That is, the information given in the margins is the nitty gritty of the business, and the name of the shop which is given prominence by its central placement is, perhaps, more abstract or general.

The pizza and deli fast food restaurant in Washington, DC pictured in 4.10 uses a characteristic polarized left–right arrangement to display its menu. On the left in the given position are food items for sale which are indicated with photos. On the right are the specific items and the crucial *new* information – their prices. You will need to look a long time to find a case in which the prices are listed on the left with the food items placed on the right.

4.09

4.10

Having said this about the relative robustness of the left–right, given–new image structure, we will need to take up this point again when we come to the problem of situated semiotics in Chapter 8 on Emplacement. In some cases such as fire exits the polarity of given–new, left–right is reversed when the exit is in the opposite direction. We saw such cases in 2.06 and 2.07 in Chapter 2. In 2.06 the given (the fire) is on the left, the new (the escape route, where one is going) is on the right. This structure is reversed in 2.07 where the exit is to the left of the viewer of the sign and the presumed fire to the right. This is a clear case where the decontextualized semiotics presented by Kress and van Leeuwen is overridden by the situated semiotics of the material world in which the sign is placed.

The Pizza Hut at Dulles Airport in Washington, DC uses a top–bottom (ideal and real) arrangement for this sign in 4.11. At the top are the company logo in both image and text. In the bottom (real) region is more concrete information including the current special and its price.

Because of the technical structure of early browsers and of html (hypertext markup language), web pages most often anchor text in the upper left-hand corner of the page which gives preference to compositions anchored in left-to-right

4.11

reading and top-to-bottom scanning. This does have the effect, however, of giving semiotic predominance to ideal and/or given information. It further favors Euro-American semiotic preferences because the center–margin composition has until recently been more difficult to produce.

Interactive participants

Participant interactions are of three types of which the third is our primary interest here. The first type are those between the producer of the image or semiotic display and the participants which are represented in the display; the second type are those among the represented participants within the picture, and the third type are those between the represented participants and the viewer/reader/user. These three types are sketched in 4.12.

These relationships parallel relationships that occur in language as can be shown with three sentences:

- *We are writing this commentary to explicate our ideas of interactive participants* (producers' relationship to the text), i.e. **we the authors write this.**

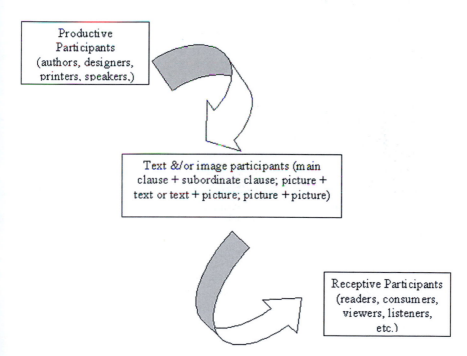

4.12

- *This opening clause is the subject of this sentence* (relationship among the participants within the structure), i.e. **X is the subject of Y.**
- *You can see in this book how to analyze interactive participant systems* (readers' relationship to the text), i.e. **you see this text.**

Participants in a picture not only exhibit narrative or conceptual relationships among themselves as we have seen above, but they also establish relationships with viewers of the image, and this is our main interest here. These relationships between pictured or represented participants and the viewer or reader are of three kinds, *contact*, *social distance*, and *attitude*. It should be clear that these relationships in images are the depiction of the social relationships outlined by Edward T. Hall beginning with his *Silent Language* as we have seen in Chapter 3. We have noted that when people approach each other to pass in the street, when they come near the boundary of social distance and personal distance, they glance down or away from eye contact with each other. This is what Goffman has called *civil inattention* – not focusing attention and being seen to be not focusing attention on the other.

With this principle operating, when we see a person looking downward at a public distance, the most common inference is that he or she is looking at the ground for some reason. When it is within social distance, the most common inference is that he or she is avoiding direct eye contact. It is this *civil inattention* that Kress and van Leeuwen call the *offer*. With one's eyes cast aside it opens the full personal front to examination by the other person socially present.

In contrast to the *offer* is the *demand* which is the direct look into the eyes of the other person. This look requires some form of social interaction. Again, this derives from social interactions in face-to-face environments. When a passerby does not look away but maintains eye contact, then we feel some obligation to enter into some sort of engagement. In other words, the *demand* is the first move in opening up interaction space in the social world.

Social distance in Kress and van Leeuwen's visual semiotics corresponds to Hall's distances and in images is represented by the size of the image within the picture frame. That is, a full head shot mimics the view you get when you are within the intimate/personal space of another person. It should be kept in mind that this is a representation; the actual visual image on the retina of a full frame photo might range from bigger than life size as when one is seated in the front rows of the cinema and a full-face shot is displayed on the screen, to very small as when one sees an advertising billboard on the highway at a great distance. An upper body shot is about the sort of image one gets within social space. A full body shot including other aspects of the environment is what one sees at a public distance.

Power and involvement relationships in the Kress and van Leeuwen system are represented by a low-angle shot and a high-angle shot, respectively. A person seen

4.13

from below looks more powerful to the viewer, perhaps because of the association of adults and children which gives this relative positioning.

The model in this advertising poster (4.13) maximizes the demand and power semiotics available through gaze, distance, and angle. She looks directly into the eyes of the viewer, she uses a pointing gesture directly at the viewer, the photo is shown from a position that puts her eye level above the viewer, it is a full-figure shot which puts her just on the edge of the social/personal distance, that is, exactly at the point where the question of whether or not there will be social interaction must be resolved, and, of course she is dressed (and only partly at that) in a Hong Kong policewoman's shirt and holds a police cap as she demands: 'I want your bra.'

In contrast with the 'policewoman' demanding the viewer's bra is this model in 4.14 for a clothing store which gives the viewer an offer. She is photographed from an angle that puts the viewer above her (involvement), the distance is social distance, that is, the viewer is within a range that requires either interaction or civil inattention, and she looks aside which provides the viewer with the license and invitation to examine her clothing.

In this chapter we have attempted to illustrate how some aspects of the interaction order are represented in visual images as analyzed in the visual semiotics of

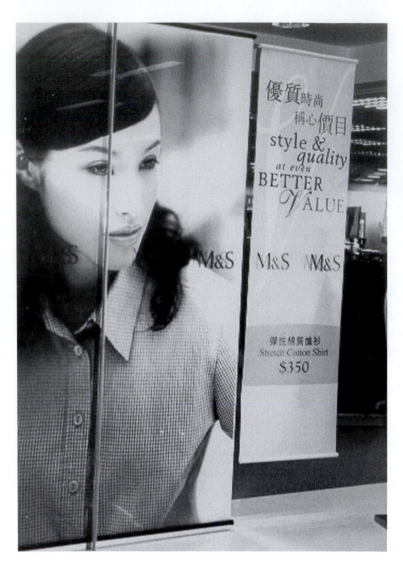

4.14

Kress and van Leeuwen. The interactive relationships represented within the frame of designed posters also obtain between the represented participants and the viewers, as shown in this last section on interactive participants. In the chapters which follow we extend the framework of visual semiotics to examine the placement of signs in the material world, showing how their meanings derive from time, space, and the social worlds indexed by language.

PRACTICE

Activity: Visual representation of narrative

Kress and van Leeuwen take up the question of narrative representations in visual images. For the purposes of geosemiotics the three most important concepts are the depiction of action – either direct action or reaction – and the invitation to action or implicit actions that we find in such 'participants' as roads and other pathways.

These school children in Umaca, Peru (4.15) are intently focused on the action of one of them writing. Her gaze as well as the gazes of all the others follow the motion of her pencil.

4.15

Assignment

Compile an illustrated poster of narrative vectors in images. These might include gaze, direction of movement of persons, animals, or inert objects such as balls or hockey pucks in sports or natural vectors such as waterfalls or objects blowing in the wind. Include a brief analysis of *how* each of these vectors is observed and *what* narrative actions the vectors create or imply. Situations such as games or sports or places such as parks and shopping malls provide relatively abundant sources of narrative actions. You might also be able to do this assignment by clipping advertising and news photos.

Observations

Are there situations and places in which narrative action is more or less abundant? One imagines the sports pages of newspapers would have more narrative action than, say, the business pages, but this needs to be tested empirically.

Activity: Modality

As Kress and van Leeuwen use the word 'modality' it signals the degree of veracity, authenticity, or naturalness of the representation of an image to the phenomenon in real life. Of course, as they point out, what is 'true' in one domain may be suspect in another. From this point of view, 'true' color when representing a succulent dish in a cookbook is likely to be done with highly saturated colors but when representing a technical object such as you would find in the instructions to operate your new video deck might be rather muted or even just an outline sketch of the functions.

Assignment

Illustrate modality operating in two different coding orientations of your choice. For example you might select images from a product repair manual to compare with images from a cookbook to see if different coding orientations are used for the production of the 'truth' about mechanical objects and about food. As an alternate, you could compare two different coding orientations in the world outside of images such as the difference in decorative schemes in a lawyer's office and in a child-care center. What aspects of color, layout, design are used to produce a sense of confidence and veracity for the care of children and for legal advice and action?

   The assignment given above can be done simply through clipping or photocopying. An alternative that can be done with a camera–software combination is to shoot a single scene with different coding orientations.

Use black and white film and color, low light and high light, different degrees of contrast and color saturation. Or produce these effects on the 'same' image using photo-processing software.

Observations

Particular coding orientations are associated with sociocultural domains both in images used to depict those domains and in the design of spaces. Observe two or three different sites to see if you can determine what color schemes, degrees of saturation and the like are used to produce the 'right' degree of modality.

Activity: Composition

A browser window is a highly complex composition with many layers within layers of structure. The screen capture in 4.16 shows at least three layers of structure:

- Outside window frame: this is set by the top (dark brown) line and the bottom toolbar line.
- Browser frame: this includes at the top the 'File' function line, the Browser function line, and the location line, at the bottom the Current status line, and along the right side the scrolling control.
- Note Six page: this is divided between the left side 'frame' with the links to pages within this website, and the right 'frame' where the content of this page is displayed.

Of course that right frame is the business of this image and is itself composed of a central figure with the *ideal* title across the top and the beginnings of the explanatory text below the figure. And, of course, here on *this* page these frame windows are set within another set of paragraphing and book layout page frames.

A few points can be mentioned here before going on to the assignment. Note that the absolute top frame is the most ideal – naming, titling, identifying: it sets the information of this page within the controlling software (Netscape). The absolute bottom line is really the bottom line as this belongs to Microsoft Windows, the operating system which controls everything else that goes on.

Those two frames, top and bottom, are also divided. At the top, on the left is the identifying logo of the software frame (given), on the right the icons which give the user the possibility of minimizing or closing it. At the bottom on the left is the first given, the 'Start' button; at the rightmost position the most real and new, the exact time of day.

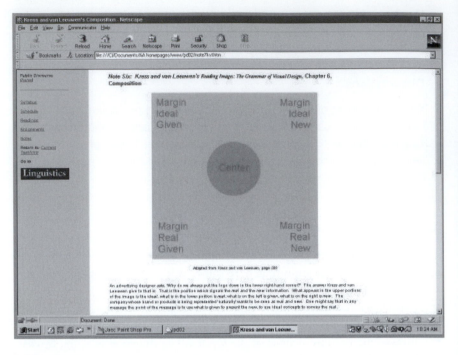

4.16

These structures play out in web-page and software design the much older principles of paragraph design. Here are two quotations from the venerable *The Elements of Style* by William Strunk Jr and E. B. White (1979 [1935]):

> The principle that the proper place for what is to be made most prominent is the end applies equally to the words of a sentence, to the sentences of a paragraph, and to the paragraphs of a composition.
>
> (p. 33)

> The opening sentence simply indicates by its subject the direction the paragraph is to take.
>
> (p. 17)

A sentence, a paragraph, or a composition begins (in languages like English which write from left to right, top to bottom) in the upper left-hand corner. It ends more toward the right, more toward the bottom. Classical web-page design continues this progression from given/ideal toward new/real though with the stricture that it works best to keep information located within a single page-image-screen-window.

We are so accustomed to the left to right, top to bottom reading pattern on the one hand and to the given–new, ideal–real information structure on the other that the section of a carry-out menu in 4.17 provides no problems in reading at all. Item numbers (most abstract) are followed by the names (*given*), then the prices (the *new* information being sought by the customer). Of course the *header* for these items ('Appetizer') must appear at the HEAD or top.

A simple reversal shows just how much we rely on these informational/ compositional structures. The menu below (4.18) with prices on the left and items on the right and with the category ('Appetizer') on the bottom not only simply *looks* wrong but requires a certain amount of extra attention even though there is really no possibility of confusing 2.50 for the item number and A1 for the price.

Appetizer

A1.	Spring Roll (2) _____	2.50
A2.	Vegetable Spring Roll (2) _____	2.50
A3.	Japanese Dumpling (4) _____	3.25
A4.	Nippon Tofu _____	2.50
A5.	Jumbo Shrimp and vegetable Tempura _____	2.50
A6.	Fried Wontons (10) _____	2.50
A7.	Lettuce Wrap Vegetable (or with Chicken) ___	3.25
A8.	Crispy Shiitake Mushroom _____	2.50
A9.	*Steamed Wonton in Hot Szechuan Sauce (10)	2.50
A10	Satay Tufu _____	2.50

4.17

Assignment

Find or create an image which clearly demonstrates each of the basic principles of composition set out by Kress and van Leeuwen, left–right (given–new), top–bottom (ideal–real), center–margin (focused and peripheral). Add to these three a fourth image which uses these principles in a more complex combination of frames within frames. Prepare a short analysis of your reasons for considering the information structure to be what you have claimed.

2.50	_____Spring Roll (2)	A1
2.50	_____Vegetable Spring Roll (2)	A2
3.25	_____Japanese Dumpling (4)	A3
2.50	_____Nippon Tofu	A4
2.50	_____Jumbo Shrimp and vegetable Tempura	A5
2.50	_____Fried Wontons (10)	A6
3.25	___Lettuce Wrap Vegetable (or with Chicken)	A7
2.50	_____Crispy Shiitake Mushroom	A8
2.50	*Steamed Wonton in Hot Szechuan Sauce (10)	A9
2.50	_____Satay Tufu	A10

Appetizer

4.18

This composition assignment can be accomplished in one of three ways:

• Locate and clip images from paper or web sources
• Find sources and use photo-imaging software to alter the information structure
• Combining camera and software, design your own images to illustrate these principles.

Observations

Your observations will be primarily focused on existing displays and images. Discourses in public such as billboards, bus-side displays, and shop-window signs are particularly rich sources of examples in which to study these principles of information structuring.

Activity: Interactive participants

The purpose of this activity is to make your own shots, either natural or posed, which will show the differences between demand and offer, the differences of perception at the three distances, personal, social, and public, and the differences between the representation of power and of involvement.

Assignment

Make several mockups of advertisements or journalistic photos which will exploit the representation of interactive participants to show different viewer–participant relationships. This can be done with camera work, by using digital photos together with some editing software, or by clipping existing photos from magazines, brochures, and other forms of advertising.

Use your observations below as the basis for taking pictures to illustrate the three types of relationship (contact, social distance, and attitude). You can either shoot separate photos at the appropriate distances and angles or use a single long shot and use cropping and other editing features to achieve effects. These photos can either be candid, naturally occurring shots or posed.

Observations

It is *very important* to observe how your camera sees an image by comparison with the eye. To make these observations do the following:

- Stand at personal–intimate distance from your subject. While focused on the eyes of your subject, note what you are able to see within your peripheral vision. Be quite exact about this. You will notice, for example, that the clarity of what you see drops off very quickly outside a fairly narrow circle of vision.
- Using your camera viewfinder, move closer or farther away from your subject until you see in the frame exactly the size image you have seen with the naked eye. What you will find is that the actual physical distance you are standing from your subject is very different. [Most likely you will be several feet farther back with the camera.] This depends to a great extent upon the lens your camera is using. If you have access to multiple lenses, also change your lenses until you get as close as possible to what you see with your eyes face-to-face.
- Repeat this procedure for social distance and for public distance.

5 Interlude on geosemiotics

5.01

Place semiotics

'Non-semiotic' spaces (prohibition)
Semiotic spaces

From the social world to images in the world

A beggar in a street in Beijing develops a recognizable role performance in the real world. For his personal front, he wears shabby clothes, he has a bandaged left ear, he kneels on the cold pavement tiles, and places his walking stick and an enamel cup for donations in front of himself. His body is oriented at a right angle to the flow of pedestrian traffic and he remains motionless until a donation is made and then clasps his hands in a gesture of gratitude and bows several times without speaking. The cup is placed well within his personal space but at a slight distance from his body so that a person making a donation will need to enter that space to do so, but need not enter *too* closely. By placing himself in the center of a busy pedestrian walkway, he has exploited the situational front or place semiotics offered by an active public space as his front stage.

A well-dressed pedestrian approaches, locates his pocket change, and then moves toward the cup to make a donation. While his hand comes to within inches of the cup, his left, trailing leg remains at an extended distance providing balance on the one hand but also marking his entrance into the personal space of the beggar as only a momentary intrusion.

We began in Chapter 2 by outlining the problem of indexicality. How does language locate entities in the world to produce meaning? More generally we might phrase this as: how does any sign point to the world for its meaning?

Just above we opened the first paragraph with the noun phrase 'a beggar in a street in Beijing'. If we were to present that sentence simply as a textual object to be read, one would be able to interpret the sentence quite well as an abstract or hypothetical statement about how some beggar, any beggar, develops the role performance required to elicit donations.

In this case, however, we are not writing about an abstract or hypothetical beggar but about the very particular one in photo 5.01. How does the reader know this? The reader knows this through indexicality. We are writing of 'a beggar'; there is a photo immediately present of a beggar. Indexicality suggests (but never absolutely limits the meaning to) that beggar in the image. As the further sentences of the paragraph develop, each point may be compared to the photo and, one detail at a time, the security of that indexical meaning is established.

In Chapter 3 we turned from the problem of indexicality to an analysis of some of the resources by which we use our bodies to produce ourselves as signs in the world. Taking our point of departure from the work of Edward T. Hall and Erving Goffman, we saw that we use our bodies to take on social role performances in the presence of others to signal to them what sort of persons we are making ourselves out to be and what actions we are taking. The distances we stand or sit apart, the way we use our eyes, how we move in space, the clothing we wear and how we wear it display the personal front we are claiming, how we expect others to respond to us, how we perceive the passage of time, and how we are defining the physical and social spaces in which we are living. In short, we produce the interaction order.

This beggar and this benefactor have been captured in this photograph in a telling moment of social life that would be recognizable to people throughout much of the world. They are using their bodies and the sign equipment of their personal fronts within this broad social space to signal to each other and to the world that they are beggar and giver at the moment of the gift. Their performances enable the indexicality of words such as 'beggar', 'contributor', 'benefactor', or 'donor', as well as somewhat more distant words such as 'well dressed', 'shabby clothes'. In these ways indexicality in language works together with the indexable in the world to produce the meaning: this is a picture of a pedestrian giving something to a beggar. While we hope it is not belaboring the point, this meaning depends on the active work of the social construction of these performances in these social spaces. That is, we feel that what we learn from Hall and Goffman and the many others who have analyzed the ways in which social performances are constructed is that 'beggar' and 'contributor' are not just inherent characteristics of these persons. On the contrary, they are actively constructed and performed at particular moments in particular spaces.

The concern then in Chapter 4 was to look rather fleetingly at ways in which pictures – images and/or texts – represent meanings. The study of visual semiotics as outlined by Kress and van Leeuwen is a study much broader than we were able to detail in Chapter 4. From the point of view of geosemiotics, our interest is somewhat more narrowly defined than theirs. We are interested in four general aspects of Kress and van Leeuwen's visual semiotics:

1   How are social relationships in the world represented in images?
2   How are social relationships between the world and the image constructed?
3   What are the concrete relationships between image representations and textual representations?
4   How do social actors in the world make use of pictures (images and texts) in taking social actions?

We have pointed out in Chapter 4 that it is worth being cautious in developing an analysis of 'caught' images by comparison with constructed ones. In this case, the image was a still capture from a video tape made of this pedestrian passageway. The video included not just this beggar but many other aspects of the scene including bookstore fronts and the activities of quite a few other participants in the scene. This image was first captured as a full screen image, largely because it was a clear, centered image of the beggar and the donor. That is to say, it was captured specifically because of the social moment of role performance it was seen to be illustrating.

After that the image was cropped to eliminate some of the 'extraneous' activity within the 'real scene' of the wide-angle video tape. Further, brightness and contrast were altered to produce a more reproducible photograph which would highlight this moment of social activity.

So to address the first of the questions in which we are interested, the social relationships in that real world moment in Beijing were represented in this case by selecting a moment of transfer, the moment when money went from hand to cup. We did not select a moment just seconds before this when no passerby was engaged with the beggar and he could be seen deeply bowed but looking rapidly left and right up and down the street to select a likely mark. After the selection of this particular mark he took on his totally passive pose to receive the gift. Once the mark had passed he resumed his active scanning and selection process.

To put this another way in the framework of Chapter 3, we might have selected a backstage moment rather than a frontstage moment to represent in this image. Our interest here was in the transaction between two social actors on the frontstage of the giving of the gift and so we selected the peak moment of that enactment. As we have said in Chapter 3, social actors produce their meanings with some grammar of indexability in the real world of social relationships.

Concerning the second question, we constructed this image; we did not just shoot it, as we have noted above. We constructed it within an 'objective' and naturalistic or documentary coding orientation. That is, we have tried to produce an image of high documentary modality. It took some time with photo editing software to produce the image reproduced here. This is decidedly not what the eye or the camera 'saw'.

Our interest in semiotic relations between images and text might not be entirely obvious on first glance because there is no text within the 'beggar' image for us to discuss. In this case we are shifting our attention. First it was the 'real' world of a beggar in Beijing. Secondly, it was the image of the action which was our interest. Now we are shifting to the image as it appears here within *this* text.

Photo 5.02 reproduces that image and the opening paragraph of this Interlude in the draft of February 22, 2002 as displayed on the screen of the word processor. It will resemble in the most crucial ways the text you see when you are reading this (but of course it will also be different in quite interesting ways). As we discussed above, the text of the opening paragraph might stand alone as text without the image. In that case it would be read as a concrete description, but nevertheless a hypothetical case presented for discussion. With the image present just above the text the same language is read as a specific description of the image (or of the events depicted in that image), not only or simply as a hypothetical example.

To put this in the terms of Kress and van Leeuwen's visual semiotics, the image occupies the ideal position and the text the real position. The text by itself might easily be read as ideal and hypothetical, but with the image immediately above, the meaning of the text is shifted to include the real meaning; this is the picture–caption relationship.

Finally we have a concern for how a picture or a visual representation is taken up as a resource for social actors in their own worlds. This is something we cannot illustrate here with this image nor can we even know. Have you as the reader of this text looked at the image first or at the text? Have you looked back and forth between image and text as this discussion has progressed? How did you locate the 'beggar' in the image? We presume this is because we have produced the beggar

INTERLUDE ON GEOSEMIOTICS

Geosemiotics in space and time

A beggar in a street in Beijing develops a recognizable role performance in the real world. For his personal front, he wears shabby clothes, he has a bandaged left ear, he kneels on the cold pavement tiles, and places his walking stick and an enamel cup for donations in front of him. His body is oriented at a right angle to the flow of pedestrian traffic and he remains motionless until a donation is made and then clasps his hands in a gesture of gratitude and bows several times without speaking. The cup is placed well within his personal space but at a slight distance from his body so that a person making a donation will need to enter that space to do so, but need not enter *too* closely. By placing himself in the center of a busy pedestrian walkway, he has exploited the situational front offered by an active public space as his front stage.

5.02

as indexable through the center placement, through the perceptual salience of that image compared to other parts of the photo. But also you will have brought to this your own history of beggars in the world, of images and their meanings, and of textual appropriation. Have you taken this up as an illustrative example of the visual semiotics of Kress and van Leeuwen or as an illustration of poverty in early twenty-first-century China?

Geosemiotics in space and time

Chapters 2 through 4 have provided the foundation for us to turn now to the main concerns of geosemiotics. Geosemiotics might be defined as follows:

Geosemiotics: the study of the social meaning of the material placement of signs in the world. By 'signs' we mean to include any semiotic system including language and discourse.

We have not called this study *geolinguistics* although we might have done that. To have called it that would have been to retain the focus on just language itself. Although our concern originates in the problem of indexicality in language and as linguists this remains a very important concern for us, indexicality in language works by pointing to a world outside of language. Language points to a world of social role performances, of personal fronts and sign equipment, of situational structures, layouts and designs of built environments. It is those sign systems in the world outside of language but to which language points or in which language is used which are our main interest. Hence the term *geosemiotics*.

Another way to say it is that *geosemiotics* is the study of the *indexability* of the material world. This is not the same as the *indexicality* of language which Hanks defines as 'the pervasive context-dependency of natural language utterances' (p. 119). A linguistic form is indexical in that it 'stands for its object neither by resemblance to it, nor by sheer convention, but by contiguity with it' (p. 119). Indexicality is the language side of this contiguity; *geosemiotics* is the indexability side of this vector of meaning.

Beginning in Chapter 6 and in the following chapters, we begin our study of place semiotics. We turn our focus away from the actions and activities of social actors in the world to a study of the material world itself and the places that language finds in it. Then finally in Chapters 9 and 10 we will return to see how these semiotic systems work together as we live our daily lives.

Semiotic vs non-semiotic spaces

Geosemiotics makes reference to the real, physical, material world in which we live our lives. We reiterate this because we find it is rather easy to slip from speaking concretely to speaking metaphorically. To ground (literally) this meaning of geosemiotics, we start with the earth itself.

The first way in which meaning is inscribed on the surface of the earth is in making a distinction between what we might call 'semiotic' and 'non-semiotic' spaces. This is absurd, of course, because any space carries meaning inherently. Nevertheless, many sociocultural systems define some spaces as prohibited for semiotic overlays. Photo 5.03 below was taken in a semiotically restricted zone, Banff National Park in Canada. Here geosemiotic intrusions are quite severely restricted to barely visible walking trails as we see across this rockface on Sulphur Mountain.

The photo taken at Huangshan National Park in China (5.04) is similar in some ways to the picture from Banff in being a mountain park preserve. Nevertheless, in such mountain parks in China they *prefer* to have writing on rock faces. This is engraved in the rock and regularly repainted to keep the writing brightly legible.

The analogous but reversed situation is seen in these two signs for the global convenience food chain store. The first (5.05) is a typical sign one would find in

5.03

5.04

5.05 (*above*) and 5.06 (*below*)

Hong Kong and which would be identifiable by potential shoppers from many places in the world. The second (5.06) is the same company's location on Wisconsin Avenue in the Georgetown area of Washington, DC. Here there is an aesthetic of very low semiotic intrusion. Only the company name inscribed very discreetly on the awning indicates what sort of store will be found in this building.

In both cases the *geosemiotic* starting point is a very general set of conventions on how and where meanings may be inscribed on the material world. This will be taken up in more detail in Chapter 8 on emplacement.

One way

Shop signs or roadway signs around the world are very useful in coming to understand what is indexable or geosemiotics. That's probably because so little language is involved that we can see fairly clearly how the different elements of the indexicality – indexable linkage are working.

A characteristic 'ONE WAY' traffic sign gives vehicular traffic regulations in three ways. There are the words 'ONE WAY' which are conventionalized as meaning 'Drive only in one direction – the direction of the arrow.' The second way in which traffic regulation is given is through the visual semiotics of the white arrow vector on a black, rectangular sign. The rectangle is widely used for traffic directions as are the white on black and the arrow vector.

This arrow vector in a white-on-black format is so powerful that a friend of one of the authors read it universally as meaning the English words 'ONE WAY'. When he was in Mexico it took some serious rethinking for him to get the Spanish word 'TRANSITO' as in 5.07 to mean 'traffic'. As far as he was concerned it meant 'ONE WAY' because in his past experience whatever letters appeared in block letters in black on the face of the traffic arrow vector meant 'ONE WAY'.

Neither of these types of meaning, however, faces up to indexicality, the third type of meaning found in this situation. 'One way' or 'transito' (traffic) still require us to know which direction in the world is the direction to drive our car. The arrow by itself without words might do the job in a sense, but not until it is located in a particular position in the material world. None of these signs means anything about where to drive until the sign is erected on a pole or fastened to the side of a building or somehow located in relation to a roadway. This sign *means*

5.07   5.08

one direction of traffic *along the nearest roadway that moves in the same direction as this sign is oriented.*

In this case the *indexable* is the roadway (not visible in these photos) and it is this roadway and all its associated meanings that give the *geosemiotic* meaning to the sign. That type of indexability is what we have called *emplacement* and is discussed in Chapter 8. Before coming to emplacement, however, we first take up the problems of code preference in Chapter 6 and of inscription in Chapter 7.

6 Place semiotics: Code preference

Indexing the geopolitical world

One of the surest ways we locate ourselves in the geopolitical world is through the signs we see here and there about us in city streets, marking road regulations alongside the highway, and labelling consumer products. The snapshot of a city street in 6.01 may not tell us exactly which city we are in but we are likely to make an immediate assumption that we are somewhere in an English-speaking community.

Similarly, the sign prohibiting smoking on the construction site shown in photo 6.02 signals presence in a Chinese community. Actually for those with the knowledge to see it, this sign is written using the simplified Chinese characters used in Mainland China (and in Singapore), not the traditional characters which are used in Hong Kong or Taiwan. In this way it indexes not only 'Chinese-speaking community' but 'Mainland China'. The sign further places this photograph in time as these simplified characters were introduced in several waves of language reform which occurred sometime after the 1949 Revolution. Thus it indexes a period of time somewhere between about 1960 and the present.

Place semiotics

Semiotic spaces
  pictures
    code preference
      center–margin
      top–bottom
      left–right
      earlier–later

6.01 (*above*) and 6.02 (*below*)

Here it is worth a momentary return to the signs in 6.01. We see the brand name Casablanca® written in a font which is not much used in our contemporary period but which was widely used at the turn of the nineteenth to the twentieth century. Was this photo taken then? Obviously it was not because we also see signs with much more recent lettering styles on the same store, not to mention a glance at the windshield of a very recent model car. Furthermore, the image is taken in color photography which was not available at the time that 'Casablanca' font might have been used as a straightforward advertising sign. In other words the font choice in this brand name is symbolic rather than indexical. It symbolizes the period of time in which ceiling fans were once popular and with which they are associated in the modern public mind. It does not index that time in the way that the contemporary fonts and signs as well as the color photography index our own period.

It is possible that we could be deceived, however, in going by the language used in and of itself. The sign for a beauty parlor shown in 6.03 is in English. It says, 'Beauty Island'. Of course it is possible that this would index an English-speaking community as did the signs in 6.01.

This sign was seen in Nanjing, China. Here we think that the use of English is much like the use of the 'Casablanca' font in 6.01. It is to symbolize rather than index. English is used to symbolize foreign taste and manners; it does not index an English-speaking community.

6.03

We believe that there are at least two clues to this in this sign. One is the name itself which, at least to our ears, is rather non-native-like in its style. 'Beauty Island' seems a bit odd as the name for a beauty salon. In fact, by the same principle that this Chinese beauty parlor has an English name, in the US one might find a European name – most likely French – to symbolize this same placement of the business within a class social structure.

The second clue is in the elaboration of the final 'y' of the word 'beauty' as the visual centerpiece of this image. The image is constructed within a circular center-and-periphery design which, as Kress and van Leeuwen have pointed out, is often used in Chinese and other Asian picture constructions. What makes this stand out as quite likely *not* a native use of the language is the emphasis that this design principle gives to the 'y'. We would not want to say that such a thing would be impossible for an English-speaking designer, but it does seem to us that other semiotic conventions such as the capitalization of only word-initial consonants works very strongly against the choice of this design principle.

From these examples we can see that the actual language used – English, Chinese, French, etc. – can either **index** the community within which it is being used or it can **symbolize** something about the product or business which has nothing to do with the place in which it is located. These same distinctions can be made through the choice of fonts or indeed preferred visual semiotic systems of construction. Our interest here in Chapter 6 is in geopolitically situated semiotic systems. That is, we will focus on the use of code preferences which depend upon and therefore which index geopolitical location.

In this discussion of code preference it is very important to remember the distinction between symbolization and indexicality as we have just discussed it. A code may be chosen because it indexes the point in the world where it is placed – this is an Arabic-speaking community (or business or nation) – or because it symbolizes a social group because of some association with that group – this is a Chinese restaurant because there is Chinese writing in the shop sign. Whether our concern is with code preference based on geopolitical indexing or with symbolization based on sociocultural associations, we must have some evidence from *outside* the signs themselves to make this determination.

Our main interest in this chapter, however, is not in the geopolitical or other sociocultural positioning of codes within a community. That is taken up in the next chapter, Chapter 7, under the heading of inscription. There we will address the question of what can be read at a more ideological level from seeing what code has been chosen to represent language in a sign placed in a particular place in the world. Here our interest is in the problem of bilingual signs or, more generally, the problem of multiple codes within a single sign or picture.

As we shall see below, the main semiotic resource by which code preference is produced when more than a single code is used is placement within the picture or in physical space. In most cases studied so far the preferred code is located above the secondary or peripheral codes if they are aligned vertically; if they are aligned horizontally the preferred code is located in the left position and the peripheral code is located in the right position. A third possibility is that the preferred code is located in the center and the peripheral code is placed around the periphery.

A point on methodology

When a text is in multiple codes (two or three or more languages such as English and Chinese) or multiple orthographies there is a system of preference. The mere fact that these items in a picture or in the world cannot be located simultaneously in the same place produces a choice system. The producers of the signs put the preferred codes in a pattern similar to the construction system discussed in Chapter 4; the significant divisions (top–bottom, right–left) are the same, though the meaning is not. The preferred code is on top, on the left, or in the center and the marginalized code is on the bottom, on the right, or on the margins.

While the code preference system works much like the construction system, probably by analogy to it, it is not really the same system. Our evidence for this is in signs such as 6.04. The book-image signs saying 'Cardiff' and 'Caerdydd' occupy the ideal portion of the sign identifying the library; the prohibition on

6.04

parking bicycles occupies the real portion in the lower half. Within those ideal and real segments there is the secondary division into preferred code (English) on the left and secondary (Welsh) on the right in the ideal segment and English on top, Welsh on bottom in the real segment.

Of course we will need to clarify more carefully that we do not really have any solid evidence about languages that have a normal text vector (direction of writing) from right to left such as Arabic, nor about how Arabic and English are displayed to show code preference where both of those languages are used. Much research remains to be done in this area. But to return to the methodological point, in places such as Hong Kong and Quebec the relative position of the two official codes is governed by law and is in agreement; that is the upper position in signs is the preferred position, the lower position is secondary as shown in 6.05. Also the preferred code in Quebec, French, must be presented as more salient than any secondary or peripheral code.

Naturally, these legal policies are frequently violated, particularly in domains at some distance from legal concern. For example, in Hong Kong street signs and governmental offices fall within these strictures, but commercial signs and private notices are not regulated by these policies. The methodological problem arises when there is no legal or policy requirement to guide the analysis. If language (or code) X is on top and Y is below it, how do we know which is the case in the following two scenarios?

- X is preferred, so we know the top is the preferred position
- the top is preferred, so we know X is the preferred code

In other words we need to have independent evidence either for the semiotic system or for the preference of the code. This is an empirical question that can be

6.05

settled largely through ethnographic means. In our research in Hong Kong and China, for example, we found there was almost a continuum of domains from tightly controlled ones to extremely loose and occasional ones. Government regulations control the code in street signs, for example, and throughout Hong Kong English is placed on top and Chinese is placed below that, this despite the fact that Hong Kong is overwhelmingly a Chinese speaking and reading speech community. This code preference rather transparently represents a carryover from some century and a half of colonial rule.

In commercial domains it is somewhat more complex an issue. If we take large shopping malls as an example, there is a continuum from those in which there is a uniform design principle which is carried throughout the mall and all official signs, that is all signs that are prepared by the owners of the mall, fit within a single design principle. One mall, Festival Walk, maintains a rigorous pattern of English on top or on the left, Chinese below or on the right as exemplified in 6.06.

In this case one might say that the principle invoked was that this is one of the newest malls in Hong Kong – it just opened as we were doing this research – and it is firmly positioned within the broadly international sphere of globalizing commerce. Characteristically the mall has many upper-end fashion shops as well as restaurants providing offerings from the major world cuisines. It might be going a bit too far to argue that this mall was firmly asserting the global status of Hong Kong and its commerce just at the historical moment when sovereignty over Hong Kong was returning to China, but there is some feeling in this mall that goes much beyond just the positioning of words in signs that the same code positioning is here indicating a global (English) vs local (Chinese) pattern of choice rather than the colonial (English) vs colonized (Chinese) pattern we see in the street signs.

Our point is that the same binary choice of English and Chinese is a semiotic code system which may be used in the service of quite different ideological positions – colonialization on the one hand and globalization in the twenty-first century on the other.

In Hong Kong the Mass Transit Railway (MTR) is another unified complex which carries throughout its entities a single semiotic system. Throughout the territory color schemes, train, station, and platform designs, colors, and materials are uniform. Likewise, the code preference system is uniform, but in the case of the MTR it is Chinese which is placed in the upper position, English in the lower (or left and right and center and periphery).

This flip-flop is perfectly consistent through these two coherently designed systems operating within the same speech community. We believe this tells us two things: first, there *is* a coherent code preference system which privileges the top, the left, and the center, and second, the code preference should not be assumed to reflect any particular community or ideology in some *a priori* way. That must be determined through further ethnographic research.

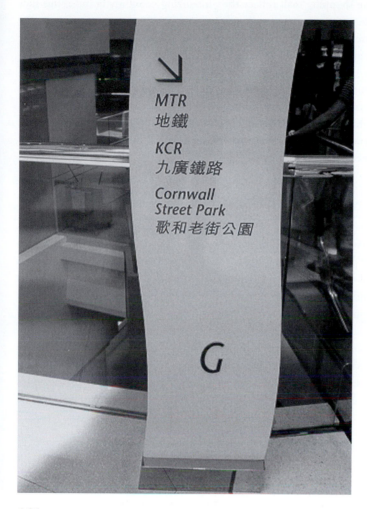

6.06

In this case of the MTR system we believe that the selection of Chinese as the preferred code does not reflect a resistance to or inversion of the British colonial history – the company is, after all, a Hong Kong government company – nor does it reflect a resistance to the forces of globalization – it is one of the sleekest and most efficient of the world's high technology metropolitan transport systems. We believe the code preference for Chinese in the MTR represents a pragmatic decision to maximize indexability for the vastly dominant Chinese-reading population of Hong Kong (about 98 per cent). Chinese is where it is because that is the code being indexed by the predominant users of the system. All the more then does the 'preference' for English in street signs reflect the colonial ideology and the English in the shopping mall reflect the globalizing economy because this flies in the face of the pragmatics of simply reading the signs.

We believe such comparative broad systems as those of a shopping mall or of the MTR (and there are many others which we have considered as well) indicate a clear code preference semiotic system, upper–lower, left–right, center–periphery. What is much more difficult to 'read' is what system of values is selecting this preference system. It might be geopolitical ideology, it might be pragmatic convenience, it might be current fashion. This aspect of the analysis cannot be 'read off' simply from seeing the code choice which has been made but must be subjected to historical and ethnographic analysis.

Code preference in space–time

In the discussion of code preference above we looked only at fixed and static relationships between signs. In some cases, however, code preferences are shown in separate signs placed in relationship to each other. For example, in Ontario, a traditionally rather Anglophone stronghold in officially bilingual Canada, both English and French road signs are given, but the first sign the motorist encounters is the English sign. French is placed on a second sign a bit further down the road (6.10 below).

Such a case crosses over from placement within a frame to placement in the world. To the extent that code preference indexes sociocultural or sociopolitical processes, we can see the potential for many of the sociopolitical processes of change in a society to be written through this system of code preferences on the times and spaces of our world.

PRACTICE

As we have said above, where there is a choice of codes available, that choice forms a code preference semiotic system. When two or more codes appear in the same picture, the choice of position is in itself a semiotic system which indexes the places in which the sign appears and is an indexable sign for social actors in that world.

Activity: Code preference as position in a frame (upper–lower; left–right)

The sign 6.07 shows French as the preferred language at a train station in Paris.

Many places in the world post signs, advertisements, and other notices in two or more languages. In some places such as Quebec or Hong Kong there are explicit government policies governing the relative positions of the two languages. In

6.07

Quebec, French must be both in the upper position and written more prominently. In Hong Kong English is in the upper position and Chinese in a lower position, but with the difference from Quebec that this applies only to such official signage as street name signs. Because of the inherent economy of Chinese writing, the Chinese takes up less space so it is not clear whether the lesser space used by the Chinese characters is also signaling lesser salience.

In Cardiff, Wales, English enjoys the privileged upper position and Welsh is placed below it on signs such as we saw above. The Japanese road sign (6.08) is not actually bilingual but uses two different writing systems, Chinese characters and Roman letters. In this case the 'Chinese' writing is on top and is significantly larger and more prominent than the Roman letters. This is markedly different from the sign for Cill Airne – Killarney in Ireland (6.09) where the Irish is given the preferred upper position, English the secondary, lower position, but the English is given much greater prominence, making it clear that the code preference system can be played off against salience.

All of these examples are texts contained within a framed sign and so one might ask if the code preference system isn't somewhat decontextualized from placement in the material world? There are two issues here. First of all, top and bottom

6.08

are placements in the material world. Note that left and right are relational terms, not related directly to the physical world. As Gregory Bateson liked to puzzle people, a mirror reverses my left and right sides but does not reverse top and bottom. This is because top and bottom are, in fact, terms which make reference to the material world whereas left and right are internally relational, not absolute. Turn the object and left becomes right.

6.09

Assignment

Make an image collage that illustrates different ways in which code preference is played off against other systems of visual semiotics such as salience. Travel about your town or city to document code preferences. These can be found in embassies and consulates, of course, but more commonly in 'ethnic' grocery stores, churches, and restaurants. Look for cases in which multiple codes are used and document which positions are used for which codes.

Observations

Are there factors such as whether the sign is on a large poster or in a printed handbill which might contribute to the difference in such systems as salience?

Activity: Code preference as earlier or later

The picture taken in Ontario (6.10) illustrates yet another way in which code preference is displayed semiotically in the world. While Canada is officially a bilingual country, on roads in Ontario the preferred English comes first into view as one drives along, the French comes later.

6.10

Assignment

If you live in a bilingual region, document road signs to see if there are instances of one language occuring sooner and another later. If not, check out websites in multiple languages to see which language occurs as the default language and which others must be selected as 'later' in the sequence of login.

Observations

What similarities can you find between highway signs and icons on the 'information highway' (www)?

7   Place semiotics: Inscription

Inscription

Among the resources of place semiotics, the topic of inscription might easily become a course in itself. In a sense it is already much more than that. The semiotic systems of inscription would include everything that printers know about the meanings of choosing and setting a typeface for a book or what designers know about using a particular typeface and color scheme for an advertisement. But beyond that, we'd include what sign painters know about how to present a banner – not just the typefaces but the type of cloth and the way it would be hung to suggest a range from the lightheartedness of a sale to the seriousness of a new exhibition at the National Gallery of Art in Washington, DC.

In a few words, we use inscription to cover all of the meaning systems that are based on the physical materiality of language (but also other code systems) in the

---

Place semiotics

Semiotic spaces
   pictures
      inscription
         fonts, letterform
         material qualities
            permanence or durability
            temporality or newness
            quality
         layering; add-ons or extensions
         state changes

world. This would include the meanings associated with the difference between a boardwalk, a gravel path, and a concrete sidewalk, between jeans and a silk suit, between a leather-bound book and a paperback, glossy paper and newsprint. For our purposes here, though, we concentrate on just a few of the meaning systems associated with the presentation of *language* in the material world. These include at least these four:

- **fonts** (or letterform) – any way in which letters or other written symbols are produced from handwriting and calligraphy through to word processing fonts and professional typefaces including size and shape or color
- **material** – the physical substances on which the inscription is made, from granite monuments to sand writing at the beach
- **layering** – add-ons/extensions of an inscription on another usually more permanent inscription such as 'on sale today' or 'limited time only'
- **state changes** – current meaning given through flashing neon lights to a lighted 'open' sign

Fonts (letterform)

Fonts, typefaces, lettering systems, calligraphy, the use of pens, brushes, pencils, typewriters, word processors – all of these produce a range of different meanings in the 'same' linguistic message.

Until a few decades ago it would have been quite an insult to send a personal letter to a friend which was not written in one's own handwriting. It was felt that much of a person's personality as well as their current state of mind could be seen in the handwriting. A typewritten note was felt to be very distant, cold, and impersonal. Such a social convention goes beyond being a convention because we feel we are seeing something about the meaning through the resources by which the language was inscribed.

Branding works partly because it is not just the name of a product which is legally protected but also the exact manner in which it is written including the color scheme. It is the distinctive font that carries this meaning to a great extent. As the fake logo (7.01) below shows, a change in font, even when the color scheme and the words are the same, brings about a significant change in meaning.

Fonts and geopolitics

In the case of branding what is at stake is a customer's or consumer's impression of the store or product being offered. In an extended body of research together with colleagues we studied the use of particular fonts in China and Hong Kong at the time Hong Kong returned from British to Chinese sovereignty. We found that

7.01

even the font chosen to write Chinese became keyed to these geopolitical developments.

Chinese is written with a set of characters which had become standardized over many centuries. This 'standard' for writing Chinese is what is used in Hong Kong and Taiwan and was used in China up until the time of the Revolution in 1949. Following that the new government undertook a massive educational and literacy campaign to simplify this writing system, much like that which was done in Japan just following the Second World War in 1946. In some cases totally new characters were created, in others they formally adopted short cuts which had become common in practical day-to-day writing. This would be much like if English writers were to shift from writing 'through' as 'thru'. This is already done on the credit cards issued by VISA, for example, but not officially sanctioned or taught in schools.

To give a single example for readers unfamiliar with Chinese, there is a company named 'Special Region Electronic Goods' the sign for which is in 7.02.

7.02

The company name which here is written in the new simplified characters is in 7.03.

7.03

This same name would be written in the traditional characters as in 7.04.

7.04

The differences are not great in this case, but many readers of one system say they cannot make any sense out of the other. The campaign to change this writing system is enforced by government law. There is a fine of ¥1,000 (about US$125) for using a traditional character in place of a legally sanctioned simplified character.

Between Hong Kong and Mainland China the border is very porous in many symbolic ways. Even long before the change in political sovereignty, beginning with the reform policy of Deng Xiaoping, people in Mainland China began to adopt a paradoxical practice. The 'new' simplified writing system is associated in their minds with the Revolution of 1949; the 'old' writing system has a double association. It is associated on the one hand with pre-Revolutionary China, the ancient Confucian literature and history. On the other hand it is associated with the newest and most modern Chinese life outside of China as located in Hong Kong, Taiwan, and overseas. So ironically, the 'old' writing system began to symbolize opening up to the outside world, to beauty parlors and karaoke lounges and to sex shops. The 'new' writing symbolized the conservative forces of the socialist state. In symbolic values using the 'old' writing to symbolize everything new in the rapidly developing economy would be approximately like our reactions would be to a sign in Gothic lettering saying 'Ye Olde Sex Shop'.

Our research project tracked the flows of these two writing systems, orthographies and their fonts, from China into Hong Kong and from Hong Kong (and Taiwan) into China during the few years just before and after the change of political sovereignty. We wanted to know if we could 'read' shifting political winds in the use of these two ways of writing Chinese. We did not know if 'traditional' writing would increase in China with more opening up through Hong Kong, or if on the contrary, 'simplified' writing would increase in Hong Kong as it became China officially.

As it turned out, there was not a great increase of traditional writing in China and almost no entrance of simplified writing into Hong Kong. The electronics shop we looked at just above (photo 7.02) was the only business we or our research assistants were able to find in Hong Kong in the year following the political change which was using simplified writing. To our surprise the most noticeable change in both places was a considerable increase in the amount of Japanese writing. This was not something we had predicted or expected.

Indexicality or symbolism?

To interpret this body of research we need to return to something we wrote at the beginning of Chapter 6 on code preference. There are two analytically distinct ways in which a sign (or a code or a font) can make meaning, one through **indexicality** and the other through **symbolization**. When a sign makes its meaning by its geophysical placement, its physical characteristics, or its placement together with another sign or object, we call that phenomenon indexicality. When a sign makes its meaning by representing something else which is not present or which is ideal or metaphorical, we call that process symbolization (of course if it is an actual picture of the thing being represented we would call that an icon).

At the beginning of Chapter 6 we commented on the use of the old-style font for writing the brand name of a ceiling fan, Casablanca® (image 6.01). We said this font symbolized the turn of the nineteenth to the twentieth century; the other signs indexed the beginning of the twenty-first century as well as a world of English-speaking customers. We had that same problem in interpreting the use of traditional and simplified writing in China. One solution is simply to say that traditional Chinese writing in Hong Kong indexes Hong Kong – that is the way Chinese is written there. At the same time simplified Chinese writing indexes Mainland China – it is the required writing system in China. Where there are departures from this, we could then speak of symbolization. Traditional writing in China *symbolizes* the discourses of China opening up to the world and global commerce, it does not *index* them. Similarly, simplified writing in Hong Kong would symbolize unification with Mainland China, it would not index that Hong Kong is China.

That is a partial solution which shows that whether we consider a sign to have an indexical meaning or a symbolic meaning depends in part on where the sign is in the world as on well as our own historical or social expectations for what would be the unmarked or default meanings in that place. We believed that traditional writing in China symbolized the reform discourse and the progressive movement toward a more globally connected economy and political life. We also believed that simplified writing in Hong Kong would symbolize the political sovereignty of China after the change in sovereignty. We were already a bit doubtful about simplified writing in Hong Kong because the only instance we could find was the one shown above the electronics store in a busy commercial district. This did not seem a likely place for the political sovereignty of China to be asserted and furthermore, it was a private commercial enterprise using this writing, and not either the Mainland government or the government of the Special Administrative Region of Hong Kong.

To test these ideas we and our colleagues conducted focus groups and interviews in which participants were asked to discuss a variety of photographs of signs taken in Hong Kong and in several cities in Mainland China. What we found was that there was an interaction among three factors, the indexical function of the sign, the symbolic function of the sign, and the sociohistorical expectations of the members of the focus group.

To give just four examples, we found that the oldest group in China felt that the choice of traditional over simplified writing was motivated by aesthetics. They said it was just more beautiful writing and so anyone would use that where they could – either being politically able or themselves having the competence with the old writing. The middle group, the one we thought of as the 'Cultural Revolution' group, made a political interpretation. They thought the use of traditional writing in China symbolized the winds of political change from a conservative revolutionary discourse to a more progressive reform discourse. The young people felt that the choice was motivated by purely pragmatic concerns such as advertising and attracting attention. They felt that a designer would use any font that might attract attention to the product or to the business and it would not matter what the font might symbolize to others. Finally, a fourth group of young people in Hong Kong thought the most important aspect was not the font itself but the quality of the sign both in terms of its materials and its design. Whatever font was used, they felt if it was of high quality it indexed Hong Kong and if it was of low quality it indexed Mainland China.

From these examples we have concluded that virtually any sign in virtually any font will have all three kinds of meaning potentially available – the meaning that comes from where the sign or font is located in the actual world, the meaning that comes from what the font, design, and materials symbolize, and the meaning that comes from the interpretive frames of the users – viewers – readers of these signs. We believe it would be futile and misguided to think that we could isolate these meanings from each other except analytically for the purposes of understanding how the semiotic systems work.

The meanings of materials

As we have just seen, the materials out of which an object is made signal much about how we are to take its meaning. A high quality manufactured sign made of durable materials and permanently fixed to a building is taken to indicate that the texts thus produced are to last the length of the building itself. Texts which are inscribed in fixed and invariable ways signal greater authority than the highly original graffiti spray-painted on city walls. Temporality can be indicated also by add-ons – signs or notices attached to or superposed on more permanent signs. This 'newly remodeled' sign (7.05) is two years old as of writing.

   Many aspects of the materiality of signs (and other objects in the world) convey meanings in and of themselves. Among those meanings are

- permanence or durability
- temporality or newness
- quality

These meanings can be conveyed through aspects such as

- medium of inscription (brush, engraving, etc.)

7.05

- material of the sign itself (brass, wood, plastic, canvas, cloth, paper)
- freshness of installation (wet paint, shiny unmarked surfaces)

The restaurant in photo 7.06 uses several of these means. The vinyl banner above the door not only reads 'Now open' but in being a clean, recent, and temporary attachment to the face of the building suggests that this has just happened. While it cannot be seen in the photo, there is a small sign on the door itself saying 'Wet Paint' which also conveys this 'just now ready for business' meaning. In the window the sign is illuminated indicating that the meaning 'OPEN' is to be read as currently functioning.

It would be premature to put forward a systemic analysis of the meanings available through these choices, but we would certainly expect permanence and durability to be conveyed through heavier, more durable, and more expensive sign materials. It is the material itself producing this indexicality. A heavy, durable, expensive material indexes a longer time of preparation and a greater expense in production which we assume conveys the intention on the part of the producer for this sign to endure over a long period of time.

Paradoxically, the same building in Washington, DC which has 'National Archives' engraved in marble indicating a permanence lasting the length of the nation also has flying over it a very flexible, flimsy, and somewhat insubstantial cloth

7.06

American flag which symbolizes a nation of permanent and enduring existence. Perhaps there are relatively few cases of institutions of such intended permanence as the State which are *symbolized* through a sign that *indexes* flux and temporality.

Layering of indexicality through add-ons or extensions

The apartment building in image 7.05 above had vacancies. An 'add-on' sign saying that it was *newly remodeled* had been attached to the large, formal building identification sign. As an add-on, it conveys that this remodeling has just happened. This sense of recency is accomplished through attaching the sign at the top of the other one where it is clearly *not* part of the original semiotic design. We call this form of inscription *layering*. That is, a sign is attached to another sign in such a way that one is clearly more recent and more temporary. The viewer of this sign may not know that when the *newly remodeled* photo was taken the sign was already about two years old. The actual newness of the sign is long gone but because it is attached as an add-on and not semiotically integrated into the 'permanent' sign, it continues to convey its newness.

A third layer of newness was added on September 12, 2001 when a US flag was attached as part of the surge in American patriotism. The flag, however, appears to convey a sort of permanent national patriotism rather than the simple add-on of the paper sticker flags pasted inside the windows of many other establishments at that time. The 'permanence' of this add-on was supported by the fixture for holding the flag which was newly and 'permanently' mounted on the frame of the building identification sign.

The end of this story will come with the end of this building, perhaps. At Christmas 2001 evergreen boughs were further added to the sign and the 'permanent' flag holder was pressed into service to anchor the evergreens. To accommodate the evergreen boughs, the flag was reattached at the back of the large sign. After Christmas the boughs were removed but also the 'permanent' flag holder, so that the flag which is still there as of this writing remains attached to the back of the building sign. Through all of this the 'newly remodeled' sign remains 'temporarily' attached as an add-on.

Layering to convey the meaning 'this is new' is done frequently on websites. Perhaps this is because of the relatively volatile nature of the medium on the one hand coupled with the inertia that often sets in once someone has designed a website but then failed to keep it up to date. Webmasters often patch a label saying 'new', usually semiotically contrasting with the rest of the web design, to signal for a returning visitor that just at that point is the part they need to consult. This layering, particularly with the patch label saying 'new', has now carried over into other domains such as we see in image 7.07 where the motorist is warned that a new definition of the geosemiotics of the roadway ahead has been created.

7.07

State changes

Many signs indicate their reading through changes of state. As we noted in 7.06 above, a fluorescent sign or a lightbox saying 'Open' on a restaurant or other business means that it is open only when the sign is illuminated. Otherwise the antonym 'closed' is to be read. Of course this is the same system we find in traffic lights which show the current reading through lighting. Although we can see the other lights, only the ones currently illuminated are to be regarded as directives for action.

Denied inscription

In Chapter 1 we noted that in many cases a sign must be inscribed as *not* to be read. Turning off the light of an 'OPEN' sign is one sort of example. In the first chapter we showed how the reading of a sign was denied by its emplacement (image 1.01).

An inscription can also be denied. Behind the large green plastic covered scaffolds in photo 7.08 workers are repairing the giant letters extolling the Chinese Communist Party.

7.08

This work is guarded from public view while the workers deface and then refurbish this inscription of paramount importance to the political structure of the nation. This is similar to the practice which now seems to be waning in which store windows were draped with cloth or paper while the 'naked' mannequins in the display windows were being dressed. One might consider this to be done out of a sense of propriety. But we should also consider that at that same time in history in Detroit the year's new car models were draped when they were sent away from the factory, even when parked on the lots of the manufacturer, until the appropriate moment for unveiling arrived on the date of the introduction of the new models.

This denied inscription can be seen to parallel Goffman's analysis of social backstage and frontstage performances. Inscriptions in signs, like role performances in people, signal their current state of indexicality. At one moment they are backstage, covered, not finished – their meanings should not be indexed; at the next moment they are unveiled, frontstage, and finished – their meanings now become available for social actors to appropriate.

PRACTICE

Inscription and role performance

Inscription in signs is much like the performance of social roles that we discussed in Chapter 3. A sign maker can make use of fonts (and designs and color schemes), materials, layers, and state changes to signal things about the meaning of the words that go far beyond what the words themselves say. These meanings can include temporality or permanence, quality, and current backstage or frontstage readings.

Activity: Inscription

The material substance of an object in the world makes a difference in its meaning. This is as true of the words that we put up in signs and notices as it is of any other objects from roadways to buildings. We could investigate this aspect of geosemiotics through the study of any form of material object we find in the world, but to keep our attention focused on language, our purpose in this activity is to see what can be learned about the meanings of words as they appear in public discourse, conveyed just through the material substance.

As we have noted above, these meanings might have to do with

- **fonts** (letterform, typefaces, sizes, color schemes, etc.)
- **materiality** (hard, soft, permanent, temporary)
- **layering**, add-ons or extension (superimposed on or clearly attached as a secondary message commenting on a more permanent or durable main sign)
- **state changes** (back lighting or drying of wet paint)

Assignment

Focus your attention on just one of the aspects of inscription (fonts, materiality, extensions, or state changes). Prepare a display (slide show, webpage, poster) that will illustrate several levels of contrast in this dimension which are created through inscription. For example, you might contrast the weightiness of signs identifying businesses based on the materials out of which the signs are made from temporary, hand-painted signs to forged brass plaques.

Observations

The easiest observations are likely to come in settings such as business districts or shopping malls where there are a variety of establishments of different degrees of permanence. You might also want to observe signs such as those on objects for sale in a supermarket or a department store. It is a very common marketing strategy, for example, to print a price and then use a felt marker to slash through that price and write a 'sale' price, even when the object has never been sold at the 'original' printed price.

8   Place semiotics: Emplacement

THEORY

Geosemiotics as a theory of emplacement

With the concept of emplacement we come to the most fundamental issue of geosemiotics – where in the physical world is the sign or image located? The first consideration is whether or not a particular place in the world is expected to have semiotic systems. We noted in Chapter 5, for example, that in North American mountain parks, we would be surprised to find writing on the faces of a mountain such as shown in the photo taken at Sulphur Mountain in Banff National Park, Canada (5.03). We contrasted that with 5.04, taken at one of China's traditional sacred mountain wilderness areas, Huangshan, which showed by contrast that writing on the rock surfaces is an essential aspect of the semiotics of wilderness there.

Photo 1.02 which we introduced in Chapter 1 of a restaurant in Kunming in Yunnan Province of China displays an anomaly but one which cannot easily be dismissed as simply a matter of ignorance of English. At the center, over the

---

Place semiotics

Semiotic spaces
        pictures
                emplacement
                        decontextualized
                        transgressive
                        situated
                                exophoric
                                situated ('feng-shui')

entrance, is the name of the restaurant, *Tai Wang Ge* which might be translated as King of the Thais' Pavilion. To the right of the name is the word 'THAILAND'. To the left of the name is the same word but spelled from right to left: 'DNALIAHT'. In passing we can note that this is not an exact mirror image as the letters stand in their normal left-to-right orientation even though the reading path, which we shall call the 'text vector', is right to left. Together this forms a pattern of symmetry about the door of the restaurant with the text vectors of THAILAND and DNALIAHT flowing away from the center point established by the door and by the name of the restaurant in Chinese characters.

As a partial window on this reverse spelling of Thailand we can look at a second photo (8.01), also taken in Kunming.

Here the large gold letters give the name of the restaurant, written in traditional Chinese style with a right to left text vector: Nan Xing Huo Guo Dian ('Nanxing hotpot restaurant'). Here we should notice that right to left writing was common if not preferred in pre-modern China. The language practices and policies of the People's Republic of China are that Chinese should now be written, like English, from left to right. In Taiwan right to left text vector writing is still very common in many contexts including such homely items as jars of canned or bottled food products. As we shall see below, the text vector, that is the direction of writing, is an important semiotic code in geosemiotics.

This sign, then, is anomalous because it has an unauthorized right to left text vector. While that might be possible on a traditional and historical site such as a temple, this is a relatively new restaurant. Furthermore, the orthography used is the authorized simplified characters which we noted in Chapter 7 would index Mainland China.

8.01

Perhaps of greater interest than this, and what caught our eye in the first place, is the phrase in smaller writing on the left side which has: 'UOY EMOCLEW GNIX NAN'. While this is not a possible sequence in the left to right text vector normally used for English, if we read this from right to left it is the nearly correct: 'NAN XING WELCOME YOU' which corresponds to the Chinese on the right side that says the same thing, in Chinese, with a text vector of right to left, *Nanxing huanying nin*. In other words, this sign has been produced, quite exceptionally for China, on a comprehensive right to left compositional vector.

In these two photos we have examples of two compositional principles for the design of signs, both of which exploit the possibility which we have in Chinese (and other languages such as Arabic) of a right to left text vector. Examples such as these lead us to see below that in some cases, images and texts make reference to the geo-material world outside the frame of the picture.

Pictures in the landscape – discourses on the earth

Browsing through a book such as Alexander's *The Timeless Way of Building* (1979) or his *A Pattern Language* (1977) we are struck by the fundamental commonsense of the approach to architecture and urban planning taken by Alexander and his group. We know many people who have used Alexander's books as a rule-of-thumb guide for redesigning their own homes to produce very humanly comfortable environments for living. Coming back to these books from the point of view of an interest in geosemiotics, we are struck by the almost complete absence of any writing or signs – discourses in place – in Alexander's many photos of 'livable' cityscapes and of homes. Among the 94 photos contained in *The Timeless Way of Building*, for example, there are only four in which any words or signs are visible and these are at a considerable distance from the camera.

There is an implied aesthetic governing both internal and external design and extending into cityscape and landscape design which values vistas without semiotic messages. To put this more accurately, there is an aesthetic sense shown in such books on urban design that it is more attractive to have vistas without words, pictures, and graphics. In urban settings such as Georgetown in Washington, DC or in Alexandria, Virginia, but also in the old towns of many European cities there is an agreed, perhaps even legislated, absence of signage representing the ever-present commercial discourses of contemporary life.

A train trip from Chicago to Portland, Oregon and a drive from Haines, Alaska to Washington, DC confirm that throughout the North American landscape, writing on the land is extremely rare. It is the odd small city which places its name, Hollywood-style, in writing on the hill above town, not the common practice, and, but for these rare signs, we could say the North American landscape outside of our cities, away from the road, and in the most elegant sections within our cities is largely free of visible discourses in place.

Contrasting with this aesthetic of non-literacy, for centuries Chinese have written upon the landscape as we first saw in Chapter 5. In the traditional sacred mountains of China one finds words and phrases written upon the rocks. In some cases these semiotized rock faces have been prepared so as not to be even legible to the human visitor to these mountains but only to some implied reader in the clouds.

In China the written form, the literate design, of visual spaces is often seen as a central aspect of their meaning. For example the geographer Tuan Yi Fu (1991) quotes from the very popular *Story of the Stone*:

> Chia Cheng reflected for a while, then said, 'The inscriptions *do* present a problem. By rights, we should ask the Imperial Consort to do us the honour of composing them, but she can hardly do this without having seen the place. On the other hand, if we leave the chief sights and pavilions without a single name or couplet until her visit, the garden, however lovely with its flowers and willows, rocks and streams, cannot fully reveal its charm.'
>
> (Tsao Hsueh-chin and Kao Hgo [sic] 1978: 226)

Tuan comments that 'the physical features of the garden are all very well, but they will seem unfinished and lacking in poetry unless the written word comes to their aid' (1991: 691). It would be misleading, of course, to make a broad and binary contrast between North American and Chinese semiotic practice. In North America we have our Mount Rushmore statuary, in China there are Buddhas carved out of rock as well.

We can categorize three general geosemiotic practices once we recognize that the most fundamental consideration is whether or not discourse in place – language in the landscape, if you like – is socioculturally authorized. For convenience we will call these three semiotic practices 'decontextualized', 'transgressive', and 'situated'.

By **decontextualized semiotics** we mean to include all the forms of signs, pictures, and texts which may appear in multiple contexts but always in the same form. The Nike 'swoosh', the characteristic 'Coca-Cola' typeface, the well-known golden arches of McDonald's are all cases of decontextualized signs which may appear in the same form on posters, packages of the products, or on the stores in which these products are sold. Of course it is not surprising that the first examples that come to mind are owned intellectual properties – brand names and logos. The goal of branding is to produce universal and decontextualized recognition of their names and products, so that their symbols become as instantly recognized as the Christian cross, the red cross, the Islamic crescent, or national flags.

But more than just these particular owned or authorized intellectual properties, we also include such decontextualized semiotic practices as the left to right text vector of English and other European languages, the right to left text vector of Arabic and some other languages, or the principles of capitalization, differently conventionalized for English and for German. In other words, decontextualized semiotics makes no reference to the place in the world where the signs appear *within the picture, image, or textual frame*. It is this sort of semiotic meaning which is largely presupposed in the visual semiotics of Kress and van Leeuwen which we presented in Chapter 4 or that of other semioticians who focus their analyses on the structure of images and texts within the borders of the image frame.

Transgressive semiotics includes any sign that is in the 'wrong' place. For this the word transgressive might be a bit harsh. We want to include here such things as the price tag which has fallen off a garment and lies on the sidewalk of a busy city street. But we would also want to include clear transgressions of semiotic expectation or intention such as the inverted 'R' in the name of a well-known toy store which symbolizes a child's writing just because it is out of its expected upright orientation. For the English reader, the two signs with which we began, DNALIAHT and UOY EMOCLEW GNIX NAN, are both transgressive of the decontextualized or universalized reading path for English.

Before going ahead we should clarify that transgressive semiotics is different from denied semiotics which we discussed in Chapter 7. A sign that is being made but not yet posted is denied its geosemiotic meaning because it has not yet been placed. Or it might be denied its meaning by being covered with a cloth or paper. A transgressive sign is a sign which is in place but which is in some way unauthorized – graffiti, trash, or discarded items are the most common examples of transgressive semiotics.

By **situated semiotics** we mean to include such common regulatory signs or notices as directions to the train in a metro system or an exit sign. Among such situated meanings, of course, are all the store names placed in such a way that one reads them as 'This is X store'. What we mean by situated semiotics is any aspect of the meaning that is predicated on the placement of the sign in the material world. This is, of course, the heart of geosemiotics.

A semiotics of decontextualization

The grammar of visual design we discussed in Chapter 4 which has been proposed by Kress and van Leeuwen is not intended to be a universal semiotic system of meaning. They make it quite clear that any semiotic system is embedded within a cultural semiotic landscape. About their own work they say,

> it is a grammar of contemporary visual design in 'Western' cultures, and
> hence an inventory of the elements and rules underlying a culture-specific

form of *visual* communication . . . This means, first of all, that it is not a 'universal' grammar. Visual language is not transparent and universally understood, but culturally specific.

(1996: 3)

We have chosen to use the word 'decontextualized' to highlight the fact that some forms of signs and discourses are severed from any placement in the real world context. When we speak of a semiotics of decontextualization we mean to focus on the semiotics of texts (or pictures or images), which are clearly set off from the world around them as bounded and separate semiotic systems. For example, Kress and van Leeuwen's visual semiotics focuses on pages from textbooks, works of art, drawings of children, photographs and a host of other pictures, but in most cases the analysis is of what is contained within the boundary of that picture. To put this in somewhat more expected terms, the grammar of visual design which we out-lined in Chapter 4 was focused on the analysis of bounded texts and pictures and did not make reference to how those texts relate to the surrounding world.

The visual semiotics of Chapter 4, then, is our starting point for looking at two problems, the problem of a transgressive semiotics – how do we construct meaning when the pictures/texts cut across other systems of meaning, and the problem of situated semiotics – how do we construct meaning out of the relationship between the text/picture and the material and physical placement of the sign in the world?

Transgressive semiotics

A group of teachers in the village of Umaca in the Peruvian Andes launched a community-wide literacy campaign. As part of this campaign, school students wrote various slogans and sayings which they then inscribed on the walls and rock faces of the community. They wrote, 'papá dame tiempo para escribir mi tarea' [Papa, give me time to write my homework], 'companeros [sic] hay que estudiar para triunfar' [Companions, we have to study in order to triumph], and 'Papá ayudame a leer y escribir' [Papa, help me read and write] (8.02).

In Ma On Shan Park in Hong Kong along a trail leading up from the Shatin side toward the saddle crossing over to the Kowloon side there are Buddhist sayings written on the rocks. They say, 'Xin zhong you Fo' [Buddha is in the heart/mind], 'Fo shan' [Buddha mountain], 'wu shin' [No mind/heart], 'kong' [emptiness], 'Chang nian Fo' [Always think of Buddha] (8.03), and other such Buddhist sayings.

We showed these photographs to American university students. Most of them said they thought these were graffiti – things transgressively written on stones and walls in public places *against the expectation* or *in violation* of a public expectation that such surfaces would be kept clean and 'unpolluted'. That is, from within the

8.02

8.03

aesthetic we mentioned above of a public space, in particular a 'natural' public space, in this community of American university students these signs were taken as transgressive, as signs which went against the grain of public decency.

This sort of characterization of a highly public-spirited UNESCO-backed literacy campaign in the Peruvian Andes on the one hand and of a spiritualized public path in Hong Kong on the other suggests, as we have said above, that there is in each community some geosemiotic system which tells members where signs and messages may appropriately appear and where they may not. Signs, however spiritual in nature they may be, are transgressive to the viewer if they appear in places not acceptable for the display of visual semiotic designs.

While we are, perhaps, accustomed to the transgressive semiotics of contemporary artists who place the common, the mundane, the erotic, the violent, and the crude into the semiotic spaces of art and high culture, examples such as these suggest that it is equally transgressive to place the spiritual, the artistic, the socially uplifting message in places in which visual semiosis is forbidden. While a public uproar is the outcome of a display of violated sacral images in an art gallery, we would imagine a much greater public outcry if sayings of Evangelical Christianity were to be painted in indelible paint on the surfaces of El Capitán in Yosemite Park.

In urban architecture there was a movement which we can see in Vienna at the turn of the nineteenth to twentieth century in which architects produced buildings with an overhanging arcade design which covered the visual presence of the commerce being carried out on the street-level floors. There was and to some extent still is within European and Western aesthetics of urban design a preference for urban surfaces without signs as an expression of high levels of elegance. As Schorske puts it in respect to Vienna

8.04

the Rathaus Quarter architects muted the commercialism of the rental palaces by the most discreet accommodation of the shops and offices on the ground floor. Whether by concealing business or store fronts beneath costly arcades in the manner of the rue de Rivoli in Paris, or by simply avoiding prominent signs, the designers assured an elegance rare even in the Ringstrasse area.

(Schorske 1981: 61,62)

This aesthetics of elegance was replicated throughout the colonized world. Turn of the century buildings in Shanghai, Hong Kong, Guangzhou, Calcutta, and even New Orleans were designed to disguise the presence of commercial enterprise within these lower floor arcades. And so it is interesting to see the transgressive semiotics of contemporary signage in Shanghai in the photograph below.

In 8.05 we see that the plans of the architects of a century ago are thwarted with signs for shops such as the *mei mei mian guan* 'Mei Mei Noodle Shop' placed on the outside of the building, outside of the arcade. These signs transgress the implicit prohibition of commercial signage in the upper regions of the building.

Our point is that the grammar of visual design, like any grammar of language, must take into consideration the placement of those structures of meaning within the larger frames of concrete placement on the surfaces of our material world. A decontextualized sign like the sign for 'Mei Mei Noodle Shop' might be entirely interpretable within the frame of the sign. But it becomes semiotically transgressive when that decontextualized semiotic object is placed within a semiotically inactive or semiotically prohibited zone in a broader geosemiotic space and, of course, that zone has changed in the 100 or so years since the design was first produced. These brief examples suggest that the starting point for interpreting

8.05

visual design cannot be the sign itself but must, more broadly, be the analysis of the geosemiotic active and inactive or prohibited zones of the world around us.

Of course, this brings us to the question of authorization: Graffiti are transgressive because they are not authorized, and they may even be prohibited by some social or legal institution. When and where language appears on the world also works within a system of meaning, in this case conveying authorization.

We should be aware as well that what is 'transgressive' at one time can become itself a semiotic system that can be used symbolically at another time or in another place. While we recognize a style of graffiti throughout the world, in photo 8.06 we see a home in the Georgetown area of Washington, DC which the owner has had painted in graffiti style. Note that this has become decontextualized transgressive semiotics here as the paint nicely stays within the boundaries of the flat surfaces of the front walls and does not cross over onto the windows as it would be likely to do in the case of genuine graffiti.

8.06

Situated semiotics

The term *feng shui* has become quite popular in recent years. Some translate this into the English 'geomancy', though this translation is at best rather approximate. Now there are magazines available in trendy, whole foods supermarkets from London to Washington to Hong Kong. Nevertheless, for all of the feng shui bandied about in the popular Western press, there is still almost no commentary on the role and placement of discourses and signs within otherwise very delicately contrived home and business environments either in China or in Western sources. In one of the very few books on the subject, Lip notes that

> Feng shui is the skill and art of design and placement with reference to nature and the cosmos . . . It is important to know that the elements of birth are closely associated with directions (for the hanging of signboards and place-ment of logos) and so when signboards of companies are hung, reference may be made to Table 2–2.
>
> (1995: 21)

Her Table 2–2 then lists the five elements (wood, fire, earth, gold, water) together with the appropriate directions (north, east, south-east, south, and west), respectively. It is left to the reader to hire a feng shui practitioner – Lip herself is, conveniently, such a practitioner – to indicate which of these elements and therefore directions would be auspicious for hanging a particular sign.

Later in the same text (1995) Lip comments in a section on the placement of signboards:

> Good signage is an integral part of building design and, therefore, should be carefully considered right at the start of the building design. Signboards should be placed after the feng shui of the entire site and building has been assessed.
>
> (p. 39)

She then makes the somewhat obvious suggestion that if a sign is at the top of a building the letters need to be large so that they can be seen from the ground.

Feng shui theory might be extremely complex or simply arbitrary and superstitious; that is beyond the scope of this analysis. What is important to us is that within traditional feng shui theory there is a basic assumption that all such analyses are concrete to a particular action being carried out by a specific person in a unique time and place. The principles that can be stated in a universalized or decontextualized way are few: *tian ren he yi* ('heaven and humans in organic harmony') or the often stated ideas that the sun should be at the front of a home, the back to the shadow, or the idea that the back of a house should be against the mountain with the front looking outward. It would be a rare home indeed – no doubt an imperial or high-ranking one – which could realize these general principles. The nitty gritty of feng shui practice is predicated on the birthdate of the owner, what that owner is trying to accomplish in erecting the building (home, business, or tomb), the dates of construction and dedication, and the exact placement of that building within a geography of not only mountains and water, sun and shadow, but also of traffic flow and of other buildings.

Exophoric and situated indexicality

In one type of sign, notices, there is normally an element of exophoric indexicality which links the internal semiotics of the sign to the external emplacement of the sign in the geosemiotic world. 'Exophoric' is a linguistic term meaning 'indexing something outside of the text'. 'Exit' signs are a clear case of such exophoric indexicality. Normally the sign itself marks that this point itself is the exit, although in some cases there is an arrow which explicitly marks the directionality of the exophoric indexicality: 'this is the way to the exit'. Other notices such as those for restrooms or no smoking regions similarly mark points outside of the frame of the sign within the geosemiotic world which is being indexed. Perhaps the most common of these explicitly exophoric signs are the ubiquitous signs along roadways indicating turns, road names, and regulated actions within those geosemiotic spaces.

Looking a bit further, one can see exophoric indexing operating in many if not all shop signs, brand names, and logos. The sign over the shops in images 5.05 and 5.06 must be read exophorically as 'This is "7-ELEVEN"' where this sign appears. Likewise, the name 'Dell®' on this computer is read exophorically as 'This is a Dell® computer.'

There is yet another type of situatedness of visual semiotics which we have observed in many cases in Hong Kong, China, and Taiwan. This is based on an exploitation of the possibility in Chinese of writing text either from left to right or from right to left in the horizontal text mode. Of course it is also possible to write Chinese from top to bottom (with either right to left column, the normal mode, or even left to right columns in somewhat rarer instances). Because Chinese has the possibility of both left to right and right to left text vectors, the text vectors themselves are exploited to situate the sign in relationship to the geosemiotic world. Generally speaking, and with very few exceptions in our data, the base of the text vector, that is the point from where the reading starts, is located at the most salient point. These 'salient points' consist of doorways, corners of buildings, as in photo 8.07, the center of the road, the front of buses, trucks, and even airplanes as we can see in image 8.08.

8.07

8.08

The distinction between situated and exophoric reference in signs can be illustrated with the naming of the planes of China Southern Airlines (photo 8.08). The name, *Zhongguo Nanfang Hangkong Gongsi*, in Chinese characters of course, on the plane exophorically indicates, as we have noted above, 'This is a China Southern airplane.' At the same time, the text vector of this identification is from front to back of the airplane. That is, on the right-wing side of the plane it is written with a right to left text vector while on the left-wing side of the plane it is written with a left to right text vector. Thus while the sign itself is exophoric in labelling the plane, the text vector identifies the front to back direction of the airplane. Such symmetrical text vectors are found frequently on trucks and buses as well.

In interviewing Chinese about where they might find right to left text vectors, when the question is asked out of context, the first response in China is that one will not find this text vector as there is a policy of writing from left to right like English. When questioned further, respondents will say that, of course, one might find this on either ancient temples and other historical sites or, in some cases, on newly built structures designed in the ancient mode. When shown the photographs of buses and trucks, people often shift logics to say that it is written from front to back because, when a bus passes one in the street, that is the natural direction of reading, from the first thing seen as it passes to the last thing seen. This does not apply, however, to airplanes which are almost always seen either stationary at docking gates or so high in the sky that there is no actual motion vector to couple with the text vector.

Interactions among geosemiotic systems

As the term 'situated vector' suggests, it is not just a question of the semiotics of the text vector *within* the decontextualizing frame of the picture, but the text vector is situated in reference to the physical object on which it is written and the orientation of that physical object in space. This is a visual semiotic system which can only be read concretely as it is situated in the geosemiotic world. While our photographs here and elsewhere do, to some extent, decontextualize these situated text vectors, they do not universalize them. That is to say, we can take a photograph of the symmetrical text vector used in writing the word 'Thailand' on the two sides of the door with which we began (image 1.02), but the vector itself remains concretely positioned in relationship to the door of the restaurant as itself a concrete, material space.

From this point we can argue that there is in many cases attested in Hong Kong, Taiwan, and China a visual semiotics of situatedness within concrete, material space which cannot be decontextualized. In this respect it was interesting to us to see the process of a shift from situated semiotics to a decontextualized semiotics take place over a single weekend in the signs giving the name and logo of a well-known Hong Kong bank, Hang Seng Bank. Throughout Hong Kong this bank had made an issue of adapting their branches to feng shui of the particular sites on which they were placed. That is, the way the name and logo were laid out were based in the concrete realities of each separate bank. Thus, the Hang Seng Bank at our university, City University of Hong Kong, had the Chinese name on the right of the main door with a right to left text vector. On the left of the door was placed the English name with the expected left to right text vector. This produced a symmetry in text vectors but in a rather unexpected way. That is, the arrows or points or ends of the text vectors pointed *to* the door, not *away* from the door as we would have expected from the many other examples of symmetrical text vectors we observed in Hong Kong. We will return to this problem just below.

On the weekend in question we noticed at a different branch that all the signs were being taken down and replaced with a new set of signs, one of which can be seen in 8.09.

While the old set could only be visualized from the anchor-holes in the marble building surface, it was clear that the new sign was producing a very different alignment. The new alignment had – and still has – Chinese on the left, written with a left to right text vector, a central logo, and then English on the right. This produces symmetry of arrangement but without situated text vectors. The text

8.09

vectors in this case are decontextualized as invariably left to right. Had Chinese been written right to left, it would have fit in with the principle we have suggested above of basing the text vectors symmetrically in the center.

We rushed back to our bank at City University and found that the sign we commented on above had been removed and in its place was the decontextualized sign we had seen going up at the other branch. Further checks around Hong Kong that weekend confirmed that in one weekend the bank had removed all of its 'feng shui' contextualized and situated signs and replaced them with an invariable and decontextualized name and logo combination sign.

We don't believe we can assume that there are general, grand, and overarching semiotic systems. Certainly the field is still too new to try to establish such systems. We prefer to follow Kress and van Leeuwen's preference for thinking in terms of small systems of meaning interacting with each other. We believe the case of this Hang Seng Bank sign both before and after decontextualization reflects a dialectic among four sub-systems of semiotics:

a text vector system,
a construction system,
a preference system, and
an indexicality (situated/exophoric or decontextualized) system.

At the most basic level, that of the text vector, there are multiple systems available throughout the world's languages: left to right (throughout Indo-European languages, but also Chinese, Japanese, and others), right to left (for Arabic, Chinese, and others), top to bottom (Chinese, Mongolian, and others), or boustrophedon (Etruscan, Greek inscriptions). When we showed the DNALIAHT photograph (1.02) with which we began to another class of university students, we were struck by how very difficult it was for the group who had no experience with writing in any other text vector system than English and European languages (left to right) to make any sense out of DNALIAHT, even though they had been primed with the understanding that there are multiple text vector systems. The most common response was to leave the text vector system unchallenged and to cook up theories about languages with *initial* 'dn' consonant series and to hypothesize that this must be a Chinese minority language. This, of course, is hardly the sort of data that would enable one to say very much about the text vector system, but it does suggest that at some psychological level, it takes considerable adjustment for at least some readers to come to suspect the left to right text vector system.

Equally anecdotal but none the less interesting is the mother of a colleague visiting the US from China who was learning to 'read' English. She used a symmetrical composition text vector. She 'read' the word 'Stonehurst' as 'the one with "st" at each end' and 'SHOPPERS' as 'the one with "s" at each end and "pp" in the center.'

Within the indexicality system the choices are either to use a decontextualized system in which no reference is made to the world outside the boundaries of the picture, or to use a system of exophoric and/or situated reference in which the sign is keyed to its physical emplacement in the world. In Hong Kong many signs are situated (and exophoric) and the unmarked text vectors have their base at the point of salience (doors, corners, front of vehicles, or the center of the street).

A third system is the construction system we discussed in Chapter 4. In Hong Kong there is a high value placed on a symmetrical (center and margin) construction. Most of the right to left text vectors (but not all) are used within this sub-system of construction.

In the fourth instance there is the code preference system which we have discussed in Chapter 6. When there are two languages in use in bilingual notices, the code preference system positions the upper-most or left-most of two languages as the preferred code, the lower or right-most language as peripheralized.

In Hong Kong at least before the change of sovereignty from Britain to China in 1997, it was recognized that there were two languages in common use and that Chinese was the main language of 98 per cent of the population. English was nevertheless the preferred code in many domains of public use. As we saw in Chapter 6, we find English on top in road signs and, in the case of Hang Seng Bank which we are examining here, English was on the left of the logo in a symmetrical English – logo – Chinese arrangement.

The dialectic, then, among a text vector system of English left to right and Chinese right to left, a construction system of symmetry of center and margin, an indexicality system of situatedness, and a preference system favoring English was played out in the old sign on the Hang Seng Bank such that the preference system of English on the left overrode the situatedness system with the result that a reversed set of vectors pointed *toward* the door rather than away from the door.

When the bank moved to decontextualize the signs, they kept the construction system of symmetry, moved Chinese to the left to elevate it over English (in keeping with the sociopolitical change) and universalized the text vector as left to right throughout for both languages. This latter move, it could be argued, is supported by (1) the globalization of universalized bank logos, and (2) the universalization of Chinese in a left to right text vector following widespread practice in China. On the first point, this universalization of logos was sweeping through several banks, notably Bank of America which had just at that time merged with NationsBank, and HSBC, the parent bank of Hang Seng Bank, which was expanding rapidly overseas. On the second point, this universalization of the text vector for Chinese is perceived as relating to the sociopolitical changes of these few years in Hong Kong.

Which way is the emergency exit?

In Chapter 2 we introduced two fire/emergency exit signs (2.06, 2.07) photographed in Hong Kong which are symmetrical. In the first the figure is shown running away from the flames on the left side toward (presumably) the exit on the right. The emergency exit in this case was, indeed, to the right of this sign as it is viewed in the picture. In the second picture the semiotics are reversed and point to the exit which was in this case on the left as viewed.

The data we had at our disposal showed this reversal as a kind of situated semiotics based on the physical location of the exit in the real world. A perusal of the catalogs (printed and on websites) of sign suppliers for both the US and the UK shows signs in both directions with the proviso in some cases that customers need to specify the directionality for their needs.

8.10   8.11

Of course this raises questions for the visual semiotics of Kress and van Leeuwen as presented in Chapter 4. As we noted there, in this case it is not difficult to argue that the flames constitute the 'given' portion of the sign and the directional arrow constitutes the 'new' portion. The sign in 8.11 as in 2.06 fits within the universalized or decontextualized given–new, left–right semiotics laid out in Chapter 4. Unfortunately, 8.10 and 2.07 go directly against that informational and constructional structure: the given is on the right and the new is on the left.

The solution we propose, as we have proposed above is simply to say that there will always be multiple semiotic systems in interaction with and sometimes in contradiction of each other. We would argue that situated semiotics always overrides any decontextualized semiotics as being more fundamentally grounded in the earth and the spaces on the earth in which we live.

As an added wrinkle to the story of the exit signs, Jewitt and Oyama (2001) have argued that the left–right (given–new) information structure is 'British' but a right–left (given new) information structure is Japanese. As evidence they cite a 'British' sign such as that in 8.11 above and a 'Japanese' sign as well as other visual semiotics in advertisements in Japan and in the UK.

We have noted that at least in British catalogs exit signs of both directions are sold. In the Japanese case we cannot confirm whether or not both alternatives are available or found in place in Japan. What is important to note, however, is that there is always a danger of overgeneralizing from closely situated semiotics to broader social, cultural, or universal categories. There will always be an inter-action among multiple semiotic systems some of which will be decontextualized, some of which very tightly situated, and some transgressive. Among these competing and contradictory semiotic interests will be a negotiated compromise situation which becomes a crucial part of the meaning of those discourses in that place.

The need for ethnography

We have gone into some detail in these two cases of the change of signage for Hang Seng Bank and of the emergency exit signs though there are other cases we might equally have discussed, because they point up four conclusions we would like to draw about emplacement of signs and discourses in geosemiotics.

Our first conclusion is that the understanding of the visual semiotic systems at play in any particular instance relies crucially on an ethnographic understanding of the meanings of these systems within specific communities of practice. As the case of the word DNALIAHT showed us, it is virtually imperceptible as an English word read with a reversed text vector to people who have little or no experience of different text vector readings while it is rather simply transparent to those who do. Only an ethnographic analysis can tell us what users of that semiotic system mean by it.

Secondly, visual semiotic systems work as interactions among small or sub-systems, not as grand, overarching semiotic systems. These sub-systems operate quite independently of each other in a dialectical and negotiated way.

Thirdly, the uses of both exophoric and situated indexicality, as they are so richly played out in Hong Kong and China but also in the directionality of such simple signs as emergency exits, call attention to a kind of geosemiotic sphere of social practices that extends far beyond the meaning systems of bounded texts to the placement or the prohibition on placement within the material spaces of our world.

Finally, there may be developing an ever wider distribution of a kind of decontextualized semiotics, a set of systems of meaning, which are hierarchically being positioned to override the concretizing, particularistic, material-based semiotics of the worlds in which we live. The use of brand names and logos is a good example of the widespread development of these decontextualized signs. In the face of this development it is important to realize that any sign whatsoever continues to give a significant portion of its meaning through the ways in which it indexes the world in which it is placed.

PRACTICE

Activity: Emplacement

How we read a sign saying 'DO NOT ENTER' depends on where this sign is placed in the world. implied is some 'HERE' in the vicinity of the sign. The purpose of this activity is to investigate the geosemiotics of emplacement by comparing signs and the world in which they are placed to see what sets of relationship are 'readable' from signs to world and from world to sign.

Assignment

Develop an analysis in two or three pages, illustrated with photos and drawings, of several signs which will show how the sign is related to the world in which its actions are to be carried out. These can be signs designed for cars, for pedestrians, for bicycles, or for shoppers and others in streets or malls. The photos taken should indicate not just the sign as in these cases but also the surrounding world in which the sign is to be interpreted. As helicopter shots are difficult to achieve, make drawings of the spaces indicating roads, paths, or other relevant possible paths of action.

Observations

In making observations see to what extent you can derive a system. For example, where are EXIT signs placed in buildings and how can one read the pathway for exiting from their placement? Are these placements governed by regulations or policy or are they purely conventional?

Activity: Transgressive and denied semiotics

Texts may violate expectations (*transgressive*) even where semiotic messages are expected so that we might find a computer terminal on the altar of a cathedral or a cell phone in a classical music concert. We know that the price tag lying soiled on the pavement is not the price of that portion of the pavement because we read it as a kind of 'meaning out of place'. As we mentioned in our opening example in the first chapter, the road sign (1.01) saying 'TRAFFIC LIGHT OUT OF ORDER SLOW' is not to be interpreted as a message to drivers. We know that because of its placement behind the fence and away from the view of drivers.

The package for 'Barcelona Salted Cashews' is transgressive in that it doesn't 'fit' in place. Lying as it does at the edge of a roadway we read it as discarded, as trash (8.12).

8.12

Assignment

Prepare a photo display to illustrate the difference between transgressive semiotics and denied semiotics. Particularly pay attention to any problematical cases.

Observations

In making observations it will be important to try to determine *for whom* some sign or discourse in place would be transgressive. Graffiti might be transgressive for municipal authorities but fully authorized within a neighborhood youth gang.

Activity: Situated semiotics

Texts such as signs may reflect the physical environment in which they are placed (*situated*). By far the most common of these are the simple directional signs we see everywhere. Interesting examples of situated emplacements are found in China where the language may be written either from left to right or from right to left. This allows the text itself to form an arrow (text vector) in the direction it is read. For example, a text may read from right to left on the right side of the bus or airplane and left to right on the other side so that the text vector (the direction of writing) indicates the direction from front to back of the vehicle as on the airplane above (8.08).

These vectors may be left to right or right to left as text alone or they may be a combination of image and text so that the image is in the 'base' position in relationship to the text or vice versa. It is common for the base of a text vector or an image–text vector to originate at the front of vehicles (pointing toward the rear), the center of the street (pointing toward the building), the corner of a building (pointing toward the front or side faces), or the center of a business such as over the door.

Arabic is written from right to left so signs are prepared that work outward from the center with Arabic on the left of center and English on the right as in this airline office in London (8.13). The text vectors form a symmetrical movement away from a base at the center:

←——— center ———→

8.13

In this case it is not clear whether or not the placement of Arabic on the left indicates or violates a system of code preference.

Assignment

Prepare a photo display to illustrate situated indexicality. If you can find cases of writing in Chinese or Arabic, try to work out which direction is the text vector and then see if the signs or texts use decontextualized or situated semiotic systems.

Observations

It is important in doing this to keep focused on the question of indexicality. For example, in a magazine look for cases which make reference to the actual piece of paper on which the sign is printed. Household utility bills will sometimes write: 'Tear on the dotted line below' which indexes that very piece of paper.

Activity: Emplacement in space and time

The most fundamental aspect of *geosemiotics* having to do with language in the material world is *emplacement*. The geosemiotic meaning of the sign depends on where on the earth it is placed. In the case of a sign showing a lighted cigarette with a red circle and a slash we can read the universal slashed red circle to mean 'Do not smoke', but it is only by reference to a physical location that we know *where* to apply this restriction. The reading is based on where in space the sign is found. In some cases a meaning is created for a zone of space through two signs marking a beginning and an end. This implies, of course, that the reader or viewer is moving in or through that space. There are also meanings based upon *when* the sign is to be followed. Many signs regulating parking, for example, are of this time-bound nature.

In some cases both time and place are important for interpretation. On a highway a sign may be placed which indicates that a business establishment is 10 minutes ahead. This implies not only the directionality of travel but the speed. One could not walk there in 10 minutes.

Assignment

Find three cases in which the meaning of a sign or a set of signs is achieved through separate placement. This might be like the case of two languages in Ontario (image 6.10) with one sign placed before the other as the 'reader' moves. It might be two signs placed on opposite sides of a doorway or entrance. It might be beginning and ends of a zone through which one passes.

An alternate assignment would be to check up on municipal department of transportation sign regulations about distances from crucial points a sign must be placed by regulation. State and Federal highway engineers do this as part of their daily work; an interview with an engineer might yield very interesting material for a discussion.

Observations

Often ambiguous or conflicting cases provide interesting data. Try to find cases in which the placement of signs is confusing or contradictory and then try to establish if it is equally contradictory or confusing to everyone or whether people have different expectations (quite without respect to legal or regulatory apparatuses).

9 Place semiotics: Discourses in time and space

THEORY

Space, time and the ecology of human action

In Chapter 8, Emplacement, we looked at some of the ways in which signs and images and other forms of written discourse come to have their meaning in part because of where and how they are placed in the material world. Signs such as registered trademarks may be standardized, carrying the same meaning wherever they are found, through a process of decontextualization or universalization. Or they may be situated, shaped by the material world in whose midst they are placed. Or again they may be transgressive, as graffiti violates sensibilities and laws of emplacement. We saw a case in which situated signs were replaced by decontextualized ones over the course of a weekend. We also considered the ways those signs index the changing world in which they are placed.

Discourses in particular places shape and are constrained by the built environment as well as the interaction order that governs the people who use urban spaces. As we discussed in Chapter 1, there are four factors to be considered in geosemiotics:

- the social actor, i.e. the habitus of individual humans,
- the interaction order in which they conduct their social lives,
- visual semiotics, i.e. the discourses of images and texts which they encounter, and
- the place semiotics in which all of this happens including all the other sign equipment and their emplacement or location in time and space in the material world.

In Chapters 4 through 8 our focus was mainly on visual semiotics, though as we have seen code preference, inscription, and emplacement all bring the semiotics

Place semiotics

Semiotic spaces
  spaces
      frontstage or public
        exhibit/display
        passage
        special use
        secure
      backstage or private
  discourses
      regulatory (e.g. municipal)
        vehicle traffic
          cars
          buses and trucks
          bicycles
          horse-drawn carts
        pedestrian traffic
        public notice
      infrastructural (e.g. municipal)
        public functional notice
        public label
      commercial (e.g. advertising)
      transgressive (e.g. graffiti)

of visual images and texts into an interaction with the place semiotics of the material world. In this chapter we now consider more directly the intersection of the interaction order and the built environment in which social interaction takes place. We examine some of the ways in which discourses come to organize the many spaces of the material world. We focus first on how the spaces of our world are organized in relationship to Goffman's interaction order – the ways in which we organize our social interactions. These intersections of multiple discourses and the interaction order in particular places form what we are calling *semiotic aggregates* – such places as restaurants or neighborhoods, street corners in cities or shopping malls. As our primary example of this centripetal aggregation of discourses we use material from a study we conducted of five street corners around the world – Hong Kong, Beijing, Washington, DC, Vienna, and Paris.

We refer to the mutual influence of discourses within a semiotic aggregate as 'interdiscursive dialogicality'. For example, on busy intersections the municipal regulatory discourse for pedestrians and motorists interacts with commercial, mass transit, and other infrastructural discourses as well as the discourses carried by the people and vehicles passing through. Such interdiscursive dialogicality is a major concept in geosemiotics which we make in line with dialectics or dialogical theory. In this we see the semiotic aggregate as a result of centripetal forces of aggregation including discourse aggregation.

At the same time, we might also follow a single discourse through the many semiotic aggregates of which it forms an element. For example, if we track the traffic regulatory discourse on an urban street corner we find it runs through all of the streets of that municipality. The stop sign on this corner is the same as the one on that corner. Further, we can track that line of discourse into the city sign shop where the signs are made or in many cases to catalogs for the companies which specialize in the sale of regulation signs to individuals, government bodies, and corporations. This same discourse would further penetrate into the city planning commission and be found in their minutes and discussions as well as in their published ordinances. From there we would also find the discourse would penetrate into the law enforcement system with a schedule of fines to be paid for violations, formal procedures for ticketing violators and the payment of fines. In some cases where points for traffic violations are accumulated this discourse might extend into the personal identity system if a person has his or her driver's license suspended because of too many points. In such a case the person would find it more difficult to cash checks or accomplish other tasks which would depend on the driver's license as official identification.

This centrifugal approach would be to carry out a part of the agenda suggested by Hägerstrand and which we discussed in Chapter 1. One might use this centrifugal strategy to follow a discourse through a particular semiotic aggregate to see how it brings history and social practice with it into the semiotic mix of resources available at any particular moment.

Geosemiotics is the study of signs in place as indices of discourses constituting this web of pathways through the material environment. There is a dynamic tension between the centrifugal forces by which discourses distribute themselves across time and space and the centripetal forces by which discourses converge in time and space to form semiotic aggregates.

Public spaces: The built environment and the interaction order

In Chapter 3 we talked about the ways in which we organize ourselves in social interactions along the lines of Goffman's interaction order. From the point of view of that chapter, we were interested in ways in which these forms of social interaction are not only indexable but constitute the social-interactional grounds for discourses which occur in place. Now we turn to the question of how these discourses and indexable social interactions are themselves placed in the material world. There is a continuum, of course, between relatively open socially available spaces such as parks, game fields, and boulevards on the one hand and relatively closed and tightly defined spaces such as a court room in which there is often an almost one-to-one match between the type of space and the social performances expected or required within it. In a public park we can walk or read as singles, converse with friends, play games, or exercise. In a court room, only citizens selected to be jury members may sit in the jury box, only the judge can take up the seat behind the bench, and only the witnesses and others called by the judge may sit in the designated seat for witnesses. The formal, legal procedures they swear to take serve to maintain these roles. Members of the jury may not write notes, and witnesses may not ask but must answer questions.

There is also a continuum in the design of public spaces between highly designed and controlled places where only certain clearly defined social actions and inter-actions may occur – a busy street intersection allows only certain types of traffic to pass in certain sign-designated times, many cities prohibit street vendors – and much more loosely designed and loosely controlled places; often these are socially marginalized places or zones such as back alleys or peripheral regions of a city.

We might think of each type of social interaction as having preferred, if not obligatory, time and space requirements. To the extent these are relatively fixed and known, the design of the built environment may well take this into consid-eration in being structured. In what follows, then, we will first discuss preferred conditions for different social arrangements and what they imply for a geosemi-otics of spaces.

From what we discussed in Chapter 3 concerning the major types of social interactions, it should be clear that no space could be designed in which each and every one of these types of interaction would be favored, let alone even be viable. Football games cannot be played in the narrow sidewalk café spaces of European cities but conversations work very well indeed there. The passage of many singles or withs through a space involving long queues is again highly problematical. Keeping contacts from rapidly evolving into uncomfortable withs is very difficult in enclosed spaces where motion is slow or stopped or an abrupt turn-about is untenable.

As we have said above, spaces may be designed ranging from very close speci-fication to the needs of particular types of social interactions to very loose, multi-purpose spaces. More to the point of the section below on the semiotic aggregate, many public spaces are not all that carefully designed in the first place. They simply reflect a loose and conflicting aggregate of considerations having little to do with the social uses of those spaces but which, in time, because they are suitable to some uses and not others come to take on those meanings quite unintentionally.

If we come at this from another point of view, we can see that public spaces – including intermediate spaces such as commercial ones (restaurants and malls) which are privately owned spaces intended for the public to use for specific commercial purposes – have at least four zones which are designed to encourage certain types of activities or perhaps to limit activities to certain types. Of course there are many more, and these are certainly not distinct categories, but provisionally it seems we could recognize these four types:

1   exhibit or display spaces
2   passage spaces
3   special use space
4   secure spaces.

There are also, of course, hidden or backstage spaces such as the service and management areas, offices, passageways, and elevators of hotels, but these lie outside of our interest in discourses in public here.

Exhibit-display spaces

Some of the spaces in which we live and act are simply to be looked at as we do other things in them or as we pass through them. Parks have garden spaces that are not to be trod upon, buildings have walls on which notices are not to be posted, and public rooms have wall decorations, planter boxes, and other barriers. Their function may be either to display or exhibit plants or other objects or simply to provide a demarcation of the spaces. What is important is that these exhibit-display spaces are set aside as not being open for public use, or at least not 'use' in the sense that we may act upon them or alter them.

We can read the social roles and performances of the men we saw in Chapter 3 (3.07) as not being simply pedestrians just because they are working on one of the most common of exhibit-display spaces, a common public wall of a building. Their actions are not transgressive (we presume) because they fall within a set of repairing actions that are intelligible to us as part of a general building maintenance discourse.

Passage spaces

Much has been written about the broad boulevards of great European cities such as Paris because they not only allow passage, but they foster a kind of slow, 'civilized' passage on foot. Many cities from Washington, DC to Beijing are now returning to their older districts to 'pedestrianize' them. That is, we are beginning to recognize the desirability of being able to walk together with others in a common social space without having to keep a constant eye out for automobiles.

9.01

Stairs are an example of a passage space which is often not explicitly marked for use but which is implicitly reserved for passage. They normally may not be used as a place to sit and are often only incidentally decorative. That is, stairs virtually always 'go somewhere', not just rise up into a wall.

The multilevel escalators in the Festival Walk shopping mall (image 9.01) not only invite passage from one level to another but are a highly decorative aspect of the design. This confounds the notion of any clear distinction between display spaces and passage spaces.

Passage spaces may be the default public use spaces in the built environment. If it is not prohibited (explicitly or otherwise) because the space is to be viewed and not entered or if the space is not marked as designated for special use (cafés, playing fields, bus stops), then it is assumed you may pass that way.

Special use spaces

High seats in a coffee shop are set in front of computers. Without labeling, this arrangement indicates that these are for internet users. Shops and restaurants are rather low in passage spaces and high in special use spaces which are marked by the disposition mostly of tables and chairs.

The cluster of seats and tables in image 9.02 is marked by City University of Hong Kong as a smoking area. With the exception of a few of these areas, the rest of the university is posted as a non-smoking area. Parks, shopping malls, universities, and other such built environments are relatively high in passage spaces.

9.02

Shopping malls throughout the world are complex and sometimes ambiguous public places. On the whole they are, in fact, privately owned for commercial purposes while making their spaces available for public uses once more commonly found in city streets and plazas.

Pacific Place is one such shopping mall in Hong Kong. On the left is a passage space which connects to an escalator to Hong Kong Park (foreground), to court buildings (left), and to the trams, buses, and MTR (Mass Transit Railway) of the external street (background) (image 9.03). Center of the picture is a large open space which is passage space at the time of this photo but often houses exhibitions from automobiles and cosmetics to Santa Claus at Christmas time.

Image 9.04 shows trams in Wanchai, Hong Kong. These trams run on ground reclaimed from Hong Kong harbor. Pedestrian passage is limited to the pavements along the store fronts and to marked pedestrian crosswalks. Exhibit-display spaces are restricted to the fronts of the stores. In such streets as these there are no other public special use spaces such as sidewalk cafés.

9.03

9.04

9.05

Secure spaces

Security in public places is an increasing concern throughout the world. The photo taken in Washington, DC (9.05) shows new structures which have been placed since September 11, 2001. These physical markers of a new national discourse of 'homeland security' are constant reminders to residents and visitors alike of much broader discourses of nationalism and terrorism, of conservative politics and globalizing commercialism.

Backstage spaces

As we said above, there are also the many backstage regions of public places – management offices, service corridors and elevators, and storage spaces for cleaning equipment which are not our direct concern except that people moving between these spaces must normally organize their personal fronts to perform the appropriate social roles within the public space.

The semiotic aggregate

We could argue that there are no spaces in the world which are discursively 'pure'. That is, there is no place where one might find a single semiotic system in place making meanings within that system and that system alone. Certainly there are places that aspire to this purity and simplicity. Bateson (1972) argued many years ago that one of the functions of the board room of a corporation is to severely limit the number of other considerations that might intrude on the purely economic deliberations. The sanctuary in a church, seminar rooms in universities, or courtrooms are among the places in which there is an attempt to closely limit the number of discourses present and the ways in which people can use those discourses in taking actions.

Even in these tightly limited examples, however, other discourses are present. A member of a jury in a court case may wear a shirt emblazoned with the commercial logo of the company that produced it. The court recorder's equipment will carry the logo and brand name of its manufacturer. The lamps will have nearly invisible markings of the company that produced the bulbs. Most places in our world are much more complex than these rarified settings and have in place at any moment a huge range of discourses which form what we would like to call a semiotic aggregate.

The many different kinds of social interactions that can take place in a crowded Saturday afternoon shopping area are supported or actually encouraged by the wide public walkways, providing passage spaces, directly in conjunction with a high concentration of big department stores and other shopping venues with their own configurations of display spaces, passage spaces, special use spaces, and backstage areas.

The many discourses which fall together in a single place such as this shopping area produce such a semiotic aggregate. We know we are in a shopping district, for example because we see signs of different shops, or by the traffic directions placed there by the city, and by the number and kinds of pedestrians we see. Each of these are separate realizations of different semiotic actions but together they form a place which we can read and which tells us, for example, what sort of shopping might be done in that area of the city. Within such a semiotic aggregate are spaces which accommodate interaction units of all sizes, from singles to celebrative occasions or platform events such as the one in image 1.03.

In Vienna's Stephansplatz, the large public square with abundant passage space is exploited by this street performer we saw first in Chapter 1 who models a statue, standing motionless and creating an exhibit-display space until a passerby puts money in the box. Then he bows slowly and shakes the hand of the donor if they offer it to him. His movement to shake hands disrupts the expected barrier between passage and exhibition and produces a hybrid space in which the street performer is partly on display and partly in social interaction with the pedestrians who pass by. Like a lecture theater in a university this platform event requires some space for the separation of the performance and the viewing audience.

The interaction order and the semiotic aggregate

A major semiotic resource in any semiotic aggregate, or at least one in which there are any humans present, is the interaction order. One looks at a place and it seems a good place to have a conversation. This might be judged from the distribution of special use spaces – chairs and tables – or from the presence of others in that space who are enjoying a conversation. It is common, for example, for people to judge the quality of a café or restaurant by the numbers of other people in withs and conversational encounters already there.

Singles in public places by and large are either in transit from one place to another, which is displayed by their direction of movement, gaze, manner of movement like Baudelaire's well-known *flâneur*, or they are stationary. If they stay in one place, they engage in work which is displayed by their tools and uniforms, they read or look at video displays, or they produce the pseudo-with by talking on a cell phone. One other role is not documented here, but they may also take 'tourist' photographs. That is, they display themselves as being engaged in appreciative looking. What the single almost never does in public is nothing. It appears to be reserved to street sleepers and other socially marginal roles to be seen in public doing nothing, often in the socially marginalized spaces mentioned above or in public parks or sidewalks at liminal, socially marginalized times.

From the point of view of geosemiotics, the problem posed for the single in spaces where others are present is how to produce a visible display of involvement that makes it legitimate to be in that space when no social interaction is available or desired. For women perhaps more than men alone in public places such as waiting in an airport lounge, reading is a primary means of remaining not only alone but inaccessible to those who might want to start a conversational encounter.

While it may seem an exaggeration to say that singles must display legitimate involvement in public places or move on, recently in Washington, DC it was noted in several newspapers that among the possible profiles of a terrorist was a person who was alone in a public space, particularly among the national monuments or public buildings, and taking notes and photographs. It was particularly suspicious if more than a single photograph were taken or if the 'tourist' would dwell on any particular space or view. Of course the authors of this text have often produced a portion of this 'terrorist' profile in compiling the photographs and observations for this book.

The single in a space occupied by others must in general show himself or herself to be in transit to another place or display legitimate reasons for being in that space and not moving along. The problem for the design of such spaces if they are to be inhabited by singles, then, is the converse. It is to produce or provide legitimate involvements for singles. This means places to sit – particularly separable seats or small tables, things to read or look at such as books, magazines, or video screens. Or work to do. A single does not occupy much material space but his or her involvements may be abundant. His or her discourse needs may be minor but the material supports may be profuse as in the coffee shop or bar where music, video displays, newspapers or other reading materials, computer terminals and the rest may come to occupy much of the physical, visual, and aural space. Further, they may well be in conflict with the social situational needs of the with or the conversational encounter.

Singles would feel out of place in many restaurants without a newspaper, and during busy times even reading would not justify occupying space allotted to larger withs. Where space is limited and there are time constraints, such as Amtrak dining cars and small restaurants in San Francisco's Chinatown or a restaurant such as the one pictured (image 9.06) on Sunday mornings, patrons are expected to share tables with strangers.

As tables are designed for people seated at them to share social if not personal or even intimate space, Americans placed together at a table tend to form a with and engage in conversation for the duration of the meal. In Hong Kong on the other hand, the practice is to ignore people not part of the with.

Assembling for tea

The social interaction that happens around a table (9.06) in a restaurant in Hong Kong is closely cogged into both the social understandings of the interaction order and the structure of the physical space and the time in which it occurs.

The restaurant in which this photo was taken is part of an urban semiotic aggregate – a main thoroughfare through an industrial neighborhood where members of the group manage wholesale or retail operations. It belongs to a chain found in several similar neighborhoods in the city. The newsstand next door lent itself to the perusal of items before purchase. This restaurant does not make it so easy for those who are passing by to examine what is on offer, being committed themselves to service encounters on the inside. Although many restaurants display menus in windows or on portable display easels, or in some cases such as in tourist areas of cities like Paris and Beijing restaurant staff urge everyone within social or even public distance to enter, this one does not provide any external menu or other itemized list of offerings.

Within this establishment which is itself a semiotic aggregate, many discourses converge, among them building codes, interior design, food distribution and service, government health inspection, and payment structures such as credit

9.06

cards. The restaurant is one kind of business in which the customer is not generally required to pay until after consumption has taken place. We know a man who in his youth before credit cards were common would regularly go to restaurants with a group of friends, none of whom had cash to pay for the meal. They would simply leave if they could or failing that, offer to wash dishes.

Visible are signs indicating exits and restrooms are found in all restaurants of this size. Also visible are sports attire and serving uniforms indexing social roles as well as serving and eating utensils common in South China. The space to the left where pitchers can be seen is a service area used mainly by staff but also by customers if the need arises to empty or fill containers of tea.

Discourse around this table is of course shaped by the arrangement of table and chairs within the space and its place within the trajectory of waitresses as well as the placement of the particular individuals around the table. In the Confucian tradition, the leader of the group whose birthday is being celebrated and the venerable elder to his right hold the place of honor facing the entrance. The empty chair to his left is occupied by the ethnographer who took the photograph. Each person shares personal space with the individuals to each side and social space with the rest of the group. Most, but not all, of the talk is loud enough to be heard by everyone around the table. A major aspect of this semiotic aggregate are the discourses brought in by customers, including in this case those of *taijiquan* (tai chi) and of business, and news in the form of newspapers.

The individuals gathered here walked a distance of about a kilometer in withs after exercising together in a nearby park. To get to the park they traveled distances ranging from less than a kilometer to ten kilometers on foot and by subway or bus for journeys of ten minutes to over an hour. In traveling they observed regulatory discourses of mass transit and pedestrian movement and largely ignored signs regulating motor vehicle traffic. The texture of paths that converge in this photograph has a complex history rooted in past situations that for the videographer go back nearly five years with some of the dozen or so people around the table and for some of them another ten years, perhaps before the restaurant was opened or at least before they first gathered there.

Being rooted in past situations also means that the teas and dishes served have a history going back at least to the restaurant closer to the park which has since closed, where the group assembled for several years. The manner in which teacups and dishes are cleaned before use is also dictated by custom and constrains table talk. So too the placement of foods on the table and their distribution among the eaters, the pouring of tea by women and other junior members of the group, the settling of the bill and dividing up the total. The total ritual takes about an hour.

This exact aggregate of persons had never been together before and was convened by S. Scollon as part of a project of putting up a website for this group of Morning Exercise Friends (www.friendsoftaichi@geocities.com). With this the tai chi discourse spread around the globe, becoming accessible to many more than the number of persons sitting here which reaches the limit of the capacity of the table. The likelihood that this group of people would meet again is constrained by the limited length of each human life, most saliently that of the balding grey-haired man who was 88 years old, and the fact that movement between Hong Kong and Washington where the authors live consumes time, as well as the limited ability of the human being to take part in more than one activity at a time due to the indivisibility of the human body.

The activity itself, having tea and dimsum (snacks) while chatting, is further constrained by the other activities each individual has planned for that day and that week and the time it takes to travel to the place where the next activity is scheduled to begin. For the man next to the old teacher, it is a van ride that consumes about 15 minutes to travel to the clinic where he resets bones and treats other injuries resulting from falls or fights. For the man in the green shirt and his wife, it is an hour bus ride to the place where they conduct their import-export business. For the old teacher whose eyesight is failing, it requires not only traveling time but arranging in advance for his student, sitting to his right in image 9.06, to accompany him and guide him in crossing intersections such as the one shown below.

Following the trajectory of the videographer back in time and space, we would find her crossing the intersection in photo 9.07 about three hours before on her way to the playing field where the group congregated. Moving forward, we might find her retracing her steps, taking a similar if not identical path back to the same intersection.

Convergence of discourses in a place

From the scene above of discourses around a table for tea, we now shift the focus from a particular kind of social interaction to a particular semiotic aggregate at least peripherally related to some of the members of the group we just glimpsed.

The corner of Tat Chee Avenue and To Yuen Street in Hong Kong's Kowloon District is at the point where the Kowloon–Canton Railway (KCR) and the Mass Transit Railway (MTR) meet underground and is thus a major transfer point between these two underground rail systems. On the surface is a bus station, and the corner supports much vehicular traffic in the form of buses and taxis as well as private cars and pedestrians. There are very few bicycles. Most of the buildings on this section of Tat Chee Avenue were constructed in the last decade of the century. On one corner is City University of Hong Kong, on a second is the Hong Kong Jockey Club's Environmental Center, and on a third is the Hong Kong Productivity Center. The fourth, above the MTR/KCR stop is Festival Walk, Hong Kong's newest shopping mall (at the time of the photographs).

To develop our idea of the semiotic aggregate we decided to focus on a very simple type of action taken in a very common setting in daily life: crossing from one side of a street corner to the other in a major city. Altogether we compared five cities which are quite different from each other and highly distinctive: Vienna, Hong Kong, Beijing, Washington, DC, and Paris. It would be difficult to mistake which one of them you were in if you were suddenly placed on one or another of

9.07

these five corners. Nevertheless, we found that they share much more than they differ in respect to the kinds of discourses which are found aggregated there and so they work as a way to think about the semiotic aggregate in general. Our interest was in seeing how these five corners are semiotic aggregates where multiple discourses converge, out of which pedestrians and others who use the corner must make sense.

We found that there are 15 reasonably distinct discourses involved in these five corners. Of the 15, eight are common to all of the corners and they fall into four general categories:

- regulatory discourses: municipal
- infrastructural discourses: municipal
- commercial discourses
- transgressive discourses

Regulatory discourses; municipal

Vehicular traffic is regulated in four of the five places with systems of traffic lights, painted vehicle traffic lanes, and directional arrows as we see in image 9.08 from Hong Kong.

9.08

The turn left (as opposed to 'bear to the left') signs carry different meanings which are, in part, signalled by their physical states as we noted in Chapter 7 on inscription. The white-on-blue arrow, as a permanent inscription carries the meaning 'always bear left at this point' (i.e. do not go straight – there is a building entrance just beyond this). The green arrow which is lit from behind carries its meaning of 'you can turn just now' because of the changing state of the lighted signs.

Here and there about the intersection are other signs which make clear at least some of these intended (and required) directions of flow. Turn arrows painted on the pavement form a second semiotic system regulating automotive traffic flow. These two systems have enforceable status. From time to time traffic police stop drivers for violations.

In all five places the license to drive a motor vehicle is linked to passing a test on these regulatory signs. In this way the discourse of vehicular traffic differs from all of the others we will take up here. No licensing is required to operate bicycles or to walk through these corners or elsewhere in these cities. We walked over signs painted on roads crossing Tat Chee Avenue for years before noticing them, observing that they were for motorists and that they were unlike signs we were familiar with.

Pedestrian traffic is somewhat more complex than vehicular traffic. Perhaps this is because two semiotic discourses converge in pedestrian traffic (as perhaps elsewhere as well), a regulatory discourse of electronic signs, road and pavement markings, and physical barriers and a sociocultural discourse of navigation across streets as part of the interaction order which, in Hong Kong, Paris, and Washington, only partly pays attention to this regulatory discourse.

The lighted green symbol of a man (is it anywhere a woman?) walking is recognizable in many parts of the world. On the corner in Hong Kong it is almost entirely ignored. We observed a couple whose ages one might estimate in their seventies arrive at this corner. The man started across, the woman tried to hold him back pointing at the red image of the standing man (in some parts of the US it is an image of a hand, palm toward the walker). The man went across anyway and yelled back for her to follow.

Of course not all, actually not many of the intersections in Hong Kong have buttons to call for a walk signal. In two periods of observation of more than an hour each we saw the button on the corner we studied in Hong Kong pushed only three times, once in the first period, twice in the second. In one case it was a child of about four who pushed this button after crossing the street and he was scolded and pulled away by his father. As we will take up in Chapter 10, an action such as crossing the street takes place not only within the regulatory structure and within the structure of the physical spaces; it also takes place within the interaction order of the presentation of appropriate social selves to others in the immediate environment, with the embodied habits of members of sociocultural groups.

The question of where to walk responds to both regulatory and voluntary semiotics. Many signs, more inside the shopping mall and university on this corner than outside of it, show the pedestrian where he or she may choose to walk. If you are going to the MTR, it is this way. The reading of this sign (9.09) presumes a degree of intention and voluntarism on the part of the reader.

In the four busy commercial districts (Vienna, Hong Kong, Beijing, and Paris) pedestrian crosswalks are clearly marked as well with zebra crossings. Of course pedestrians often pay no closer attention to these legal markings of their regulated pathways than they do to the signs regulating when they may walk. In all five cases pedestrian traffic is of a rather different order than vehicular traffic, both in terms of social practices and in terms of legal enforcement of regulations. More often it is the traffic itself to which pedestrians pay attention, looking for cars or buses, not the regulatory signals. Pedestrian signals are being read *not* as authorization to pass but as an indication of whether or not cars and buses might be present.

These comments need to be tempered by saying that there is still a range of social practices in evidence on these corners. The pedestrian who goes against the walk light is common in Hong Kong but actually quite rare in Vienna in our observation. In Jyväskylä, Finland from our hotel window we have observed pedestrians patiently waiting for the light to authorize them to cross a street when there were

9.09

no other people present anywhere in visible distance and there were also no cars or other traffic visible in any direction. In Portland, Oregon on the other hand we have known a man to be arrested for jay-walking at 2 o'clock in the morning when there were no cars in the street.

Public notices inform the public either about conditions or regulations that are present in that place. In Vienna, for example, is the sign (9.10) forbidding the posting of bills.

The electric signal boxes in Hong Kong have similar notices in vertical black lettering saying to post no bills. On the corner we studied, next to this 'post no bills' notice is a notice which is also posted on each of the 12 poles of the electrical signal equipment on the corner. As the main signal box is not labeled for function, it is the flash of orange color on each piece of signal equipment that gives a semiotic unity to this constellation of apparatus.

In addition to the notice which gives the times at which the mail in the mailbox in Washington will be picked up is a 'Customer Information' notice which tells the public to take certain kinds of mail directly to the Post Office and not to deposit it here.

While we have tried to define the term 'Public Notice' as having to do only with information, this is clearly a matter of informing the public about regulations. Still there seems to be an important difference between informing the public about regulations and a posted directive to carry out the law. In fact, the Federal

9.10

Highway Administration terms regulatory signs and other signals 'traffic control devices'. That is, a 'Do Not Walk' sign takes the form of a directive to the person looking at it. A notice would say more discursively, 'Pedestrians may not cross at this point when the signal light prohibits crossing.' It is a fine distinction but has pragmatic significance.

For our point of view here, public notices fall into this second category of informing the public about conditions or regulations which apply within a particular place. Like pedestrian signals, they require no licensing to interpret nor are they much enforced. Furthermore, public notices are written to be viewed at close range. Often they have extended and complicated texts. To put it quite simply, they are discourses which may be easily ignored.

Non-linguistic signs occur frequently on the four busiest corners but also on the more residential corner in Washington. In Hong Kong like in Paris there are fence barriers which prevent pedestrians from straying from the regulated pathways.

In Hong Kong and in Washington, DC there is another non-linguistic sign, the fire hydrant. While this might not be thought of as a sign, it should be remembered that in all five places it is illegal to park a car in front of or within a certain distance of a fire hydrant. In some cases this is posted with another sign, but in most cases the fire hydrant itself is the regulatory sign.

All these sub-discourses we have just considered – vehicular traffic, pedestrian traffic, public notices, and non-linguistic notices – are loosely grouped as municipal regulatory discourse. As we have noted, we cannot easily lump these together as there are important differences between those regulations which are enforced through a licensing process and those which are not and between those for which large posted signs indicate expected actions and those which must be read in close proximity to the notice.

Our point here is not to make any clear distinction among discourses nor to finally determine exactly how many there might be in any particular semiotic aggregate. We simply want to demonstrate that there are multiple, partly overlapping, but nevertheless distinct discourses operating within this semiotic aggregate.

Infrastructural discourses: Municipal

All of the discourses we have considered above carry some regulatory weight. That is to say, not only have they been produced by some municipal regulatory body but any person who goes against them might potentially at least be legally sanctioned. There are other public discourses, however, for which there is no legal sanction but which exist for other reasons than to regulate the public.

Public functional notices are directed much more closely to a specific audience such as workers who maintain the municipal infrastructure of water, power, and gas. One does not imagine most pedestrians would have much idea what these are

about, but various utilities workers would know where to get access to underground lines and the like as in image 9.11 in Nagoya.

Cable TV has several large cement plates in the pavement in front of City
University in Hong Kong. The water supply utility has both metal plates with
embossed identifications and next to some of them are spray painted further
markings in red. Pedestrians simply walk over these and in our observation, none
have given so much as a glance to these bits of municipal infrastructural discourse.

Like the water supply and other plates in the pavement, the markings on utility
poles carry specialized infrastructural meanings which are largely opaque to and
ignored by pedestrians.

While of very minor semiotic importance, it seems fair to say that a city without
these notices and plates in the pavement would be surprising. The City of Nagoya,
Japan makes each of these pavement-embedded plates a work of art with an
embossed dragon or other design (9.11, 9.12). Each of them is original and without copy elsewhere in the city (insofar as we could determine). This suggests that
even though these public signs are to be functionally ignored by most who see

9.11

9.12

them – pedestrians, drivers, and the like – they are still considered to be a significant aspect of the semiotic make-up of the experience of walking in the city and so are given artistic value even when they are assumed to be simply backgrounded in most cases. The rectangular sign indicates a channel for fire hoses, the dragon symbolically representing 'dragon head', the word for fire hydrant.

Public labels such as street signs are commonly found on these corners. These signs are indexical in that they label the streets on which they are posted. Perhaps the most elegant in our sample are the ones in Paris (image 9.13).

9.13

Commercial discourses

Commercial discourses are present on these corners in the form of shop signs and other identifications of businesses. Unlike many other corners in Beijing, the one we have studied is relatively clear of advertising. Nevertheless, there is a massive billboard erected on top of the building structure advertising the restaurant down below. At the street level one sees the two stone lions indicating 'something Chinese is to be expected around here' (and probably not much more) but in this case coupled with the four-lantern balcony display above, there can be little question that it is a restaurant.

In Paris the camping goods shop uses both the words of the company name (*AU VIEUX CAMPEUR*) and an image logo (9.14) to signal its presence in this semiotic aggregate.

9.14

Transgressive discourses

Transgressive notices range from graffiti to printed and posted notes such as the one in 9.15 advertising the domestic worker services of Athena on the corner in Hong Kong.

Despite the public notices to 'Post No Bills', the fixtures of this intersection have an interesting array of private services advertised there. These notices are transgressive in the sense that they have been specifically prohibited by the Hong Kong Governmental notices.

One finds here on this corner that a Ms Wong and a Ms Lee are seeking employment. Athena is offering her services as a domestic worker. Another unidentified person will buy and sell household appliances. This is written on the base of the signal operations box. And lessons in Putonghua are on offer. One notice even angrily promises death to a family. In Paris the group called 'The Federation of Anarchists' has posted its transgressive notice on the street name identification sign.

Are these notices read and by whom? They could only be read by pedestrians because of the placement and the size of the print. Perhaps these, rather than the

9.15

walk/stop signs are what pedestrians are noticing as they wait for the traffic to clear.

More than the content, it is the marginalized placement which signals the private and transgressive nature of these adverts. Some are handwritten, and all appear on the back or on the side of signs or are superimposed on other semiotic surfaces.

These five street corners in five cities of the world are distinctive in many ways, but, as we have seen, they also share much with each other in that this array of discourses is recognizable on each of these corners. We could argue that among the factors which make these places recognizable as urban street corners is this semiotic aggregate of regulatory, infrastructural, commercial, and transgressive discourses.

Distribution of regulatory discourses

We have seen the convergence in space and time of multiple discourses to form semiotic aggregates at street intersections of bustling metropolitan areas and in a restaurant for a group of friends who exercise together. Now we will explore some of the pathways by which a particular discourse arrives at one of these places. While we could choose any one of a number of discourses (taijiquan, commercial, infrastructural, etc.) we will return to look in particular at the signs of regulatory discourses as we suggested in opening this chapter.

The streets and pavements belong to the municipal government and are regulated by that government through quite universal procedures of law-making, posting and signaling, and law enforcement.

A city such as Hong Kong or Vienna or Washington, DC will have an entire regulatory apparatus for controlling street traffic which produces the laws on one end and the posting of stop signs, traffic lights, and painted lines on the street on the other. Throughout the city these signs and signals and their application will be 'universal'. That is, each of these signs will be the same in shape, color, design, and degree of enforcement. Across wider jurisdictions such as the United States these signs and signals are regulated by a federal authority.

In the US the semiotics of signs, signals, and markings is spelled out for traffic engineers in the *Manual for Uniform Traffic Control Devices* (MUTCD), published by the Federal Highway Administration (FHWA) division of the Department of Transport. The manual's audience includes

> the insurance industry, law enforcement agencies, academic institutions, private industry, and construction and engineering concerns.
>
> (http://mutcd.fhwa.dot.gov/kno-overview.htm 5/25/02, 3:19 p.m.)

Different types of signs such as warning or regulatory signs are required to have distinctive shape and color that indicate what class of sign they are. According to the Manual,

> REGULATORY signs instruct drivers to do – or not do – something.

Under the heading 'Purpose of Traffic Signs', it states,

> Traffic signs are devices placed along, beside, or above a highway, roadway, pathway, or other route to guide, warn, and regulate the flow of traffic, including motor vehicles, bicycles, pedestrians, equestrians, and other travelers.

It makes abstract statements about placement:

> Signs should be placed only where warranted by facts and engineering studies. Signs should be placed as necessary for safety and proper regulation of traffic. However, the use of too many signs in a given location may reduce the effectiveness of all the signs at that location.

Here it says nothing about the presence of non-regulatory signs in the same location with traffic signs. It lists conditions signs must satisfy:

> Signs, like any other traffic control device, must meet five fundamental requirements:
> * fulfill a need
> * command attention
> * convey a clear, simple meaning
> * command respect from travelers
> * give adequate time for proper response

Simultaneous with this regulatory discourse will be the development of the commercial discourses within which businesses buy property, open stores, post signs, and seek to attract customers. There will be tight lines drawn between public property and commercial property and the degrees to which these might overlap.

In some areas there is a clear regulatory dialogicality. A store-front sign might protrude into the public street or not depending on municipal regulations. The government will make a ruling about legal shop signs. As we saw in Chapter 7 on inscription, in China and in Quebec (as well as in many other places) the government has made rulings concerning not only the size and shape of shop signs that protrude into public spaces but also concerning the languages used and the type of lettering that is authorized.

Governments also have rulings regarding the posting of bills and posters on public and private land. The *Laws of Hong Kong*, Volume 11, CAP 132, Part IX, 104E (4), for example, defines 'bills' and 'posters' as including

> any word, letter, model, sign, placard, board, notice, device or represen-tation and also includes any advertisement painted on any wall, fence, railing, post, rock, road-cutting or tree.

(pp. 42–43)

The *Laws of Hong Kong* also defines where signs, bills, and posters may be erected and how they are to be treated differently on public and private land. It also outlines the duty to maintain signs in a 'clean and tidy condition' (p. 41). Note that the law prohibits painting advertisements but not religious exhortations on rock.

In the US a catalogue for *Emedco Innovative Signs & Safety Solutions* advertises 'special compliance deals' on its cover. An advertisement for a handicapped parking sign shows the tag 'Complies with the Americans with Disabilities Act Title III Regulation'(2002 Catalog Y42E-P5:2y).

In the catalog traffic signs come in three materials designed to withstand particular weather conditions. The page showing STOP signs includes MUTCD Stop Sign Regulations for octagonal shape, white border and wording on red background, reflective or illuminated, minimum and recommended size, and specifications for placement on the right of the traffic lane, as close as possible to the intersection. 'Do Not Enter' signs come in four sizes depending on where they are posted, smaller ones for parking lots and private property.

There is thus a close interdiscursivity between the federal regulatory discourse and the sign manufacturing industry. Between the 1988 edition and the millennium there was major revision.

In Hong Kong, improvements to traffic control devices were proposed after a motorist knocked over a sign post, which fell on a child and killed it, in the neighborhood of the corner shown in photo 9.07. After a comprehensive review, signals and markings were redesigned and new devices proposed.

This interdiscursivity reveals a dynamic tension between the centrifugal spread of regulatory and commercial discourses and the centripetal convergence of discourses in semiotic aggregates where people live and act.

Aggregation as meaning: Interdiscursive dialogicality

We have founded this book on an interest in indexicality in Chapter 2. Language points to the world outside of itself for much of its meaning. In Chapter 3 on the interaction order we saw that social actors take each other into consideration in producing their own social performances in the presence of others. In Chapter 7 on Inscription and Chapter 8 on Emplacement we saw that much of the meaning of a sign from a STOP sign to the texts printed on the pages of a book is given by its physical placement in the material world. Then in this chapter we have seen that the interaction order – our interpersonal social groupings from singles to platform events – is, in a sense, 'written' into the public spaces we build and inhabit. Now we are in the position to see that other discourses and semiotic systems are themselves 'entities' in the world which give meanings to each other by processes of indexicality. That is, part of the meaning of any one of the discourses on any of these street corners is derived from its conjunction with the other discourses which are also present there.

The reason the corner in Beijing is different from the corner in Vienna or in Paris cannot be located specifically in any one of the discourses or signs present at that corner. The difference is located in the aggregate of discourses, semiotic means, and the actions taken there. These discourses themselves have become signs in this physical space. We could refer to this property of the semiotic aggregate as *interdiscursive dialogicality*.

The term 'interdiscursivity' has been widely used to capture the idea that one discourse has become influenced by another. Usually what is meant is that one discourse begins to incorporate characteristics of another. For example, in a study of medical discourse in the UK researchers argued that it had been progressively interdiscursive with business discourse. What was earlier spoken of within medical discourse as 'the most effective treatment' of an illness had come to be spoken of as 'the most cost-effective treatment'. In the same way some universities have shifted from speaking of students as students or learners and begun to speak of them as 'clients' (in an interdiscursivity with the professions or business) or as 'products' (in interdiscursivity with manufacturing). Conversely, the US railway corporation Amtrak calls its customers 'guests' and by doing so alters the service it provides from transportation to food and housing.

The idea of interdiscursive dialogicality goes beyond this concept of inter-discursivity to capture the cases that we have seen here in which several discourses co-exist simultaneously in a particular semiotic aggregate but none of the discourses is really internally altered by the presence of the other discourse. They operate quite independently semiotically, nevertheless, their co-presence produces a kind of dialogicality between them so that each takes part of its meaning from the co-presence of the other.

It is interdiscursive dialogicality that gives the semiotic aggregate its most interesting characteristics but which is most difficult to capture. We have a tendency in our academic disciplines to keep our focus limited to our professional expertise. As we will argue in Chapter 10 which follows, we believe that in order to understand how social actors act in the day-to-day world of crossing the street or in any of the very many other situations in which we find ourselves, we will need to give much closer examination to the semiotic aggregates within which we live. Language in the material world exists mainly within such complex semiotic aggregates.

PRACTICE

Discourses in places can be viewed from either one of two points of view, a centrifugal one which focuses on the discourses which flow into, through, and out of any particular place and a centripetal one which sees any particular place as an aggregate of discourses or what we would call a semiotic aggregate. This practice section will present two activities, the first concerned with the semiotic aggregate and the second with the distribution of discourses across space and time.

Activity: The semiotic aggregate

A semiotic aggregate is the result of the convergence, intentional or not, of multiple discourses in a particular place. In the photo (9.16) taken at the corner of 36th and Prospect in Washington, DC several independent discourses can be seen. There is the national patriotic discourse displayed in the flag flying from the building, a restaurant. On the corner commercial discourse is represented in the sign identifying the restaurant. Municipal regulatory discourses are visible in the license plate on the car parked at the curb, in the red 'DO NOT ENTER' sign to the one-way street, and in the cross walk markings on the street. At the corner the street intersection is labelled with posted green signs – 36th and Prospect. Finally, the neighborhood, the Georgetown district of Washington is marked with the brick sidewalks which are characteristic throughout the district.

This semiotic aggregate is relatively simple as such things go. A semiotic aggregate might also be very complex as in this case from Hong Kong (image 9.17) which almost defies analysis. We find it impossible to count the signs in this photo, but we estimate over 50 of them advertising everything from medical clinics to a bookstore. A slightly different angle would, of course, further expose municipal discourses controlling traffic and yet other discourses.

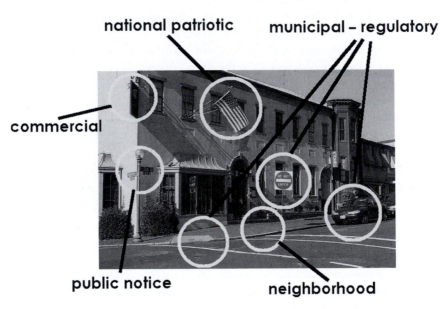

9.16

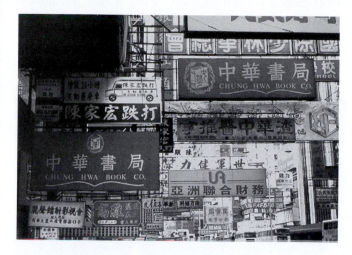

9.17

Assignment

Select a semiotic aggregate which interests you and make an attempt to isolate and document the multiple discourses you find there. Make a photo-montage which illustrates at least the most general categories of discourses you find.

Observations

Photography is useful in this case as you might take a wide-angle shot of the whole aggregate and then separate, individual shots of the representations of the separate discourses. Be sure to identify discourses which are represented not only by words and images but also by the built environment and by the social interactions (the interaction order) found at that place.

Activity: The distribution of a discourse across space and time

The opposite force from the centripetal one of the semiotic aggregate is the centrifugal force of a particular discourse. Paris has a distinctive 'feel' about it for visitors and residents alike. One of the discourses which make up this character is the design of the street signs. The Paris street sign is highly distinctive with its white letters on a blue background with a green border decoration as we saw in image 9.13.

This distinctive street signage is found throughout the city of Paris. Throughout the world this design is used to signal the 'Parisian' character of a restaurant. Just to the right of the door of a restaurant in Washington, DC in photo 9.18 is a small sign suggesting that this restaurant is found on a street in Paris which happens to have the same name as the restaurant.

9.18

Assignment

Select a discourse in which you have an interest and try to follow it out through the various places where it occurs. Document the different physical manifestations of this discourse in these different places.

Observations

Try to identify what it is about this discourse that makes it recognizable in different semiotic aggregates. Bear in mind that it might be color and typography in one place, lexical style in another, and yet some other semiotic element in another place.

10 Indexicality, dialogicality, and selection in action

Action in the social world

In his very influential book *A Grammar of Motives* Kenneth Burke comments that we think of our world and of our actions through what he called *representative anecdotes*. That is, he believed that there is an underlying metaphor or generative narrative that organizes our thinking in almost everything we do. In trying to understand human action Burke argued that we (Westerners) work with the representative anecdote of God's creation of the universe. We have a tendency to talk and think about any action within the framework by which the Book of Genesis in the Bible tells us that the universe was created. The creative entity brings everything out of nothing and into existence through an act of conscious will. God says, 'Let there be . . .' and there it is.

Perhaps Burke is right in this because there is a tendency in common thinking about action as well as in some social scientific accounts of human action toward the idea that the social actor consciously decides to do something and then simply does it. A simple action such as crossing the street which we discussed in Chapter 9 is often talked about as if someone simply decides, 'I'll cross the street,' and then just sets out to do that.

This is not the view of human action we have taken in this book. While it might be hard to articulate the representative anecdote – we will leave that to our readers – we can say that we see human action arising, largely unconsciously, out of prior experience, habits, and prior actions within the particular places we inhabit. We cross the street because here we are on a walk and we have arrived at this corner and will simply continue when we can. That is, we see human action as part of a continuous flow of process which, as Hägerstrand has pointed out, begins at birth and continues through on a trajectory to death.

Further, as we have discussed beginning in Chapter 1 and then have expanded in Chapter 3, we see human action as deeply embedded in the interaction order as a complex set of performances. These performances position us in relationship to the other social actors in our presence as well as in relationship to all of the other discourses in place as the place semiotics of that spot on the earth where the action is occurring. That is, at any moment in real time we can think of the action that is taking place arising out of the intersection of these elements:

• the social actor and his or her habitus,
• the interaction order,
• the visual (and other discursive) semiotics available for appropriation, and
• the place semiotics which necessarily includes all of the regulatory, infra-structural, commercial, and even transgressive discourses positioned in that place.

Taken together these four elements form a nexus of action as we have sketched out graphically in 1.04 and which we repeat here.

A person comes to the moment of crossing the street, as we have suggested above, with a personal history of knowledge and experience, a set of habits, a set of intentions (however vague or undefined they may be). Perhaps the person is only aware that he or she intends to cross to the other side of the street at that point as may be the case on 10.01.

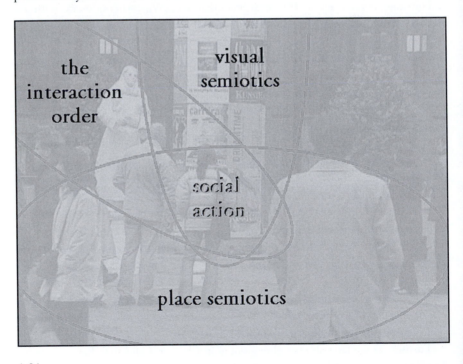

the interaction order

visual semiotics

social action

place semiotics

1.04

10.01

This first consideration is the habitus of the social actor himself or herself. Am I the sort of person who waits for the walk light or do I cross when the road is free of traffic? Am I the sort of person who worries about whether others are watching me or not? Do I even notice? Am I having trouble because of an injury and so have to be careful not to have to run or move quickly? Am I in a hurry to get to a meeting with a friend or am I taking a leisurely stroll? All of these very individual and personal considerations would make a difference in how a person would come to the corner and how he or she would treat the problem of crossing the street.

It should not be forgotten as well that this is not simply a matter of personal and autonomous choice. As Goffman has argued, there is nothing we do that does not at least 'give off' expression of our role performances and positions. This person arriving at the street corner is not only waiting for the walk light or not, he or she is also signaling to others whether or not he or she is the sort of person who waits and in so signaling is either contesting or ratifying the regulatory and other discourses present in that place.

A person alone with a lot of time might pause to read the notices for domestic worker services but one in a hurry would rush past. A person who habitually waits for the light to change would have more time to read notices posted there, even if he or she was in a hurry. Perhaps in this we see a partial explanation of the most distinctive aspect of the corner we studied in Vienna and which we discussed in Chapter 9. This was the abundance of posted notices stuck to every available space. We also observed that pedestrians in Vienna seemed reluctant to cross the street except when the green pedestrian light authorized them to pass. Also on that street corner are bus stops in four directions as well as trolley stops in two directions.

A typical person coming to this corner would have a considerable amount of time to wait until the signal changed to allow him or her to cross the street. Thus we see one form of dialogicality between the habitus of the social actor and the discourses that may be present in a place.

At the same time the person who comes to cross the street is a social person within some interaction order. He or she may be walking together with a friend or going somewhere as a single. That status as a social person will make some difference to how he or she sets about crossing the street. As we have noted in Chapter 3, Goffman identified at least 11 kinds of interaction units from the with to the celebrative occasion. As we noted, a with is a form of the interaction order in which members of the with exercise special privileges in claiming each other's attention while granting to the rest of the world what Goffman calls civil inattention. Two people engaged in a conversational with might approach a corner and be quite oblivious to the social situation or the regulatory structure at that moment.

In making observations on many street corners around the world we have observed that it is common for a with to parcel out this duty among members as they reach the street corner. Quick glances are exchanged even as the conversation continues to see if anyone is paying attention to the problem of crossing the street. If it is seen that one is taking care of this function, the others simply focus their attention on that person and follow her/his lead in crossing, quite oblivious to the lights or to the traffic. As Goffman has noted, their full attention is given over to each other.

If we imagine a Finn and a Hong Konger together in a with either in Finland or in Hong Kong we can imagine a dynamic tension between the habitus and the interaction order. The habitus of the Finn would cry out to wait for authorization to cross roads, no matter what the traffic conditions might be. The habitus of the Hong Konger would be to simply cross when possible, no matter what the regulatory conditions might be. For both of them the main consideration would be to maintain the attention of each on the other.

As we have discussed in Chapter 9 on Discourses in Time and Space, on that street corner there might be as many as a dozen or more discourses with many particular messages at the corner to which the pedestrian might need to attend. For our purposes we may just set aside all of the discourses which are not relevant to this action of crossing the street – the advertising on shop fronts across the street, the discarded food packages next to the trash can, the sign giving the name of the street, the note saying post no bills on the electrical box running the traffic signals, the poster announcing a coming theatrical performance, the gas, water, cable TV, or other manhole covers, the music playing in a passing automobile, the no-parking signs for cars, or the bus stop sign one is standing next to. But, of course, these discourses will be present, even if only as the background which provides the place semiotics of a busy urban intersection.

Among those discourses are ones which signal the sociocultural organization of that particular society. Are there traffic regulations? How are they posted and signaled? Is there law enforcement and is it taken seriously? Where and when is it legal to cross within this road regulatory and social structure? Of course it could be argued that these are really two very separate systems. One is legal and regulatory, the other is embedded in social practice. In one case it is encoded in municipal statutes that one can or cannot cross the road at this point. In fact it has been much of the central business of this book to discuss how these signs come to take up meaning when they are actually in place.

More subtly, the discourses in place at this point are just how people 'here' do things, no matter what the legal structure might say. These discourses are as much in the habitus of the individual person as in social environment in the form of the actions of others who are present. While this is an important distinction, from our point of view in *Discourses in Place*, it is not one that we need to take up in more detail here though it was a major concern in the work of Edward T. Hall which we discussed in Chapter 3. For us the main point is that at any intersection there will be sociocultural expectations, sanctions, enforcements, and transgressions in play.

From the point of view of Goffman's social situation the main consideration is simply whether or not there are other people present and what those people are doing. A Finn who would never think of crossing a street against the light at home might be on vacation in Hong Kong. He or she might simply be swept across the street against the light in a crowded mob of pedestrians in Central against which resistance would be futile. Alternatively, a Hong Konger in Finland might feel quite uncomfortable stepping out to cross the street if several other people are standing there waiting for the signal, even if those others are all strangers. This apprehension about doing something that others are not doing is likely to be enhanced by the presence of a law enforcement officer as part of that social situation.

Finally, in taking this action there is the physical, material world itself that the pedestrian must consider. Are there specified walkways for pedestrians? How wide is the roadway? Can it be crossed in one go or is there a place to wait in the center? What is the weather?

A good reason why the Finns we mentioned in Chapter 9 are so careful to obey pedestrian traffic regulations could simply be that for much of the year the roads in Finland are covered with ice, the footing for a pedestrian is slippery, and oncoming cars would find it very difficult to stop in a short distance. While none of these conditions ever obtain in Hong Kong, nevertheless we found that pedestrians in Hong Kong focus more directly on the actual physical objects in the road – cars, trucks, buses, and other pedestrians. At the same time a tropical downpour of rain during a typhoon brings pedestrians to a run across streets quite oblivious to either pedestrian signals or vehicular traffic. We believe that such an action as crossing the street, wherever in the world one might be, must be very basically predicated on the physical conditions of the road, the presence of vehicles, and the general atmospheric conditions that would make it a possibility to cross or a necessity to wait.

Action and identity

In Chapter 2, we discussed the indexicality of language and other signs in the world, how for example a sign saying 'MEN AT WORK' takes its meaning from where it is placed on a street or highway, how it is oriented in relation to the flow of traffic, what time of day and what day of the week it is, from a discourse of traffic regulation. Such a sign indexes a discourse of authority, of government road maintenance, whether federal, state, county, or municipal. When we see such a sign we look for men or women on the road, for cones or other barriers, for machinery or broken pavement. If it is evening or a holiday and there are no signs of work being done we keep on driving.

There is a double indexicality in that there is a discourse which produces the sign as well as discourses for interpreting the sign. The following statement from a US Department of Transportation website indexes an American identity for users of the website as well as the administrators who put the website together. It indexes a 'language' of 'traffic control devices' by which traffic engineers communicate to drivers how they are to drive.

> We love to drive! Americans relish the freedom of climbing in a vehicle and hitting the road. And as we drive, we rely on a complex series of visual cues to help us make the journey safely. The signs, signals, and pavement markings that guide us are called traffic control devices. These devices are the language that communicates to drivers along the Nation's roadways. They tell us to slow down for the sharp curve on a two-lane rural byway. They make it possible for us to drive 100 km/h (65 mi/h) on the highway separated from other lanes of traffic by only a narrow yellow line. They tell us when and where to stop, and where we should think twice before we park. And they communicate with us in Mobile and Minneapolis, New Orleans and New York, in Seattle and Savannah.
>
> (http://mutcd.fhwa.dot.gov/kno-overview.htm)

As we noted in Chapter 9, the semiotics of signs, signals and markings is spelled out for traffic engineers across the country in the Manual on Uniform Traffic Control Devices (MUTCD).

A driver who disregards a road work sign may index to a police officer someone who has been drinking if there are in fact men at work. For such a driver the sign may not have played its indexing role. An officer who stops a driver when there is no work going on on the roadway, on the other hand, indexes an overzealous officer perhaps trying to make money for the municipality by issuing unwarranted tickets. Or, late at night it might index an officer bored on the job and trying to stay awake.

Any action (e.g. walking against the light or with the light, in the zebra crossing or outside of it, etc.) provides a double indexicality. On the one hand this action indexes the person, that is the habitus. This is a local, a foreigner, a person of good character or not, a law-abiding citizen or a rogue, a friend who considers other members of the with first or a bad social risk. By the actions of the individual in interaction with these multiple semiotic systems we index the always invisible habitus and those other amorphous psychological and characterological states:

Physical world: Doesn't care about weather, or is hyperfastidious
Discourses in place – social situation: A scofflaw or a law-abiding citizen, attentive to decorum
Interaction order: Cares for her/his friends
Habitus: A person of good character

By behaving in particular ways the person 'gives off', to use Goffman's terms, personal cues about the social role performances one is making and thus indexes these invisible psychological and sociocultural states.

On the other hand, this is always ambiguous because of the double indexicality we have referred to just above. By crossing a street in a particular way the social actor also indexes the discourses which are in place at that moment and in that place and this indexing can take on various forms from ratification to contestation. If a person approaches the corner, glances in the direction of the pedestrian signal which is signaling 'wait' at that moment, and comes to a standstill until the signal indicates 'walk', that person through that normative behavior indexes and ratifies the regulatory municipal authorities from the town council through law enforcement officers which have placed that pedestrian signal on that corner and who enforce its directive force. This is further ratified if she or he steps out on the 'walk' signal into the marked zebra crossing area and strides purposefully across to the other side.

Ambiguity arises, of course, when the non-normative occurs. If a different pedestrian arrives on the corner in the same moment but simply ignores the 'wait' signal and walks across the street we do not know where to attribute this violation of norms. By this double indexicality of habitus and social regulation, all we can infer is that this person does not stop for a 'wait' signal. If this is in Finland, because of the broad normative social organization patterns, we can assume such things as that this person is a foreigner on the one hand (and therefore the habitus is excusable) or a Finn on the other (and therefore one makes attributions to bad habitus).

In writing this book itself, we have indexed ourselves first as pedestrians and second as drivers. We started our research in geosemiotics as residents of Hong Kong traveling to cities in China and Finland. We did this work primarily as pedestrians and users of public transportation such as subways and buses. We then moved to Washington, DC, where we found many more signs for motorists than for pedestrians. After teaching a course using these materials, we were given a catalog that sells signs not only for traffic control but for industrial safety and security. From this catalog we learned of the manual for uniform traffic control devices.

We find that the semiotic systems of the physical world, the discourses in place and the social situation, the interaction order and habitus change as we go from being pedestrians to motorists. As drivers, we cannot be as attentive to others in the vehicle with us as we can as pedestrians walking in a with. We must attend to the physical world at greater distances and higher speeds. We flout regulatory signs and traffic signals at greater risk. We need higher degrees of training to be licensed as drivers, while we need no special training to walk in cities around the globe. Our interpersonal distances are constrained by the design of the vehicles we ride in rather than the design of sidewalks and passageways. We take different actions that require different sociocultural organization and call on different aspects of habitus. Thus our actions are inherently productive of identity because they index the discourses in place.

Action and indexicality

In taking action, whether on foot or in the driver's seat, there is more at stake than indexing what kind of a person one is. It matters where on earth one is. When a Hong Konger in China persists in walking on the left even though hundreds of people are streaming toward him he makes movement difficult for himself. When an American in London looks left before crossing a street she may be run over by a car coming from the right. Even within the United States there are different laws governing right of way in the east and in the west of the country. One of the authors driving from Michigan to the west coast nearly hit a pedestrian in Montana, unaware that the laws of that state give right of way to the pedestrian unlike Michigan state law at that time which gave right of way to motorists.

Of course road signs as well differ from place to place. A woman originally from Western Europe where regulatory signs differ from the United States where she currently resides, when back in Europe failed to observe a sign indicating one-way traffic and had to back up in a hurry when a bus appeared before her on the narrow road.

We can summarize this discussion of action and indexicality with three principles of geosemiotics:

1 the principle of **indexicality**: all semiotic signs, whether embodied or disembodied, have as a significant part of their meaning how they are placed in the world.
2 the principle of **dialogicality**: all signs operate in aggregate. There is a double indexicality with respect to the meaning attached to the sign by its placement and its interaction with other signs. Each sign indexes a discourse that authorizes its placement, but once the sign is in place it is never isolated from other signs in its environment, embodied or disembodied. There is always a dynamic among signs, an intersemiotic, interdiscursive dialogicality.
3 the principle of **selection**: any action selects a subset of signs for the actor's attention. A person in taking action selects a pathway by foregrounding some subset of meanings and backgrounding others. Action is a form of selection, positioning the actor as a particular kind of person who selects among different meaning potentials a subset of pathways.

We can illustrate these principles with the simple action of stopping at a stop sign. A woman we know lives in a residential neighborhood of Ann Arbor, Michigan. As a mother of three school-aged boys, she was concerned about the safety of the neighborhood children and together with a neighbor had taken action that resulted in the municipal authorities having a sign placed where the two mothers had determined it was necessary. Because she had been aware of the dangers of this intersection, she had developed a firm habit of watching carefully for other cars and for children at this intersection whenever she drove through it.

One day soon after the placement of the new sign, on her way home, the woman drove straight through the intersection right past the stop sign. In taking this action she backgrounded the stop sign and by failing to notice it, she indexed actions she herself had taken in the past. That is, in her mind the action continued to index her prior behaviors of watching for children and cars, not for the regulatory stop sign. On seeing that she had failed to notice the sign in place she chastized herself for not being a good example in obeying a sign she herself had been instrumental in having installed.

The stop sign clearly indexed where a motorist should stop on the street. The aggregate of signs at the intersection had changed when the sign was put in place a short time before the woman drove past without noticing the new sign. The new stop sign was the only regulatory sign at the intersection, and the woman had been accustomed to paying attention to people and cars when driving through, not to traffic control devices. In driving past the stop sign the woman backgrounded the stop sign and foregrounded the empty street. Only on reflection did the driver realize that there was a double indexicality with respect to her previous action in lobbying for the placement of the sign and her current action as a driver ignoring the sign.

We have said that a social actor undertaking a simple action such as crossing the street or driving through a street intersection acts at the conjunction of four meaning systems: the habitus of the social actor, the interaction order, the visual semiotics, and the place semiotics of the discourses in place. Following Hägerstrand, we would argue that each of these main systems has a materiality and a history that converges at any point at which action is taken. The habitus of the individual social actor is accrued over his or her lifetime of experiences in the world and continues on its trajectory beyond the point of any action. Of course that moment of action becomes part of the ongoing development of the person's habitus.

In the same way the interaction order – a with, a queue, a conversational encounter, or a platform event – comes into existence as a convergence of separate individuals for a period of time, has its own history, and then dissolves to become part of the history of the separate individuals.

The discourses in place, both the visual semiotics and the broader place discourses we have discussed, in any concrete space tend to have a slower periodicity than the social interactions that occur in those places. The signs might be located in a city for years, the buildings perhaps for centuries. Each of these discourses would have its own history, its own trajectory by which it came to be in that place, perhaps through architectural plans or municipal ordinance. And these concrete discourses would reflect more conceptual characteristics of the societies in which those physical structures were built.

Finally, in some ways the natural world is both the most slowly changing and the most rapidly changing of these elements. Any place in the world is likely to stay in a relatively stable relationship to mountains and rivers in the vicinity. Many cities of the world are built at the confluence of rivers, for example, or on natural harbors. When these relationships change through floods or volcanic eruptions the results are catastrophic to the built human and social environment precisely because of the very long periodicity of these changes which allows the built environment to ignore such forces for decades or even centuries. At the same time a pleasant conversation in an outdoor café in Vienna can be instantaneously disrupted by a rapidly developing afternoon storm of wind and rain driving the customers all indoors for shelter.

Each of the factors or semiotic resources of an action is independent of the others but at the same time, each is in some way keyed to the others as the nexus within which that action takes on the meaning that it has in this world.

The future of geosemiotics

It will be abundantly clear to the reader that in this book we have only begun the roughest sketch of a field of study that we are calling geosemiotics. The name is not important, of course. What is important and what we hope to have accomplished through these examples and through our discussion is to suggest a number of the ways that language is located in the material world. The discourses in place everywhere in our world bring with them both potentials for action and constraints upon possible meanings and interpretations. We believe that in order to bring about the changes that we would like to see in our world, it will be not just useful and interesting, but essential for us to continue to make these analytical linkages among what have mostly been separate disciplinary interests in the interaction order of face-to-face communication, the visual semiotics of signs and images and texts, and the placement of these discourses in the physical spaces in which we live and act.

Glossary

Action   in social sciences this often implies a concern with processes that occur across time rather than an attempt to analyze a system as fixed or static.

Add-ons/extensions   layering of an inscription on another usually more permanent inscription such as 'on sale today' or 'limited time only'.

Agency   the quality of being an agent; greater or lesser agency may be ascribed to actions partly depending on how much conscious intention is ascribed to the social actor.

Agent, agency   a term derived from grammatical analysis meaning the person (or other entity) which is the instigator (conscious or not) of the action indicated by the verb; hence, any social actor who is thought of as doing something or taking an action.

Analytical   in visual semiotics, the relationship among participants in a picture that shows a categorical relationship between or among them.

Assembly   the process of creating a semiotic aggregate or a semiotic complex; in some cases assembly is centralized in some authority and in other cases it is serendipitous and accidental.

Auditory space   the structuring of the space around us on the basis of what we can hear.

Backstage   the social role performance that others are expected to ignore or disregard; contrasts with frontstage.

Body idiom   Goffman's preferred term for 'body language' (also **nonverbal communication** in some uses); all of the movements and placements of the body one may use to produce the personal front.

Body language   the general term for all of the movements and placements of the body one may use to produce the personal front.

Celebrative occasion   a social interaction which is tightly ritualized such as weddings, awards ceremonies and the like where the actions of all participants are governed by prior scripts for performance.

Center–margin composition   when a picture is organized around a central salient portion of the image that central image or text is the focal point, often abstract such as a logo, and the material around the periphery is secondary or more specific and concrete.

Centrifugal a force that flows outward from the center; used in this case to refer to the fact that at any place the discourses that form a nexus there flow outward into other places and spaces.

Centripetal a force that flows inward toward the center; used to refer to the concentration of multiple discourses that form a semiotic aggregate.

Civil inattention ignoring and being seen to ignore the visible and audible behavior of others in the same social space but with whom one has no currently ratified social relationship.

Co-presence meanings 'given off' or 'given' through the human body such as gestures, movements, or postures. See also **embodied expression**.

Code preference the relationship between two or more languages in bilingual (multilingual) signs and pictures; the preferred code is on top when horizontally divided and on the left when vertically divided. This preference system has not yet been researched for languages with right to left text vectors (e.g. Arabic) and may be reversed when vertically divided with preferred codes on the right, secondary codes on the left.

Coding orientation the conventional set of ways in which modality is produced in a particular semiotic domain; for example, scientific documents tend to use diagrams to produce high modality, travel brochures tend to use full color photography to produce high modality.

Composition in visual semiotics, the meanings produced by the relationships in space within a picture. Three main systems are the ideal–real, the given–new, and the center–margin relationships.

Contact a fleeting social interaction that is produced by glances of mutual recognition but which is not allowed to segue into more fully developed forms such as the with or the service encounter.

Conversational encounter a with which has as its main focus of attention the production and the maintenance of a state of talk among a relatively small group.

Decontextualized semiotics all the forms of signs, pictures, and texts which may appear in multiple contexts but always in the same form; also called **universalized semiotics**.

Deictic adverb a word referencing a place ('here', 'there') the meaning of which can only be determined by looking at something in the world outside of language.

Deixis the property in language of pointing to the world outside of language.

Demand an interactive participant relationship in which the participant in the image looks directly into the eyes of the viewer.

Demonstrative   a word referencing an object, sometimes classed as a demonstrative pronoun, which functions as an index (such as 'this', 'that', 'these', 'those') the meaning of which can only be determined by looking at something in the world outside of language.

Denied semiotics   any sign that is 'canceled' or signaled as being out of order or not to be read.

Design   used by Kress and van Leeuwen to mean the level between discourse and production in which meanings are encoded into specific modes. Corresponds to Goffman's 'authorship'.

Dialogicality   the property of all discourse that it responds to prior discourse and anticipates subsequent discourse; discourse always 'speaks to' other discourses (derived from Bakhtin).

Discourse   in the narrow sense, language in use; in the broader sense, a body of language use and other factors that form a 'social language' such as the discourse of traffic regulation, commercial discourse, medical discourse, legal discourse.

Disembodied   signs that are not embodied or somatic, that are not part of or do not involve the human body.

Display space   a space designed to be observed but not entered into; also called exhibit space.

Ecological proximity   a distance close enough to another person that observers will judge two or more persons to be 'together'; a highly variable cultural construct.

Embodied expression   meaning 'given off' or 'given' through the human body such as a gesture, movement, or posture. See also **co-presence** and **somatic expression**.

Emplacement   the act of placing a sign in a physical location to activate its meaning; the meaning that derives from such an action; the study of such meanings.

Ethnography, ethnographic   the study of human behavior and action and sociocultural systems which is done through participant-observation using a wide range of research tools for observation. Normally carried out over an extended period of time such as an annual cycle.

Exhibit space   a space designed to be observed but not entered into; also called display space.

Exophoric indexicality   a sign which points to something outside of its own physical position; an exit sign.

Extrasomatic   signs that are not somatic, that are not part of or do not involve the human body; also '**disembodied**'.

Face-to-face communication   communication which takes place without any mediating technology. See also **co-presence**.

Feng shui   (pronounced approximately 'fung' [rhymes with lung] 'shway' [rhymes with way]); a complex system originating in China in which fate and fortunes are examined and optimized through developing a knowledge that combines astrology with the concrete spaces in which human actions are located.

File or procession   a group which moves together, whether more or less loosely formed as military parades or groups of tourists.

Font   any way in which letters or other written symbols are produced from handwriting and calligraphy through to word processing fonts and professional typefaces including size and shape or color; meanings range from the highly conventionalized letterforms of academic texts to innovative designed fonts in advertising and other graphic design.

Frontstage   the social role performance that others are expected to pay attention to; contrasts with **backstage**.

Geosemiotics   the study of the social meaning of the material placement of signs and discourses and of our actions in the material world.

Geosemiotic zones   broad areas such as an urban neighborhood or a mountain wilderness preserve in which there is an explict or tacit agreement about how semiotic messages will be presented.

Give expression   the intentional production of a meaning for another person to note.

Give off expression   the unintentional production of a meaning which another person might note.

Given–new composition   in a vertically divided picture, the left portion carries the given information and the right portion carries the new information; this is particularly susceptible to reinterpretation where the dominant writing system is read from right to left as in Arabic.

Grammar of visual design   based in the work of Kress and van Leeuwen, a formal and systemic account of the meaning potential systems available in particular cases.

Habitus   the accumulated experience and knowledge both conscious and unconscious of a social actor which is theorized as the primary source of human action.

Haptic (or tactile) **space**   the structuring of the space around us on the basis of what we can touch.

Hybrid   a mixture of multiple semiotic resources which produces a new possibility. See also **interdiscursivity**.

Icon   a sign that gives its meaning by looking like the object it refers to.

Iconicity   the property of being an icon.

Ideal–real composition   in a horizontally divided picture, the upper portion carries an ideal meaning while the lower carries a real meaning.

Index   a sign that is connected or points to its object of reference.

Indexicality   the property of the context-dependency of signs, especially language; hence the study of those aspects of meaning which depend on the placement of the sign in the material world.

Inscription   all of the meaning systems that are based on the physical materiality of language (signs and pictures) in the world; includes at least fonts, materials, add-ons or extensions, and state changes.

Interaction order   Goffman's rough categorization of the forms of social interactions we produce when we come together; these include the following: single, with, file or procession, queue, contact, service encounter, conversational encounter, meeting, people-processing encounter (gatekeeping encounter), platform event (watch), celebrative occasion (each separately defined in this glossary).

Interactive participants   in visual semiotics, any element of a picture (image or text) which is designed as being in relationship with a viewer or reader outside of the picture.

Interdiscursivity   the interactive influence of one discourse upon another. See also **hybrid**.

Interpersonal distance, **intimate**   the culturally specific space within which we feel an intimate relationship with another person; for the Americans Edward T. Hall studied that was touch to 18 inches.

Interpersonal distance, **personal**   the culturally specific space within which we feel a personal relationship with another person; for the Americans Edward T. Hall studied that was 18 inches to 4 feet.

Interpersonal distance, **public**   the culturally specific space within which we feel a public relationship with another person; for the Americans Edward T. Hall studied that was 12 feet to 25 feet.

Interpersonal distance, **social**   the culturally specific space within which we feel a social relationship with another person; for the Americans Edward T. Hall studied that was 4 feet to 12 feet.

Involvement   a term used by Goffman to indicate the specific stances taken by a person toward any current activity or activities; a dominant involvement is the activity which may interrupt any others, e.g. waiting for a train; a subordinate involvement may take place in a hiatus of a dominant involvement – reading while waiting; a main involvement is what one is doing just now (reading) and a side involvement might be carried on simultaneously – humming a tune.

Landscape   the sociocultural (hence ideological) meaning given to or implied by a geosemiotic zone or a visual representation of such a zone as in landscape painting.

Literate design   the overall 'face' of a public place or urban setting; the ways in which written codes form a semiotic aggregate at a particular place.

Marginal code (also **secondary** or **peripheral**)   the non-preferred code in bilingual or multilingual signs.

Material   the physical substances on which the inscription is made from granite monuments to sand writing at the beach; more durable materials tend to indicate more permanent meanings.

Meeting   a more tightly structured encounter which normally has a declared purpose with a ratifiable set of participants, relatively clear beginnings and endings, and most often a chair or facilitator.

Methodology   a formal set of procedures which are integrated with a theory as a means of deriving valid and reliable data to test the theory.

Modality   the property of showing the degree of validity or truth value in a picture through such means as color saturation, or the use of diagrams as opposed to photographic images. This can be interpreted only within a specific coding orientation.

Monochronism   the practice of doing, or preferring to do, one thing at a time; also called **monofocality**.

Monofocality   the practice of doing, or preferring to do, one thing at a time; also called **monochronism**.

Municipal–infrastructural discourse   the entire discourse from meetings of government bodies or utilities companies through to the placement of signs governing actions such as the placement or maintenance of power or gas supplies throughout a city.

Municipal–regulatory discourse   the entire discourse from meetings of government bodies through to the placement of signs governing public actions such as vehicular traffic or pedestrian traffic.

Narrative   in visual semiotics, the relationship among participants in a picture that shows a relationship of action between or among them.

Natural world   a sociocultural construct which purports to make reference to a world 'untouched' by human design.

Non-semiotic space   a space conventionally prohibiting the posting or construction of signs; in the US and many parts of the Western world national or wildlife parks are such non-semiotic spaces.

Non-verbal communication (also **nonverbal communication**)   a cover term sometimes used to cover all somatic or embodied communication which is not expressed in language. See **body idiom**.

Offer   an interactive participant relationship in which the participant in the image looks aside or away from the viewer.

Olfactory space   the structuring of the space around us on the basis of what we can smell.

Participant-observation   the primary research strategy of ethnography in which the ethnographer takes on a meaningful role within the sociocultural group being studied.

Passage space   a space designed to facilitate or allow passage from one space to another, a corridor or a stairway.

People-processing encounter (gatekeeping encounter)   a social inter-action which is polarized into those who have some power to define significant outcomes for those others who normally must provide some account of themselves. Job interviews and the issuing of traffic violation tickets by the police are examples.

Peripheral (secondary or marginalized) code   in bilingual (multilingual) signs, the code in the right or lower position is secondary or marginalized by comparison with the code in the upper or left position.

Personal front   the 'identity kit' that one produces to take on the performance of a social role.

Personal pronoun   a word ('I', 'you', 'they') which refers to a person, the meaning of which can only be determined by looking at something in the world outside of language.

Picture   in visual semiotics, any image or text or combination of image and text that forms a coherent single-framed sign.

Place   the human or lived experience or sense of presence in a space; a term much discussed and debated by cultural geographers and others; contrasts with space.

Place semiotics   a loose (non-theoretical) set of semiotic systems including code preference, inscription, emplacement but also anything in the built environment or possibly even the weather or regular climate patterns which contribute to the meaning of the place.

Platform event   someone or a small group performs as a spectacle for others to watch whether on an elevated platform or encircled by the group of watchers. Elsewhere we have called this a 'watch' to parallel Goffman's with.

Polychronism   the practice of doing, or preferring to do, more than one thing at a time; also called **polyfocality**.

Polyfocality   the practice of doing, or preferring to do, more than one thing at a time; also called **polychronism**.

Preferred code   in bilingual (multilingual) signs, the socially preferred code is placed in the upper or leftward position; but research remains to be done for right-to-left text vector languages such as Arabic.

Private legal notice   a sign which appears in public and which is legally sanctioned such as the name of a shop or its advertisements. Such private signs are sometimes restricted by public law such as with restrictions on the use of particular languages, obscenities, the sizes and shapes and extensions into public space that are sanctioned.

Private transgressive notice   any sign from graffiti to posted notices for events that is placed in public in contravention of prohibitions such as 'post no bills'.

Public functional notice   a sign that appears in public but which is addressed to a specific audience of infrastructural officials and workers such as the identification label on a traffic light.

Public label   a sign which identifies a public space or property such as the name of a street or of a park.

Public notice   a sign that informs the public either about conditions or regulations that are present in that place.

Queue   an aggregate of people, mostly not known to each other, who co-ordinate their activities so that they will arrive at some transaction point in a sequence.

Real time   a problematical concept which is commonly used to mean the sense of time people have while in face-to-face communication; often used in opposition to technologically mediated or recorded time.

Represented participants   in visual semiotics, any element of a picture (image or text) which is designed as being in relationship with another element in that picture.

Role performance   the meaningful display of the signs and actions appropriate to a recognizable social role such as mother, bus driver, or teacher.

Secure space   a space set off by security barriers or gates and checks.

Semiotic aggregate   separate realizations of different semiotic actions but which together form a composite meaning which we can read and which tells us, for example, what sort of shopping might be done in that area of the city.

Semiotic complex   an attempt to control the aggregation of signs and semiotic systems, that is, to produce an overarching system that limits to some extent the multiple systems that can occur within it such as in many shopping malls.

Semiotic practices   regular, habitual ways of making meanings among some sociocultural group.

Semiotic space   a space conventionally allowing the posting or construction of signs; contrasts with **non-semiotic space**.

Semiotic systems   a broad and very general term that covers any code or mode that can be used to convey meaning including whole systems such as language, fashion design, or architecture or sub-systems such as the given–new information system or color.

Semiotics   the study of the social production of meaning through signs.

Sense of time   the psychological feeling of how time is passing or how we use time in communication.

Service encounter   the social arrangement that occurs when we procure and are delivered some service such as buying a cup of coffee at a counter or exchanging a bus ticket with the driver as we board a bus.

Sign   in semiotics, a material object that indicates or refers to something other than itself; includes **icons, indexes,** and **symbols.**

Sign equipment   all of the physical and personal materials and objects one has at one's disposal to produce a social role performance including the body but also including clothing, hair style, or objects such as handbags.

Single   a person who is by himself or herself in a social space among others.

Situated indexicality   a sign such as some observed in China and Hong Kong in which the text vector itself indicates physical characteristics of the object on which the sign is placed; for example, the name of the bus company reads from the front toward the rear of the bus on both sides.

Situated semiotics   a sign which is designed to make reference to the characteristics of the object on which it is placed; 'feng shui' semiotics.

Situated vector   a line of gaze, an arrow, a reading path or text vector that is aligned with a directionality in the world outside of the image or picture.

Situational front   everything that facilitates a social role performance that lies outside of the personal front; this includes the spaces, objects, layouts, and other people present at the performance.

Social actor   the agent or instigator of an action; this term implies a major component of sociocultural habitus is part of any action taken.

Somatic expression   an embodied expression such as a gesture, posture, or movement. See also **co-presence.**

Space   refers to the objective, physical dimensions and characteristics of a portion of the earth or built environment; often defined by sociopolitical ideologies and powers; contrasted by geographers with **place.**

Special use space   a space designed for some conventional function such as a sidewalk café, a plaza, an entranceway, or a playing field.

State changes   the current meaning of a sign is given by such means as flashing neon lights or a lighted 'open' sign.

Symbol   a sign that is conventionally associated with its object of reference.

Symbolic   the property of being a symbol.

Tense   the property of language that makes reference to time such as past, present, or future which has an indexical function based on the 'present' meaning 'now'.

Territoriality   the phenomenon observed by ethologists that organisms from birds to mammals such as humans use the specific spaces their bodies inhabit as meaningful semiotic systems.

Text vector   the normal or conventional reading direction of text in a language; English has a text vector from left to right, Arabic is from right to left, traditionally Chinese could be left to right, right to left, or top to bottom.

Thermal space   the structuring of the space around us on the basis of the heat or warmth we feel.

Three-dimensionality   in geosemiotics, the characteristic of having meanings that depend on distribution in space (as opposed to the two-dimensionality of signs, images, and notices).

Time adverbial   a word such as 'then' or 'now' which indexes a moment in time that must be understood from something outside of the language.

Time urgency   the psychological sense (displayed somatically through 'nervous' gestures, etc.) that things need to be done more quickly.

Timescale   a rhythm and extension across time which is appropriate to some particular phenomenon; for example, a dinner works on a timescale which is relatively much shorter than the growing season in the temperate zones.

Transgressive semiotics   a sign which violates (intentionally or accidentally) the conventional semiotics at that place such as a discarded snack food wrapper or graffiti; any sign in the 'wrong place'.

Universalized semiotics   a sign which is designed to appear in exactly the same form wherever it occurs; e.g. a logo, or a shop, brand, or product name. A sign which is intentionally not sensitive to its emplacement in the world, not situated. It is, of course, always situated in any event. Also called **decontextualized semiotics**.

Vector   movement in a direction in a picture or text; shown by gaze, body movement or pointing.

Visual semiotics   the study of the ways in which visual images produce social meaning; a term from the work of Gunter Kress and Theo van Leeuwen.

Visual space   the structuring of the space around us on the basis of what we can see.

Watch   someone or a small group performs as a spectacle for others to watch whether on an elevated platform or encircled by the group of watchers. Goffman uses the term 'platform event'.

With   two or more individuals who are perceived as being together with each other as the main focus of their mutual attention.

References

In the first section below we have prepared notes on the main sources we have used in writing this book. In order to avoid excessive footnoting and citation in the main text of the book, general comments on those sources are provided here. The second section gives the actual citations for all sources used in the main text as well as in these notes.

NOTES ON REFERENCES USED

Preface

The critique of simplistic concepts of information has been developed by Brown and Duguid in a number of papers (Brown 1997; Brown and Duguid 1991, 2000a, 2000b, 2001, 2002). Most central to our thesis in this book is their idea that information is nothing when it is not placed within what they call a network of practice.

We are indebted to Illich's *Shadow Work* (1981) and *Gender* (1982) for the insights into the history of grammar in the production of the nation state. Harvey's *The Condition of Postmodernity* (1989) has proved to be a major work in the definition of our understanding of our contemporary postmodern world.

Chapter 1: Geosemiotics

The story about California nudist beaches is from Hanauer (2002).

Charles Sanders Peirce (1839–1941) and Ferdinand de Saussure (1857–1913) are generally thought of as the founders of the field of semiotics though the term was coined by John Locke (1632–1704) two centuries earlier (Edgar and Sedgwick 1999). For our purposes the work of Peirce is more central because of his concern with indexicality (Hanks 1990, 2001).

Michael Billig's *Banal Nationalism* (1995) is widely read for insights on the subtle, almost invisible ways in which the sociopolitical structures of our society are indexed in common day-to-day discourse. Fairclough (2001), Kress (1996), Lemke (1995), Meyer (2001), van Leeuwen (1996), and Wodak (2001) are useful sources on critical discourse analysis and the strategy of making visible the workings of sociopolitical forces through discourse. M. A. K. Halliday's foundational work (1978) argued that language is a social semiotic system. That is to say, language is a system in which structuring of meanings, the production of meanings, and the exchange of meanings cannot be separated. Consequently, in such a social semiotic system the study of any signs or messages is inherently the study of sociocultural and sociopolitical relations and processes of power distribution. We position our own work here within this general conception of social semiotics.

The terms 'somatic communication' and 'extra-somatic communication' were first used in Scollon and Scollon (1995) to avoid confusion with the metaphorical extensions that had arisen with Goffman's (1959) nearly synonymous 'embodied' and 'disembodied' expression. Csordas (1994, 1999) has also used the term embodiment and conducted extended research into the ways in which we attend *with* the body *to* the bodies of others. This theme is taken up as the subject matter of Chapter 3 on the interaction order.

Hägerstrand's work in the 1940s (Hägerstrand 1975; Carlstein, Parkes, and Thrift 1978a, 1978b) is fundamental in human geography or what is now perhaps more often called cultural geography (Crang 1998; Mitchell 2000). As Giddens (1984, 1991) has noted, we have yet to develop a fully integrated social science that takes both space and time into account. We are indebted to Gu Yueguo for calling our attention to Hägerstrand's work via the work of Giddens. Geosemiotics, in our view, is a move to approach this problem from an understanding of discourse.

Elsewhere we have put forward an action perspective on discourse under the rubric of mediated discourse analysis (R. Scollon 1998a, 1998b, 2001a, 2001b; S. Scollon 1998, 2001, 2002; S Scollon and Pan 2002) which we see as co-articulated with the geosemiotics we develop in this book. In terms of mediated discourse analysis geosemiotics is an extended development of the concept of the cultural tool or mediational means.

The concept of habitus has a long history beginning for us with the writings of Elias (1994, 2000) and Nishida (1958), though in the latter case the term used was *historical body*. More recently Bourdieu (1977, 1985, 1998) has written extensively on the role of habitus in practice theory (S. Scollon 2001, 2002). While Piaget did not use this term (Flavell 1963; Piaget 1971), his work makes it clear that he views human action as a dialectic between internal structures of human history and experience and the external world. In this respect (but of course not in all ways) we see Piaget's work as in concord with that of Vygotsky (1978) though just how these internal structures should be analyzed and how they originally develop and are maintained is different in their psychologies.

Bateson (1972) argued on this point that if there is one thing we know about human psychology it is that we do not have conscious access to our intentions, a point much more fully developed by the discursive psychologists (e.g. Harré 1994, 1998; Harré and Gillett 1994).

Norris (forthcoming) has developed the concept of 'modal density' with which she argues that in any single action a social actor focuses attention among an indefinitely large number of multiple modes for its expression. Modal density refers to the process by which either multiple modes are focused in the production of a unitary expression on the one hand or by which a single mode is strongly intensified. Schmidt (2001) includes a full literature review of research on the structures of attention.

The notion of the semiotic aggregate which we mention in passing in Chapter 1 but which is taken up more centrally in Chapter 9 is not a new concept except perhaps in wording. The idea is based on the fundamental principle in dialectics that no entities are unitary but are, in fact, the conjunction of flows of processes. Harvey (1996) has a particularly clear discussion of the main principles of dialectics which we have found very useful in our thinking.

Chapter 2: Indexicality

Charles Sanders Peirce is most often associated with the development of philosophical concerns with indexicality (e.g. 1955). While many linguists have had an interest in indexicality this interest has perhaps been most fully developed among linguistic anthropologists. Hanks (2001) is a succinct and apt statement of the central issues which, of course, relies on his own other work (e.g. 1987, 1990, 1996), as well as the work of many others (e.g. Silverstein 1976, 1996; Silverstein and Urban 1996; Irvine 1996; Haviland 1996, 1998, 2000; Danziger 1998).

Billig's (1995) argument in *Banal Nationalism* is that the 'nation' is indexed in quite subtle ways; for example, when a weather report gives 'the' weather, there is a particular sociopolitical entity implied much in the same way that a particular nation is indexed when a newspaper comments on what 'the' President has said today.

Chapter 3: The interaction order

Our use of the work of Edward T. Hall is based on two early books, *The Silent Language* (1959) and *The Hidden Dimension* (1969). Goffman's most important works for our purposes are *The Presentation of Self in Everyday Life* (1959), *Behavior in Public Places* (1963), *Relations in Public* (1971), and *Frame Analysis* (1974). While both scholars had long and productive careers, these early works set out the main frameworks which were elaborated in later projects and writing. The specific forms of interaction order given are from Goffman's presidential address to the American Sociological Association, 1982 (Goffman 1983).

The collaboration of Jurgen Ruesch and Gregory Bateson at the Langley Porter Clinic was an important moment in the development of social interactional studies and studies of nonverbal communication (Ruesch and Bateson 1968 [1951]; Ruesch and Kees 1956; Bateson 1972). While much younger than these researchers, Erving Goffman was part of this research group for a time.

The observations on how Anglo-American and African-American workers 'read' each other's behaviors are from Frederick Erickson's public lectures and have been confirmed with him through personal communication (email to Ron Scollon, February 18, 2002, 11:30 am). Erickson's *The Counselor as Gatekeeper: Social Interaction in Interviews* (with Jeffrey Shultz: 1982) remains the basic resource for an understanding of how such mis-read interpretations construct prejudicial outcomes in institutional gatekeeping encounters. See also Erickson (1976) for important analyses of the relationships between microethnographic and macro-ethnographic studies.

Walter Ong's thoughts on literacy and orality are from his book *Orality and Literacy* (Ong 1982). Geaney (2000) notes that the Chinese philosopher Xunzi took just exactly the opposite position from that of Ong in arguing that sound is the unifying sense, not vision. This is a caution that such broad synthesizing comments are always likely to be more ideological than empirical.

Chapter 4: Visual semiotics

We have used the framework of visual semiotics put forward by Gunther Kress and Theo van Leeuwen (1996, 2001) as our point of departure in developing our ideas about geosemiotics. It will be clear that we have used only portions of their much more extended framework and that we have gone considerably beyond what has been proposed by them.

The comments concerning American and British concepts of sincerity are from Mead (1977). The discussion of modality in European art is found in Janson (1962).

Chapter 5: Interlude on geosemiotics

Published research in geosemiotics, at least using this terminology, is relatively new. The authors have worked together with Yuling Pan and Xiaping Pan (R. Scollon and S. Scollon 1998, 1999; S. Scollon and R. Scollon 2000; S. Scollon and Y. Pan 1997; X. Pan and R. Scollon 2000; Pan 1998). We have also learned much from projects done by our students de Saint-Georges and Norris (de Saint-Georges and Norris 1999; de Saint-Georges 2000; Norris 2000), Johnston (2000), and Zavala (2000). This work has covered the three areas we discuss in Chapters 6, 7, and 8, that is, code preference, inscription, and emplacement.

Chapter 7: Place semiotics: Inscription

We are grateful to Natalie Richter for pointing out to us the spelling 'thru' on the VISA cards in our wallets. Some of these issues concerning inscription have also been taken up in R. Scollon (2000a, 2000b, 2001c).

Chapter 8: Place semiotics: Emplacement

Gu Yueguo of the Chinese Academy of Social Sciences suggested that we use 'situated' in our discussion here. The use of the term 'notices' is from Lock (1999).

Chapter 9: Place semiotics: Discourses in time and space

Human geographers have long had a primary interest in the ways in which assemblies come together. Hägerstrand (1975, 1978) insisted on the necessity of integrating both space and time in geographical studies as early as his work in the 1940s. Cosgrove (1984) observed that social formations are inscribed on our landscapes. More recently cultural geographers (e.g. Crang 1998; Mitchell 2000; Pile and Thrift 2000) have reiterated the fundamental inseparability of space and time in their analyses. Tuan (1969, 1991, 1996) along with others (e.g. Agnew and Smith 2002) has been concerned to move geography beyond objectivistic views of space and the historical ties of this concept to nationalistic power and ideology into an understanding of place as the lived experience of human agents. Our interest here is in making a linkage between these movements in cultural geography and discourse analysis.

Harvey (1996 as well as in other places) has outlined crucial principles of a dialectical analysis of flows and processes. We have found his chapter on dialectics (his Chapter 2) most useful in developing our thinking on the semiotic aggregate.

REFERENCES CITED

Agnew, John A. and Jonathan M. Smith (2002) *American space/American place: Geographies of the contemporary United States*. Edinburgh: Edinburgh University Press.
Alexander, Christopher (1979) *The timeless way of building*. New York: Oxford University Press.

Alexander, Christopher, Sara Ishikawa, Murray Silverstein (1977) *A pattern language: Towns, buildings, construction*. New York: Oxford University Press.

Bateson, Gregory (1972) *Steps to an ecology of mind*. New York: Ballantine.

Billig, Michael (1995) *Banal nationalism*. London: Sage.

Bourdieu, Pierre (1977) *Outline of a theory of practice*. 'Richard Nice,' tr. Cambridge: Cambridge University Press.

Bourdieu, Pierre (1985) The genesis of the concepts of habitus and of field. *Sociocriticsm 2* (December 1985):11–24.

Bourdieu, Pierre (1998) *Practical reason: on the theory of action*. Stanford: Stanford University Press.

Brown, John Seely (1997) *Seeing differently: Insights on innovation*. Boston: Harvard Business School Press.

Brown, John Seely and Paul Duguid (1991) Organizational learning and communities of practice: Toward a unified of working, learning, and innovation. *Organizational Science* 2(1):40–57.

Brown, John Seely and Paul Duguid (2000a) Foreword. In Martin Kenney (ed.) *Understanding Silicon Valley*. Stanford: Stanford University Press, ix–xvi.

Brown, John Seely and Paul Duguid (2000b) Balancing act: How to capture knowledge without killing it. *Harvard Business Review*, May–June:73–80.

Brown, John Seely and Paul Duguid (2001) Knowledge and organization: A social-practice perspective. *Organizational Science*, 12(2):198–213.

Brown, John Seely and Paul Duguid (2002) *The social life of information*. Boston: Harvard Business School Press.

Burke, Kenneth (1969 [1945]) *A grammar of motives*. Englewood Cliffs, N.J.: Prentice-Hall.

Carlstein, Tommy, Don Parkes, and Nigel Thrift (1978a) *Human activity and time geography*. New York: John Wiley and Sons.

Carlstein, Tommy, Don Parkes, and Nigel Thrift (1978b) The Lund school: Introduction. In Tommy Carlstein, Don Parkes, and Nigel Thrift (eds) *Human activity and time geography*. New York: John Wiley and Sons, 117–121.

Cosgrove, Denis E. (1984) *Social formation and symbolic landscape*. Madison: University of Wisconsin Press.

Cowan, Ruth Schwartz (1983) *More work for mother*. New York: Basic Books.

Crang, Mike (1998) *Cultural geography*. London: Routledge.

Csordas, Thomas J. (1994) *Embodiment and experience: The existential ground of culture and self*. Cambridge: Cambridge University Press.

Csordas, Thomas J. (1999) The body's career in anthropology. In Henrietta L. Moore (ed.) *Anthropological theory today*. Oxford: Blackwell, 172–205.

Danziger, Eve (1998) Introduction: Language, space and culture. *Ethos* 26(1):3–6.

de Saint-Georges, Ingrid (2000) Discussing images: pictures reception and appropriation in focus groups. Paper presented at the Georgetown University Roundtable, Washington, DC, May 4–6.

de Saint-Georges, Ingrid and Sigrid Norris (1999) Literate design and European identity: Visual practices of an imagined community. Paper presented at the International Visual Sociology Association Annual Conference, Antwerp, July 14–18.

Durán, Manuel, Gloria Durán, and Charles E. Kany (1978) *Spoken Spanish for students and travelers*. Lexington, Mass: D. C. Heath and Company.

Edgar, Andrew and Peter Sedgwick (1999) *Key concepts in cultural theory*. London: Routledge.

Elias, Norbert (2000 [1994]) *The civilizing process: sociogenetic and psychogenetic investigations*. 'Edmund Jephcott', tr. with some notes and corrections by the author. Revised edition: Eric Dunning, Johan Goudsblom, and Stephen Mennell (eds). Oxford: Blackwell.

Erickson, Frederick (1976) Gatekeeping encounters: A social selection process. In Peggy Reeves Sanday (ed.), *Anthropology and the public interest: Fieldwork and theory*. New York: Academic Press, 111–145.

Erickson, Frederick and Jeffrey Shultz (1982) *The counselor as gatekeeper: Social interaction in interviews*. New York: Academic Press.

Fairclough, Norman (2001) Critical discourse analysis as a method in social scientific research. In Ruth Wodak and Michael Meyer (eds), *Methods in critical discourse analysis*. London: Sage, 121–138.

Flavell, John (1963) *The developmental psychology of Jean Piaget*. New York: Van Nostrand Reinhold Company.

Geaney, Jane (2000) The sensory experience of writing in early Chinese philosophical texts. Paper presented at the Association for Asian Studies Annual meeting, San Diego, March 9–12.

Giddens, Anthony (1984) *The constitution of society*. Cambridge: Polity Press.

Giddens, Anthony (1991) *Modernity and self-identity*. Cambridge: Polity Press.

Goffman, Erving (1959) *The presentation of self in everyday life*. New York: Doubleday.

Goffman, Erving (1963) *Behavior in public places: Notes on the social organization of gatherings*. New York: Free Press.

Goffman, Erving (1971) *Relations in public*. New York: Harper and Row.

Goffman, Erving (1974) *Frame analysis*. New York: Harper and Row.

Goffman, Erving (1983) The interaction ritual. *American Sociological Review* 48:1–19.

Hägerstrand, Torsten (1975) Space, time and human conditions. In A. Karlqvist, L. Lundqvist, and F. Snickars (eds), *Dynamic allocation of urban space*. Farnborough: Saxon House, 3–12.

Hägerstrand, Torsten (1978) Survival and arena. In Tommy Carlstein, Don Parkes, and Nigel Thrift (eds), *Human activity and time geography*. New York: John Wiley and Sons, 122–145.

Hall, Edward T. (1959) *The silent language*. Garden City, New York: Doubleday.

Hall, Edward T. (1969) *The hidden dimension*. Garden City, NY: Doubleday.

Halliday, M. A. K. (1978) *Language as social semiotic*. London: Edward Arnold.

Hanauer, Gary (2002) Nude Beach 2001, Muir Beach Update. www.sfbg.com/nude01/muir.html Site visited Saturday, February 9, 2002, 5:47 pm.

Hanks, William F. (1987) Discourse genres in a theory of practice. *American Ethnologist* 14(4):668–692.

Hanks, William F. (1990) *Referential practice: Language and lived space among the Maya*. Chicago and London: The University of Chicago Press.

Hanks, William F. (1996) *Language and communicative practices*. Boulder, CO: Westview.

Hanks, William F. (2001) Indexicality. In Alessandro Duranti (ed.), *Key terms in language and culture*. Oxford: Blackwell, 119–121.

Harré, Rom (1994) Is there still a problem about the self? *Communication Yearbook* 17:55–73.

Harré, Rom (1998) *The singular self: An introduction to the psychology of personhood*. London: Sage.

Harré, Rom and Grant Gillett (1994) *The discursive mind*. Thousand Oaks, CA: Sage.

Harvey, David (1989) *The condition of postmodernity*. Oxford: Blackwell.

Harvey, David (1996) *Justice, nature and the geography of difference*. Oxford: Blackwell.

Haviland, John B. (1996) Text from talk in Tzotzil. In Michael Silverstein and Greg Urban (eds), *Natural histories of discourse*. Chicago and London: The University of Chicago Press, 45–78.

Haviland, John B. (1998) Early pointing gestures in Zincantán. *Journal of Linguistic Anthropology* 8(2):162–196.

Haviland, John B. (2000) Pointing, gesture spaces, and mental maps. In David McNeill (ed.), *Language and gesture: Window into thought and action*. Cambridge: Cambridge University Press, 13–46.

Hodges, John C., Hary E. Whitten, Winifred B. Horner, Suzanne S. Webb, and Robert K. Miller (1990) *Harbrace college handbook*. Fort Worth, TX: Harcourt Brace Jovanovich College Publishers.

Illich, Ivan (1981) *Shadow work*. Salem, NH and London: Marion Boyars.

Illich, Ivan (1982) *Gender*. New York: Pantheon.

Irvine, Judith T. (1996) Shadow conversations. In Michael Silverstein and Greg Urban (eds), *Natural histories of discourse*. Chicago and London: The University of Chicago Press, 131–159.

Janson, H. W. (1962) *History of art: A survey of the major visual arts from the dawn of history to the present day*. Englewood Cliffs, NJ: Prentice-Hall Inc. and New York: Harry N. Abrams, Inc.

Jewitt, Carey and Rumiko Oyama (2001) Visual meaning: a social semiotic approach. In Theo van Leeuwen and Carey Jewitt (eds) *Handbook of visual analysis*. London: Sage 134–156.

Johnston, Alexandra Marie (2000) Signs of recovery?: Reading politics and economics in the street signs of Beirut. Paper presented at the Georgetown University Roundtable, Washington, DC, May 4–6.

Kress, Gunther (1996) Representational resources and the production of subjectivity. In Carmen Rosa Caldas-Coulthard and Malcolm Coulthard (eds) *Texts and practices: Readings in critical discourse analysis*. London: Routledge, 15–31.

Kress, Gunther and Theo van Leeuwen (1996) *Reading images: The grammar of visual design*. London: Routledge.

Kress, Gunther and Theo van Leeuwen (2001) *Multimodality*. London: Edward Arnold.

Lemke, Jay L. (1995) *Textual politics*. London: Taylor and Francis.

Lemke, Jay L. (2000a) Across the scales of time: Artifacts, activities, and meanings in ecosocial systems. *Mind, Culture, and Activity* 7(4):273–290.

Lemke, Jay L. (2000b) Opening up closure: Semiotics across scales. In Jerry L. R. Chandler and Gertrudis Van de Vijver (eds), *Closure: Emergent organizations and their dynamics*. New York: Annals of the New York Academy of Sciences, Vol. 901:100–111.

Li, Fang Kuei (1946) Chipewyan. In Harry Hoijer (ed.) *Linguistic Structures of North America*. New York: Viking Fund Publications in Anthropology, 6:398–423.

Lip, Evelyn (1995) *The design and feng shui of logos, trademarks, and signboards*. New York: Prentice Hall.

Lock, Graham (1999) Semiotic resources on the Hong Kong Mass Transit Railway. Paper presented at the International Systemic Functional Congress, Singapore, July.

Mead, Margaret (1977) End linkage: A tool for cross-cultural analysis. In John Brockman (ed.), *About Bateson*. New York: E. P. Dutton, 171–234.

Meyer, Michael (2001) Between theory, method, and politics: positioning of the approaches to CDA. In Ruth Wodak and Michael Meyer (eds), *Methods in critical discourse analysis*. London: Sage, 14–31.

Mitchell, Don (2000) *Cultural geography: A critical introduction*. Oxford: Blackwell.

Nishida, Kitaroo (1958) *Intelligibility and the philosophy of nothingness*. Tokyo: Maruzen Co. Ltd.

Norris, Sigrid (2000) Visual semiotics: A reflection of sociopolitical currents in Germany. Paper presented at the Georgetown University Roundtable, Washington, DC, May 4–6.

Norris, Sigrid (forthcoming) Multimodal discourse analysis: A conceptual framework. In Philip LeVine and Ron Scollon (eds), *Discourse and technology: Multimodal discourse analysis*. Washington, DC: Georgetown University Press.

Ong, Walter J. (1982) *Orality and literacy*. New York: Methuen.

Pan, Xiaping and Ron Scollon (2000) Reading multimodal, multicoded texts: The problem of meaning in a contemporary hybrid system – shop and other signs in Hong Kong. Paper presented at the 7th International Pragmatics Association Conference, Budapest, July.

Pan, Yuling (1998) Public literate design and ideological shift: A case study of Mainland China and Hong Kong. Paper presented at the 6th International Conference on Pragmatics, Reims, France, 19–24 July.

Peirce, Charles S. (1955) Logic as semiotic: The theory of signs. In J. Buchler (ed.), *Philosophical writings of Peirce*. New York: Dover Publications, 98–119.

Piaget, Jean (1971) *Structuralism*. New York: Harper and Row.

Pile, Steve and Nigel Thrift (2000) *City a–z*. London: Routledge.

Reed, Irene, Osahita Miyaoka, Steven Jacobsen, Paschal Afcan, and Michael Krauss (1977) *Yup'ik Eskimo grammar*. University of Alaska, Alaska Native Language Center and the Yup'ik Language Workshop.

Reichard, Gladys A. (1951) *Navajo grammar*. Publication of the American Ethnological Society, XXI. New York: J. J. Augustin Publisher.

Ridington, Robin (1990) *Little bit know something: Stories in a language of anthropology*. Iowa City: University of Iowa Press.

Ruesch, Jurgen and Gregory Bateson (1968 [1951]) *Communication: The social matrix of psychiatry*. New York: W. W. Norton & Company.

Ruesch, Jurgen and Weldon Kees (1956) *Nonverbal communication: Notes on the visual perception of human relations*. Berkeley and Los Angeles: University of California Press.

Schegloff, Emanuel (1972) Notes on a conversational practice: Formulating place. In Pier Paolo Giglioli (ed.), *Language and social context*. Harmondsworth: Penguin Books, 95–135.

Schmidt, Richard (2001) Attention. In Peter J. Robinson (ed.), *Cognition and second language instruction*. Cambridge: Cambridge University Press.

Schorske, Carl E. (1981) *Fin-de-siècle Vienna politics and culture*. New York: Vintage Books.

Scollon, Ron (1998a) *Mediated discourse as social interaction: The study of news discourse*. London: Longman.

Scollon, Ron (1998b) Mediated discourse and social interaction. *Research on Language and Social Interaction*, 32(1 and 2):149–154.

Scollon, Ron (2000a) Hidden dialogicality: When infelicity becomes infringement. In Malcolm Coulthard, Janet Cotterill, and Frances Rock (eds), *Dialogue analysis VII: Working with dialogue*. Tübingen: Max Niemeyer Verlag, 425–439.

Scollon, Ron (2000b) Methodological interdiscursivity: An ethnographic understanding of unfinalizability. In Srikant Sarangi and Malcolm Coulthard (eds), *Discourse and social life*. London: Longman, 138–154.

Scollon, Ron (2001a) *Mediated discourse: The nexus of practice*. London: Routledge.

Scollon, Ron (2001b) Action and text: Toward an integrated understanding of the place of text in social (inter)action. In Ruth Wodak and Michael Meyer (eds), *Methods in critical discourse analysis*. London: Sage, 139–183.

Scollon, Ron (2001c) Multilingualism and intellectual property: Visual holophrastic discourse and the commodity/sign. *Georgetown University Round Table on Languages and Linguistics 1999, May 6–8, 1999*. Washington, DC: Georgetown University Press.

Scollon, Ron and Suzanne Wong Scollon (1995) Somatic communication: How useful is 'orality' for the characterization of speech events and cultures? In Uta M. Quasthoff (ed.), *Aspects of oral communication*. Berlin: DeGruyter, 19–29.

Scollon, Ron and Suzanne Wong Scollon (1998) Literate design in the discourses of revolution, reform, and transition: Hong Kong and China. *Written language and literacy*, 1(1):1–39.

Scollon, Ron and Suzanne Wong Scollon (1999) Physical emplacement of texts in shop signs: When 'NAN XING WELCOME YOU' becomes 'UOY EMOCLEW GNIX NAN'. Paper presented at the III Conference for Sociocultural Research, Campinas, Brazil, July, 14–16, 2000.

Scollon, Suzanne (1998) Identity through the embodiment of authoritative gesture: The practice of taijiquan in Hong Kong. In D. Ray Heisey and Wenxiang Gong (eds), *Communication and culture: China and the world entering the 21st century*. Amsterdam: Rodopi Editions, 181–204.

Scollon, Suzanne (2001) Habitus, consciousness, agency and the problem of intention: How we carry and are carried by political discourses. *Folia Linguistica XXXV/1–2*:97–129.

Scollon, Suzanne (2002) Political and somatic alignment: habitus, ideology, and social practice. In Ruth Wodak and Gilbert Weiss (eds), *Theory and interdisciplinarity in critical discourse analysis*. London: Palgrave.

Scollon, Suzanne and Ron Scollon (2000) Inscription and the politics of literate design. Paper presented at the Georgetown University Roundtable, Washington, DC, May 4–6.

Scollon, Suzanne and Yuling Pan (1997) Generational and regional readings of the literate face of China. Paper presented at the Second Symposium on Intercultural Communication, Beijing Foreign Studies University, October 10–15.

Scollon, Suzanne Wong and Yuling Pan (2002) Saa Taaigik: A metaphor for conflict management. In David C.S. Li (ed.), *Discourses in search of members*. Lanham, MD: University Press of America, 423–450.

Silverstein, Michael (1976) Shifters, linguistic categories, and cultural description. In K. Basso and H. Selby (eds), *Meaning in anthropology*. Albuquerque: University of New Mexico Press, 11–55.

Silverstein, Michael (1996) The secret life of texts. In Michael Silverstein and Greg Urban (eds), *Natural histories of discourse*. Chicago and London: The University of Chicago Press, 81–105.

Silverstein, Michael and Greg Urban (1996) The natural history of discourse. In Michael Silverstein and Greg Urban (eds), *Natural histories of discourse*. Chicago and London: The University of Chicago Press, 1–17.

Strunk, William Jr and E. B. White (1979 [1935]) *The Elements of Style*. New York: Macmillan.

Tsao, Hsueh-Chin and Kao Hgo [sic] (1978) *A dream of red mansions*. 'Yang Hsien-Yi and Gladys Yang', tr. Beijing: Foreign Languages Press.

Tuan, Yi Fu (1969) *China*. Chicago: Aldine Publishing Company.

Tuan, Yi Fu (1991) Language and the making of place: A narrative-descriptive approach. *Annals of the Association of American Geographers* 81(4):684–696.

Tuan, Yi Fu (1996) *Cosmos and hearth*. Minneapolis: University of Minnesota Press.

van Leeuwen, Theo (1996) The representation of social actors. In Carmen Rosa Caldas-Coulthard and Malcolm Coulthard (eds), *Texts and practices: Readings in critical discourse analysis*. London: Routledge, 32–70.

Vygotsky, L.S. (1978) *Mind in society: the development of higher psychological processes*. Cambridge: Harvard University Press.

Wodak, Ruth (2001) What CDA is about – a summary of its history, important concepts and its developments. In Ruth Wodak and Michael Meyer (eds), *Methods in critical discourse analysis*. London: Sage, 1–13.

Zavala, Virginia (2000) Public images of literacy in Andahuaylas. Paper presented at the Georgetown University Roundtable on Languages and Linguistics, May 4–6, Washington, DC.

Index